CW01209541

Issues in Second Language Proficiency

Issues in Second Language Proficiency

Edited by

Alessandro G. Benati

continuum

Continuum International Publishing Group

The Tower Building	80 Maiden Lane
11 York Road	Suite 704, New York
London SE1 7NX	NY 10038

© Alessandro G. Benati and contributors 2009

All rights reserved. No part of this publication may be reproduced or transmitted in any form or by any means, electronic or mechanical, including photocopying, recording, or any information storage or retrieval system, without prior permission in writing from the publishers.

British Library Cataloguing-in-Publication Data
A catalogue record for this book is available from the British Library.

ISBN: 978-0-8264-3515-6 (Hardback)

Library of Congress Cataloging-in-Publication Data
The Publisher has applied for CIP data.

Typeset by Newgen Imaging Systems Pvt Ltd, Chennai, India
Printed in Great Britain by the MPG Books Group, Bodmin and King's Lynn

In memory of my mother
Anna Maria Ferrari

"Piccola anima smarrita e soave, compagna e ospite del corpo, ora t'appresti a scendere in luoghi incolori, ardui e spogli, ove non avrai piu` gli svaghi consueti. Un instante ancora, guardiamo insieme le rive famiiari, le cose che certamente non vedremo mai piu`. . . Cerchiamo d'entrare nella morte a occhi aperti"

From *Memorie di Adriano* (pp 275.276)
by Marguerite Yourcenar. Einaudi 1974.

Contents

Contributors ix
Acknowledgements xiii

Introduction

1. Attaining Second Language Proficiency 3
   Alessandro Benati, University of Greenwich, United Kingdom

Part 1: Theory and the Dimensions of Second Language Proficiency

2. What Is 'Priming', And What Might Priming Techniques 9
   Be Able to Tell Us About L2 Learning and Proficiency?
   Emma Marsden, University of York, United Kingdom

3. Cross-linguistic Influence In L2 Verb Frames: The Effects of 24
   Word Familiarity and Language Proficiency
   Christopher J Hall, York St John University, United Kingdom, and
   Areli Reyes Durán, Universidad Autónoma de Tlaxcala, Mexico

4. The Role of Working Memory in the Development 45
   of L2 Grammatical Proficiency
   Clare Wright, Newcastle University, United Kingdom

Part 2: Factors Contributing to the Attainment of L2 Proficiency

5. Statistical Learning And Innate Knowledge in the Development 63
   of Second Language Proficiency: Evidence From the Acquisition
   of Gender Concord
   Roger Hawkins, University of Essex, United Kingdom

6. Metalinguistic Knowledge: A Stepping Stone Towards 79
   L2 Proficiency?
   Karen Roehr, University of Essex, United Kingdom, and
   Gabriela Adela Gánem-Gutiérrez, University of Essex, United Kingdom

7. The Development of Vocabulary Proficiency in Relation 95
   to Learning Style
   Paul Booth, Kingston University, United Kingdom

8. Second Language Reading Proficiency and Word Recognition: 116
The Concept of Saliency and Its Application Across Different Scripts
Mick Randall, British University in Dubai, Dubai

9. L2 Proficiency: Measuring the Intelligibility of Words and 132
Extended Speech
Sara Kennedy, McGill University, Montréal, Canada

10. English With a Native-like Accent: An Empirical Study on Proficiency 147
Tanja Angelovska & Angela Hahn, University of Munich, Germany

Part 3: Attaining L2 Proficiency in the Classroom

11. Formal Intervention and The Development of Proficiency: 169
The Role of Explicit Information
Bill VanPatten, Texas Tech University, United States of America

12. Secondary and Cumulative Effects in Attaining L2 Proficiency 189
in the Classroom: The Acquisition of French
*Alessandro Benati, University of Greenwich, United Kingdom, James Lee,
University of New South Wales, Australia and Cécile Laval,
University of Greenwich, United Kingdom*

13. Models of Speaking and The Assessment of 202
Second Language Proficiency
Peter Skehan, Chinese University of Hong Kong, Hong Kong SAR

14. Researching Task Difficulty: Towards Understanding L2 Proficiency 216
Parvaneh Tavakoli, London Metropolitan University, United Kingdom

15. On Transfer, Proficiency and Cross-individual/Aggregate 233
Sla Differences: Examining Adjectival Semantics In L2 Spanish
*Pedro Guijarro-Fuentes, University of Plymouth, United Kingdom,
Tiffany Judy, University of Iowa, United States of America and
Jason Rothman, University of Plymouth, United Kingdom*

Index 255

Contributors

Tanja Angelovska holds an MA in English Linguistics, Language Teaching, and German Linguistics from the University of Munich and is currently completing her Ph.D. She has taught courses in Applied Linguistics, Corpus Linguistics, Sociolinguistics and Psycholinguistics.

Alessandro Benati is Head of the Languages and International Studies Department at the University of Greenwich in the UK. He has researched and taught in the area of second language acquisition and processing instruction. He is co-author with James Lee of various books on the processing instruction model.

Paul Booth is a Senior Lecturer at Kingston University and is currently working towards a Ph.D. His research interests include second language vocabulary development and learning style.

Areli Reyes Durán is an Associate Professor of Applied Linguistics and Modern Languages and Coordinator of the Language Centre at the Autonomous University of Tlaxcala in Mexico. She has an MA in Applied Linguistics from the Universidad de las Américas Puebla, Mexico.

Gabriela Adela Gánem-Gutiérrez is a Lecturer in Applied Linguistics in the Department of Language & Linguistics at the University of Essex. Her research interests are explicit L2 learning, sociocultural theory and CALL.

Pedro Guijarro-Fuentes is a Senior Lecturer in Spanish and the BA Modern Languages Programme Manager at the University of Plymouth where he teaches Spanish and area studies. His research interests are in the interdisciplinary field of Spanish applied linguistics, SLA, sociolinguistics, psycholinguistics and bilingualism. His main current research projects include among others the study of copula verbs *ser/estar* and the acquisition of spatial prepositions by L2 learners of both English and Spanish, projects funded by the British Academy and the Art and Humanities Research Council. He has authored and co-authored numerous articles and book chapters, and his research has appeared in different international, refereed journals such as *Language Learning*, *Bilingualism: Language and Cognition*, *Cognition*, *International Journal of Applied Linguistics*, *Spanish in Context* and *International Journal of Bilingualism* among others.

Angela Hahn is Professor of Applied Linguistics at the Department of English and American Studies of the University of Munich and Head of the University Language Centre (FFP). Her main research interests include Second Language Acquisition, Phonology, Contrastive Linguistics, Corpus Linguistics, (Computer-mediated) Language Learning and Teaching, and Varieties of English. Her current research interests focus on phonological acquisition processes of learners supported by learning platforms.

Christopher J. Hall is a Senior Lecturer in English Language and Linguistics at York St John University. He studied at Newcastle, York and Southern California, and lectured in Mexico for 20 years before returning to the United Kingdom in 2007. His publications include *Morphology and Mind* (Routledge, 1992) and *An Introduction to Language and Linguistics. Breaking the Language Spell* (Continuum, 2005).

Roger Hawkins is a Professor in the Department of Language and Linguistics, University of Essex. He has published *Approaches to second language acquisition* (with Richard Towell – Multilingual Matters), *Second language syntax: A generative introduction* (Blackwell), *French Grammar and Usage* (with Richard Towell-Hodder) and numerous articles. He co-edits the journal *Second Language Research* (with Michael Sharwood Smith).

Tiffany Judy is a first-year Ph.D. candidate in the Department of Spanish and Portuguese at the University of Iowa. Her areas of interest are adult second and third language acquisition of syntactical and semantic properties. Her research and studies focus mainly on Spanish and Portuguese.

Sara Kennedy holds a Ph.D. in Second Language Education from McGill University in Montréal, Canada. Her research focuses on intelligibility of second language speech, effects of classroom instruction, particularly the teaching of oral skills, and the role of language experience in the development of speaking ability. She has extensive experience teaching English as a second and foreign language.

Cécile Laval is Senior Lecturer in French in the Department of Languages and International Studies at the University of Greenwich in London, United Kingdom. She obtained a doctorate in applied linguistics (2008) from the University of Greenwich. She has researched and published in the area of second language acquisition and processing instruction.

James Lee is Head of the Department of Spanish and Latin American Studies at the University of New South Wales, Sydney, Australia. He is the author of *Tasks and Communicating in Language Classrooms* (McGraw-Hill, 1999).

Emma Marsden is a Lecturer in the Centre for Language Learning Research in the Department of Educational Studies at the University of York, United Kingdom. She has worked on several Research Council funded projects investigating learning and teaching foreign languages in England. In 2005, she co-convened, with Professor Rosamond Mitchell, the BAAL Language Learning and Teaching Special Interest Group.

Mick Randall is currently Dean of Education at the British University in Dubai where he teaches ELT on the M.Ed. He has taught in the Middle East for many years and his doctoral research was into word recognition in English and Arabic. He has recently published a book *Memory, Psychology and Second Language Learning* with John Benjamins.

Karen Roehr is a Lecturer in Applied Linguistics in the Department of Language & Linguistics at the University of Essex. Her research interests are implicit and explicit L2 learning and the role of individual differences in adult second language acquisition.

Jason Rothman is an Assistant Professor of Hispanic linguistics and language acquisition at the University of Iowa. Mainly, his work focuses on the acquisition of syntax and semantics from a generative perspective across children and adults, including several types of bilingualism. Some recent articles have appeared or are to appear in *International Review of Applied Linguistics, Applied Linguistics, Language Acquisition, Second Language Research, Language and Linguistic Compass, EuroSLA Yearbook* and *International Journal of Bilingualism.*

Peter Skehan teaches at the Chinese University of Hong Kong. He has published in the areas of language testing, second language acquisition, and foreign language aptitude. He is currently directing research projects on task-based performance, and is particularly interested in the role of lexis in second language performance as well as the development of models of second language speaking.

Parvaneh Tavakoli received her MA in TEFL from Iran University of Science and Technology and her Ph.D. in Applied Linguistics from King's College London. She has taught and conducted research both in Iran and the UK since 1995. Her main research interests are task-based language teaching and learning, language testing and assessment and ESOL. At present, she is a senior lecturer at London Metropolitan University.

Bill VanPatten is Professor and Director of Applied Linguistics and Second Language Studies at Texas Tech University. He has published widely in the fields of instructed SLA and SLA more generally. His current projects include work on sentence processing in monolingual, and early- and late-bilingual populations, as well as the use of online methods to investigate input processing.

Clare Wright is a final year Research Council-funded Ph.D. student at Newcastle University, working with Vivian Cook and Martha Young-Scholten on linguistic and cognitive factors underpinning second language development. She has also taught English for 11 years to international postgraduates, and is particularly interested in the interface between memory and language at advanced levels of proficiency.

Acknowledgements

The chapters published in this volume are based on presentations at the British Association of Applied Linguistics Language Learning and Teaching Special Interest Group Annual Meeting held at Greenwich on the 1-2 July 2008.

First of all I would like to express my gratitude to Karen Roehr for helping me to organize this Conference. Without her help, advice, suggestion and hard work the conference would not had taken place.

A special thank you for Emma Marsden, Roger Hawkins, Tony Lilley and Martin Bygate for providing help with reviewing abstract submitted to the conference.

Thanks also to Gurdeep, Colleen, Murali and everyone at Continuum for making this volume happen.

I am also grateful to Bill VanPatten, Roger Hawkins and Jan Hulstijn for presenting their work as plenary speakers at the Conference. I would also like to thank Bill Van Patten for his advice, suggestions and help on this volume.

A final thank you to the British Association of Applied Linguistics, Baroness Tessa Blackstone and Professor Joanne Finkelstein at the University of Greenwich and everybody in the Department of Languages and International Studies at the University of Greenwich for their valuable support and for making this Conference happen.

Introduction

Chapter 1

Attaining Second Language Proficiency

Alessandro Benati
University of Greenwich, United Kingdom

The theme of the 2008 annual meeting of the British Association of Applied Linguistics, Language Learning and Language Teaching Special Interest Group was *Attaining Second Language Proficiency*. The theme was chosen to give an opportunity to present and discuss research concerned with language learning and teaching. This research has been conducted in order to measure how, why and when L2 learners improve their proficiency in a target language, and this volume explores the topic from different perspectives. Within this framework, it addresses various issues concerning the development of L2 proficiency which for the purpose of this volume have been classified into three main areas:

– theory and dimensions of second language proficiency;
– factors contributing to the attainment of second language proficiency;
– attaining second language proficiency in the classroom.

Part One of this volume is concerned with issues related to the theory and dimension of second language proficiency.

Marsden's chapter explores how priming techniques might shed some light on factors that are considered crucial in order to understand the development of L2 learning and language proficiency. Marsden seeks to evaluate the possible role of priming techniques in research investigating developmental changes to input processing mechanism in the oral mode. She concludes that there is need for more 'ecologically favourable designs' which as argued by Marsden involves 'relatively long study phase followed by a multiple item test phase'. Her chapter provides a very useful review of literature concerning the use of priming for the research into L2 learning and offers specific suggestions on how priming techniques might provide an insight on how proficiency is attained.

Hall and Reyes's chapter presents the result of a study which explores and assesses the relative effects of word familiarity and general proficiency on crosslinguistic influence at the level of verbal frames. The main finding from this study shows that as the level of proficiency increases in L2 learners, they become reliant on their L1 for frame information. Hall and Reyes argue that the results of their study have direct implications on how we view and measure proficiency. These findings raise interesting questions at theoretical level on the way proficiency is attained and measured and at pedagogical level on the way vocabulary is learnt and taught.

Wright's paper reflects on the role of working memory in the development of L2 grammatical proficiency. Wright reports on a semi-longitudinal study investigating possible correlation between working memory and individual differences as factors responsible for the development of language proficiency among adult Chinese speakers of English. Findings from this study reveal the existence of 'patterns of individual variation in acquisition of English wh-questions, but also evidence of different patterns of processing in different modes (oral vs. written) and for different types (subject vs. object extraction). Wright's study indicates that there is a correlation between working memory and L2 grammatical proficiency.

Part Two deals with various variables which might affect the attainment of L2 proficiency.

Hawkins's chapter addresses the role of statistical learning and innate knowledge in the development language proficiency. Hawkins considers the relative role that learning of statistical properties of input might play in the development of L2 proficiency in generative theories of second language acquisition (SLA). He suggests that both statistical learning and linguistic knowledge have an important role in language acquisition. Hawkins analyses and discusses a possible model where both these elements can interact with each other. In this chapter Hawkins proposes a model which will help us understand how English verb morphology is learnt.

Karen Roehr and Gabriela Adela Gánem-Gutiérrez's chapter analyses the role of metalinguistic knowledge as a factor contributing to the attainment of language proficiency. They present the main findings from a small-scale empirical study investigating the use of metalinguistic knowledge by learners of German and Spanish. The data indicated that there is a clear correlation between metalinguistic knowledge and the ability of L2 learners to use metalinguistic knowledge to accomplish language tasks. The two authors address the important issue of the role of metalinguistic knowledge in instructed language learning.

Booth investigates the possible relation between L2 learners' knowledge of vocabulary and individual differences in learning styles. For Booth, lexical development is a complex and dynamic process, and differences in learners' approaches to language learning may shape their lexical development. Booth argues that that analysis-oriented learners tend to be more consistent in their lexical development than memory-orientated learners who tend to show greater fluctuations. Booth's chapter provide the readers with the view that 'understanding how learners vary in their approaches to L2 learning can help us to understand differences in learners' lexical development.'

Randall examines the cognitive aspects of reading in language proficiency. Randall discusses the dichotomy between top-down and bottom-up methods of processing print and argues that bottom-up processes are an essential factor for the development of second language reading proficiency particularly in the case of Arabic language.

Randall further argues that word recognition is probably the major factor in L2 reading. In addition he explores the role of different saliency factors in the process of word recognition and reading. This chapter provides methodological suggestions which might help L2 readers notice salient features in the input and become more proficient readers.

Kennedy measures the intelligibility of words and extended speech (word-level intelligibility vs. discourse-level intelligibility) in the development of L2 proficiency. The purpose of Kennedy's study was to investigate the possible link between the two levels of intelligibility with the intent to develop a discourse-level intelligibility measure. The main findings from this study show that L2 learners reached the same level of intelligibility as native speakers at discourse level but not at word level. The analyses of the results presented in this chapter showed that 'word level intelligibility measures do not accurately reflect the intelligibility of extended speech in authentic communication.'

The last chapter in this part is by Angela Hahn and Tanja Angelovska who investigated how native speakers might perceive and assess foreign accented and near-native speech. Results from this study investigating L2 spoken proficiency showed to significant differences between native and non-native performances. This study makes a contribution to the research field on ultimate attainment in L2, particularly by comparing adult L2 spoken performance to L1 performance of English.

Part Three is concerned with studies investigating various factors responsible for how learners might attain L2 proficiency in the language classroom. The first chapter in part three investigates the effects of explicit information across three instructional approaches.

VanPatten reports on an investigation comparing the effects of explicit information on the outcomes of three different interventions designed to focus on form: processing instruction (PI), dictogloss (DG) and meaning-based output instruction (MOI). The main findings from this study reveal a pattern for the role of explicit information across the three instructional treatments. VanPatten concludes that the function and role of explicit information seems to vary with the approach used. While explicit information appears to be crucial in the context of DG, for instance, the success of PI and MOI is apparently less dependent on this component, with PI less influenced than MOI. His conclusion is that not all grammar treatments are equal, that some are more biased towards explicit learning than others.

Benati, Lee and Laval's chapter investigates the possible secondary and cumulative effects of the processing instruction approach. Research on processing instruction has so far investigated primary effects. In this chapter, Benati, Lee and Laval provide evidence that L2 learners who have been taught to rely on and process French *imparfait* as a tense and aspect indicator, can transfer that training to another word final verb morpheme (French subjunctive). The chapter also explores the question of whether learners can transfer their training on processing verb morphology to appropriately process a syntactic structure: the French causative construction with *faire*. This chapter opens a new line of research into processing instruction secondary effects.

Skehan's chapter explores the assessment of oral second language proficiency in relation to areas such as SLA, psycholinguistics and the analysis of speaking as a process. This chapter presents the Levelt model of speech production and findings in the area of second language task-based spoken performance. Skehan's chapter concludes that four influences (complexifying, pressuring, easing, and focusing) can be effectively adopted in measuring L2 proficiency.

In her chapter, Tavakoli argues for the importance of defining and determining task difficulty. She present the results of a study investigating the way task difficulty is perceived and defined by L2 language learners and teachers. The main findings indicate that both L2 learners and teachers 'agree, to a great extent, on what contributes to the difficulty level of a task and the criteria they consider in determining task difficulty'. This study offers a good insight into cognitive models of task difficulty and provides important evidence on how using tasks may facilitate the development of second language proficiency.

Finally, Guijarro-Fuentes, Judy and Rothman's chapter investigates the acquisition of adjectives in instructed (SLA). The results from this empirical study showed that there is a clear role for the L1 in the developmental sequence of L2 acquisition. The authors also argued that individual characteristics play a role in the development of L2 proficiency. Overall, the findings from this study provide further evidence in support for the role of L1 in the developmental sequence of SLA.

Part One

Theory and the Dimensions of Second Language Proficiency

Chapter 2

What Is 'Priming', and What Might Priming Techniques Be Able to Tell Us About L2 Learning and Proficiency?

Emma Marsden
University of York, United Kingdom

Abstract

There have been many calls to develop ways of measuring implicit learning processes. One possibility is the use of priming techniques. This chapter describes what priming is, and reviews the various paradigms, methods and theoretical frameworks that are related to priming research. It includes an overview of the kinds of L2 research which have used priming, focusing in particular on a few studies which have investigated input processing. The chapter concludes with a discussion of some of the problems and possible future directions of using priming techniques for informing our understanding of how L2 proficiency is attained.

Introduction

This chapter has three main aims. The first section describes what priming is, and describes some of its theoretical and methodological underpinnings. The second section provides a brief overview of some second language (L2) research which has used priming techniques. The third section reviews in a little more detail some studies investigating the effects of different exposure conditions on L2 priming and, in particular, the orientation of attention during L2 input processing. The conclusions consider some of the challenges of using priming techniques in L2 learning research, and some possibilities for their use in future research.

What Is Priming?

This section aims to clarify some key terminology, and discusses basic theoretical underpinnings and methodological frameworks associated with priming research.

Key Terminology

Priming is the term used to describe the phenomenon that prior exposure to something influences subsequent responses to the same or related things. Language can be primed, so that exposure to a linguistic feature influences subsequent speed of responding to that feature, often called the reaction time or response latency. Also, prior exposure to a linguistic feature can influence the nature of subsequent responses to that feature. For example, it can affect subsequent accuracy of use, amount of use, preference for, or opinion about that feature. The initial exposure can be referred to as the 'initial presentation', the 'prime', the 'stimulus', the 'study phase' or the 'training phase'. The subsequent exposure is sometimes called the 'response', the 'test' or the 'target' (note how this use is not identical to the standard use of the term in instructed SLA research). Responses, during the test phase, can be observed in production or comprehension of the target. It is these responses which tell us whether there were any priming effects. Priming effects can be positive (facilitative), speeding up reaction times or leading to greater accuracy, more frequent usage or more positive opinions about the target. They can also be negative (inhibitory), slowing down reaction times or leading to less favourable opinions or usage.

In order to measure the effects described above, the 'response' and/or 'reaction time' data can be compared to responses to items which were not presented previously. These items are sometimes referred to as 'unseen', 'unheard' or 'unrelated'. Less commonly, comparisons could also be drawn with other kinds of baseline data, such as responses to targets which had been primed under different types of prior exposure conditions, and this is discussed in more detail in the section 'Using Priming to Research the Effects of Different Exposure Conditions on Priming'.

Theoretical Underpinnings: Processes Underlying Priming Phenomena

Priming techniques can be used as an implicit measure of the extent to which forms in the input are activated within the hearer/reader (Priming, 2004; Reber, 1995). Priming is generally considered to be an implicit, automatic process. It is usually assumed that the participants have little or no awareness of its occurrence (McDonough & Trofimovich, 2008). Priming effects are regarded as evidence of an activation model of storage and access to language representations, and evidence that networks of representations are linked (Harley, 2001). As listeners (or readers) are exposed to a certain form in the input (lexical item, inflection, syntactic pattern, etc.), then the neurological representations of that form are activated (are given 'energy', Harley, 2001, p. 417) via the resources available in working memory. Over the course of time, a representation may receive increasing amounts of activation, and this is thought to lower its activation threshold i.e. it can be activated with less energy.

Activation is thought to occur at different levels of linguistic representation: semantics, syntax, morphology and phonology (Pickering & Branigan, 1998). For example, it has been demonstrated that words sharing derivational morphology (Marslen-Wilson, Ford, Older & Zhou, 1996) and inflectional morphology (Silva & Clahsen, 2008) prime each other reliably. Activation at other levels of representation has also been demonstrated via priming effects, at the semantic, syntactic, word (auditory and visual), phonological (or phonemic) and phonetic (or feature) levels. As a particular representation of a form is more activated, the more likely it is that this activation will persist and be detectable in priming effects.

In principle, priming effects *per se* need not be explained by one specific model of language representation. For example, there is no agreed perspective on whether priming effects suggest that humans possess a universal and innate representation of grammar, or whether grammatical representations emerge as a result of usage in the input. However, priming evidence can be used to support particular models; for example, it has been used to support a Construction Grammar explanation of grammar (Chang, Bock & Goldberg, 2003; Gries & Wulff 2005; Wulff & Gries, in press;). Priming evidence has also been used to research holistic versus decompositional routes for storing and accessing morphology (see section 'Overview of Some L2 Priming Research To Date' below).

Nevertheless, if we are to use evidence from priming to support models of *learning*, this does require the assumption that priming effects reflect learners' storage and access of linguistic representations and, critically, that these processes contribute to acquisition mechanisms. However, this is perhaps uncontroversial as all L2 acquisition theories, as McDonough and Trofimovich (2008) point out, 'share the premise that knowledge must be represented and accessed during parsing and production' (p. 6). It seems, then, that priming evidence could, depending on the specific findings of individual studies, be compatible with a range of different perspectives on language acquisition as it does not, *a priori*, assume one specific model of acquisition.

Critical for the use of priming effects to support language *learning* theories is that priming effects have been found to be persistent, and it is widely considered that they are a window into implicit memory and learning processes (Bock &

Griffin, 2000; Savage, Lieven, Theakston & Tomasello, 2006; and for reviews see McDonough, 2006; McDonough & Mackey, 2008; McDonough & Trofimovich, 2008; Schacter & Tulving, 1994; Trofimovich, 2005 & 2008). For example, auditory word priming effects have been found to last over delays of minutes (Church & Schacter, 1994), days, and weeks (Goldinger, 1996), suggesting that such effects have a long-term memory component likely to be used for learning.

Types of Priming

There are thought to be several different types of priming and priming effects, and several different ways of testing for priming effects. A few of these are summarized here, and see McDonough and Trofimovich (2008) for a fuller account of auditory, syntactic and semantic priming. The aim in the current chapter is simply to define, very briefly, some key concepts, terminology and techniques.

Repetition priming is the observation that an initial presentation of a stimulus can influence the response to that *same* stimulus when it is presented at a later time. This stimulus and the target are related by their physical form. This could be a word, a morpheme, a syntactic structure, or a phonemic or an orthographic feature etc. Syntactic and acoustic priming are types of repetition priming. Semantic priming is the observation that responses to a word (or a picture) can be influenced by previous exposure to a stimulus whose *meaning* is related to the target (see McNamara, 2005). In semantic priming experiments, the prime and the target are usually physically different, though not always (see for example Felser & Roberts, 2007).

In priming studies, the presentation of the stimulus is often manipulated, so as to reduce the awareness that participants may have of relationships between the prime and the target. In masked priming studies, the visual prime is 'invisible', i.e. the prime is presented so quickly, that the participants are not conscious of it; then participants must make a judgement on a visual target. Cross-modal priming refers to the phenomena whereby the processing of a visual target is facilitated if it is preceded by auditory presentation of an identical or semantically related word (Neely, 1991).

Types of Tests for Priming Effects

Clearly, different tests are used to address specific research concerns, such as whether processing time and/or accuracy of response data are required, or whether production and/or comprehension processes are to be involved (see McDonough & Trofimovich, 2008 for more details). This section outlines some of the most frequently used test types.

During a test phase, priming effects can be observed in the production of the target. For example a participant may show a greater tendency to *use* a form, in terms of amount and/or accuracy and/or speed. Priming effects can also be observed in the responses to the target in the input. For example the participants may have a greater tendency to hear, read, like or identify the target, and/or be faster in their responses. This could include tasks such as lexical decisions (with questions such as: is this a word or a non-word? alive or not alive? French or English?). Perceptual identification tests present the target word or sentence either under white noise (in the aural modality) or under visual masking (in the written modality). The participants are then either offered a forced choice as to what they heard (or saw), or they are asked simply to reproduce what they thought they heard (or saw). Other test tasks include naming a picture, reading a word out loud, repeating a word they listen to, completing a word fragment (cl_ck) or completing a word stem (cl_ _ _). During most tests, participants are asked to complete each item as quickly as possible.

To date, there has been a somewhat dichotomous view of two types of priming phenomena. One, exemplified by semantic priming described above, can be referred to as conceptual priming. The other can be referred to as perceptual priming, which is thought to involve the analysis of the form of the stimulus, and has been found to be sensitive to the modality and exact format (e.g. acoustic properties such as voice type) of the stimulus. These two views of processing have been associated with specific types of priming and specific tests for priming effects, for example lexical decisions for semantic priming, and identification tests for perceptual priming. However, the separation of processing 'form' and 'meaning' may not be so clear cut (see for example VanPatten, Williams, Rott & Overstreet, 2004), and so methodological paradigms associated with this distinction are probably becoming less significant (e.g. Arnotta, Chenerya, Murdocha & Silburnb, 2005, used lexical decision tests to investigate syntactic priming).

Designs of Priming Studies

Obviously, the design of studies is motivated by the research questions being asked. However, although most priming studies are carried out in laboratory, computer-based environments, some research designs seem to have more potential to be related to instructional events than others. Some priming studies can consist of one prime item followed immediately by one test item eliciting the response to or the production of the target (e.g. Silva & Clahsen, 2008), or the prime and the target can be within the same sentence (e.g. Felser & Roberts, 2007). Such designs could perhaps be seen as comparable, in teaching terms, to presenting an item and then immediately asking for some response to it or use of it. However, several syntactic priming studies have investigated whether priming can influence the use of the target over longer periods of time, and some studies investigate priming in human interaction (for a review, see McDonough & Mackey, 2008). Also, some studies provide a longer training phase consisting of several exemplars of the prime, and then a test phase including several test items (e.g. Trofimovich & Gatbanton, 2006; Marsden, Altmann & St Claire, 2005). Such designs could, arguably, be more comparable to providing an input flood of exemplars during instruction, and then asking learners to use or respond to the target and assessing their performance to evaluate the learning phase.

Overview of Some L2 Priming Research to Date

Although priming has been well-attested for over a hundred years (Cattell, 1888, cited in Harley, 2001), it is only recently that it has been incorporated into L2 research. Indeed, Libben & Jarema (2002) argued that one of the threats to the validity of psycholinguistic priming research to date is that it has not been sufficiently generalized to samples of language users other than normal adult natives. They suggest that developing bilinguals are one sample of the language-using population who could inform our interpretation of priming evidence. In this section, I review some L2 priming research to date, although presenting the findings of each of these studies is beyond the scope of this chapter. Instead, my main aim is to illustrate the ways in which priming has been used, and the kinds of L2 research agendas in which priming evidence is being put forward. As becomes clear below, research with L2 participants has mainly looked for cross-linguistic priming i.e. the prime and the target are in different languages (L1 then L2 or *vice versa*). Research using within-L2 priming is much less common, though a few examples are emerging in the literature.

There has been a considerable number of studies using priming techniques to investigate the nature of the bilingual mental lexicon (e.g. Grainger & Frenck-Mestre, 1998; Dong, Gui & MacWhinney, 2005; Schwartz & Area da Luz Fontes, 2008). Some of this research investigates the existence and nature of conceptual and/or perceptual (orthographic or phonetic) links *across* the L1 and the L2. Another branch of this research investigates whether semantic links between words are the same *within* both languages. The researchers often measure whether the responses is different as a function of whether the stimulus and/or the target are in the L1 or the L2. This line of research is almost always at the word level (rather than sentence or discourse level), although there has been some cross-language research investigating whether L1 and L2 share the same store for syntax. For example, Hartsuiker, Pickering, and Veltkamp (2004) and Schoonbaert, Hartsuiker, and Pickering (2007), used cross-linguistic priming evidence to support a shared-syntax account. In general, this cross-language research is carried out via visual presentation, therefore requiring literacy in one or both languages.

A relatively active area of priming research, particularly in the L1, is that testing for decompositional and/or holistic routes for storing and accessing morphology. This has included both derivational (e.g. *-ness*) and inflectional morphology (e.g. walk, walked; buy, bought) (see e.g. Marslen-Wilson, 2007). There has been some recent work along similar lines but looking at L2 to L2 priming. Silva and Clahsen's (2008) masked priming study found that inflected forms were primed among L1 natives, but not among second language learners (L2ers). They conclude that L2ers rely more on lexical storage and less on decomposing morphology than natives. Typical of this research agenda, their study used visual presentation and focused on inflected words in isolation.

Recently, L2 researchers have used a priming technique to investigate online parsing. Felser and Roberts (2007) used a cross-modal picture priming task to investigate the reactivation of antecedent indirect objects. This task had not, to the authors' knowledge, been used with L2ers before. It relies on the semantic priming phenomenon. During aural presentation of sentences, a picture was presented visually at strategic points: either at gaps where the antecedent was hypothesized to be integrated into the sentence parse, or at another, control (or baseline) point. The pictures were either identical to or semantically unrelated to the antecedent. In this study, the participants were told that they had to decide as quickly as possible whether the animal or object in the picture was alive or not alive. The findings suggested that the advanced L2ers did not behave like natives in their activation of wh-dependencies.

In an ongoing programme of research, McDonough, Mackey and colleagues are addressing the role of priming during production within interactional contexts. The studies address whether when learners hear a syntactic form they are more likely to then use this form. Their research has focused on a range of syntactic features among L2 learners of English: McDonough (2006) on dative constructions; McDonough and Mackey (2006 & 2008) on question development; Kim and McDonough (2008) on L2 passives. In these studies, the researcher had a script during an interaction task. The script prompted the researcher to use a specific form. It was found that English prepositional datives (e.g. he gave the book to the boy) and the syntax of questions and passives could be primed in this way among second language learners, but not double object datives (e.g. he gave it the boy). Gries and Wulff (2005) and Wulff and Gries (in press) also gathered production to production syntactic priming evidence from advanced German learners of English, and used this to argue that priming of verb gerund and infinitival complement constructions (e.g. try rowing; tried to row) was greater when the same lexical 'carrier' item that was experienced in the prime is used in the participants' production. They argue that these findings suggest that syntactic constructions are part of L2ers interlanguage, compatible with construction grammar theories of language acquisition.

Summing up the above, priming evidence has been used in L2 research to support a range of hypotheses relating, for example, to the mental lexicon, storage of morphology, parsing, and the use of syntax. However, little research to date has looked into the effects on priming of different exposure conditions during the study phase. The following section reviews this area of research.

Using Priming to Research the Effects of Different Exposure Conditions on Priming

Several calls have been made to adopt more implicit methods to investigate input processing and the effects of different types of input manipulations. For example, Robinson (2003) suggested that 'measures such as those adopted in implicit memory studies . . . may be more sensitive measures than those requiring on- or off-line production and verbalisation of the contents of awareness' (p. 639), and Segalowitz (2006) recommended the use of 'finely grained cognitive and perceptual measures' (137). Despite these and other similar calls, there has been very little research into the effect of different input conditions on whether particular linguistic features can be primed. In L1 research, several findings suggest that different manipulations of exposure to spoken words do not affect the influence of priming. For example, Schacter and Church (1992) found similar priming effects regardless of whether adult native listeners had previously heard a word under instructions to estimate how many meanings it might have or under instructions to make a judgement about its clarity (see also Church & Schacter, 1994). Church and Fisher (1998) also found that semantic processing did not interfere with word priming among L1 learners (see also Smith, 1991).

The impact of orientation of attention on priming effects was, albeit indirectly, addressed in Heredia and McLaughlin (1992)'s visual word-priming study among adult English – Spanish bilinguals. In one of their experiments, all participants were exposed to lists of English words during the study phase. Then, during the test phase, participants did one of two tasks: they either had to carry out a fragment completion task in English (i.e. within language priming), or they had to use the English fragment to generate the equivalent Spanish word (i.e. within-followed by cross-language priming). Heredia and McLaughlin found that having to translate the completed fragment during the test phase (which probably involved conceptual processing of the word) eliminated any processing benefits for having seen the word during the exposure phase. That is no priming effects were found in the translation-at-test condition.

Some within-language L2 research has been carried out in a related area. Trofimovich (2005), Trofimovich and Gatbanton (2006) and Trofimovich (2008) investigated the effects of different exposure conditions on the auditory priming of lexical items. (These studies also investigated the sensitivity of L2ers to acoustic properties of the input, such as gender of the voice, though this aspect of the studies is not reviewed here). In these studies, participants were assigned to one of two study conditions. In one condition they had to rate the clarity of a word (considered to promote perceptual processing) and in the other they had to rate the pleasantness of the meaning of the word (considered to promote semantic processing). In the test the participants had to listen to a number of words (half of which were unheard and half of which had been primed), and then repeat these words as quickly as possible, providing reaction time data. Together the studies point to a number of observations. Trofimovich (2005) found that a semantic orientation did not influence auditory word priming effects among the intermediate learners' L2 Spanish nor in their L1 English. Trofimovich and Gatbanton (2006), however, manipulated another variable: low versus high pronunciation accuracy, as rated by native speakers for the degree of foreign accent in their L2 speech. They found that for participants with low pronunciation skills in their L2, a semantic orientation to the words during exposure eliminated priming effects. When the exposure and test was in their L1, a semantic orientation did not reduce priming effects compared to an orientation to form. For the high accuracy pronunciation group, prior exposure to words lead to significant priming effects in both their L2 and their L1 *regardless* of the orientation to form or meaning.

Also investigating whether the orientation of attention during aural input processing influences priming effects is a study by Marsden et al.(2005). Three different levels of proficiency were used: Beginner L1 English learners of French with approximately 100–200 hours exposure to classroom instruction; Intermediate L1 English learners of French with approximately 700 hours classroom instruction and adult French Natives. The exposure phase was different to Trofimovich and colleagues's studies in two main ways. First, the feature under investigation was not a word, but a verb inflection (-ons, the French verb inflection for the first person plural in the present tense). Second, the two exposure conditions were at the sentence level. In one condition, participants had to focus on sentence meaning by judging whether it made sense e.g. 'nous jouons au fromage' (we play+1.pl. cheese) or 'nous regardons la tele' (we watch+1.pl. telly), a task which has been used in previous studies to orient attention to sentence meaning (Daneman & Carpenter, 1980; Walter, 2004). In the other exposure condition, participants had to orient their attention to the inflection: they had to judge whether the speaker was talking about something they do with other people in sentences such as 'jouons au tennis' (play+1.pl. tennis) or 'regardez la tele' (watch+2.pl. telly). The test phase was designed to measure whether learners had activated representations of the inflection differently as a result of being in different study phases. One test was a lexical decision in which half the words ended in the verb inflection which had been primed (e.g. arrichons), and half the words ended in a range of different unheard inflections (e.g. arrichera). Participants had to decide whether the word was real or not. The other test was a perceptual identification test, in which participants were asked what they had heard under white noise (e.g. they heard 'nous jouons au tennis', with the 'jouons' under white noise; then they heard 'jouons' or 'jouer' and had to choose which they had heard). Both the reaction times and the actual responses suggested (with the exception of the actual responses for the perceptual identification test) that for beginners, focusing their attention on the verb inflection resulted in more activation of the target inflection than equivalent exposure to the inflection while trying to understand sentence meaning. This could be compatible with Trofimovich's observation that for certain learners, a semantic orientation at the study phase does reduce the perceptual processing of form. Marsden et al. also found that for intermediates and natives there was no difference in priming effects between the focus on form condition and the sentence meaning condition. They offer several explanations for their findings, including that at higher proficiency levels participants may have had more resources available to process verb inflections (Bates & Goodman, 1997; VanPatten, 2002), or that they may already have had some representation of the target form which was primed to the same extent in both exposure conditions (Schmidt, 2001). Another explanatory factor may be that the redundancy of the bound inflection (e.g. *-ons* co-indexed with the subject) in the sentence meaning condition reduced the activation of the form for the beginners but not for the higher proficiency participants (VanPatten, 2002, 2004 & 2007, and for related arguments see Deutsch & Shlomo, 1994; Leeser, 2007; Marsden, 2006).

Given that this line of research is still emerging, it is too early to bring the findings together with confidence. It may be that the effect of orientation to L2 input on priming is dependent on modality, and/or the nature of the feature being primed (e.g. lexical, morphological), and/or the proficiency of the learner. In visual processing, Heredia and McLaughlin's study suggests that a semantic orientation may interfere with word priming, although this finding was based on manipulating orientation during the test, rather than the exposure phase, and it was with adult bilinguals, rather than learners. In auditory processing, there is evidence that semantic processing can cause interference with priming words among low-intermediate learners who have weak phonological processing skills (Trofimovich & Gatbanton, 2006) and with priming verb inflections among beginner learners (Marsden et al., 2005). To date, the evidence suggests that for L2ers with better phonological skills (Trofimovich & Gatbanton, 2006), for L2ers with higher proficiency (Marsden et al.; Trofimovich, 2005), for L1 adult natives (Church & Schacter, 1994), and for L1 learners (Church & Fisher, 1998), auditory repetition leads to priming effects which are unaffected by the orientation of attention during exposure. The researchers involved in these studies make their own suggestions about areas which remain to be addressed by priming research investigating the orientation of attention during input processing.

Conclusions: Problems and Future Directions

If we are to use evidence of priming to inform language learning and teaching theories, there are several issues that require attention. One is the design of the studies. Increasingly, research designs are used which do resemble, albeit to a limited extent, instructional events. For example, Trofimovich's and Marsden's studies operated a relatively long study phase followed by a multiple item test phase; and Mackey and colleagues's studies also partially simulated learning events. These are clearly ecologically favourable designs compared with the more main stream cognitive psychology designs in which a very brief exposure is followed by an immediate test. However, the longer exposure and test designs may not always be appropriate. For example, repeated exposure to the same morphological or syntactic feature followed by multiple test items may affect the internal validity of a priming study. For example, it is not known whether there is a cumulative effect of the exposure and/or the test items, and such issues remain to be addressed by future research.

As discussed in the section 'What is priming?', priming is often considered to be evidence of automatic or implicit processing, with little or no awareness from the participants. However, detecting priming effects is not actually an 'on line' measurement, and so does not, unequivocally, tap directly into the real-time processing event alone. In terms of researching L2 learning, this may be problematic as L2ers often have some metalinguistic knowledge which may become more accessible during off line processing. Future research should determine the possible role of awareness during priming experiments, as the paradigm has emanated from work with adult natives where explicit knowledge may be less prevalent. Another related problem is that priming effects may be influenced by long-term memory representations, rather than being a pure indication of implicit, automatic processes directly involved during the exposure phase. If we want to observe changes in input processing over time as a function of proficiency level, we may not want to confound evidence of learners' long-term memory representations with evidence of online input processing. For example, McDonough and Trofimovich (2008) note that questions have been raised as to whether reaction times are appropriate indirect measures of linguistic knowledge for language users who have not fully acquired the target language (Crain & Thornton, 1998). Indeed, some priming research has already shown different outcomes depending on the measure used, for example measures of electrical activity in the brain (event related potentials) pattern differently to reaction times as a function of the language (Kotz, 2001) or proficiency level (Elston-Güttler & Friederici, 2005; Kotz & Elston-Güttler, 2004). In Marsden et al.'s study summarized above, it was found that the reaction times and the accuracy of identification in the perceptual identification task did not pattern in the same way across different proficiency levels. Other types of psycholinguistic L2 research have indicated dissociations between linguistic knowledge and processing as measured by reaction times. For example, Juffs (1998) and White and Juffs (1998) argued that their accuracy data reflected underlying competence of argument structure whereas their reaction time data reflected ease of processing (see also Murphy, 1997). In future research using reaction times as evidence of priming, it is clear that other outcome measures should also be adopted, to further explore relations between language performance, representation and reaction times. In addition, research needs to address the impact that different exposure and testing tasks have on claims about priming.

L2 priming research to date generally uses words or morphosyntax that are not necessarily new to the participants. Also, participants have tended to be fluent bilinguals or advanced learners, rather than beginners. This limits the extent to which such evidence informs us about the role priming may have in how new language is learnt. Addressing this gap could involve priming completely novel constituents (perhaps using artificial or semi-artificial languages) or using complete beginners, while manipulating factors such as phonological or morphosyntactic similarities with the L1, attentional orientation and/or linguistic context.

The research reviewed the final section above is beginning to address questions about the influence attentional orientation may have on within-language L2 priming, and the role this may have in attaining proficiency. It seems that priming techniques could inform our understanding of whether so-called semantic processing (e.g. conceptual processing, or reliance on lexical, paralinguisitc, contextual and world knowledge cues) affects perceptual processing in an L2. In particular, more research is needed on processing a wider range of morphosyntactic features in the input, for example using constituents that are co-indexed across contexts of more than one word. Also, it would be useful to simulate different types of comprehension situations, in terms of learners' attentional orientation, the task in hand and the linguistic context. Finally, to validate L2 priming evidence about input processing, other psycholinguistic techniques are likely to be necessary, such as phoneme monitoring and word spotting, in a variety of attentional and linguistic contexts in both oral and written modalities.

References

Arnotta, W., Chenerya, H., Murdocha, B., & Silburnb, P. (2005). Morphosyntactic and syntactic priming: An investigation of underlying processing mechanisms and the effects of Parkinson's disease. *Journal of Neurolinguistics*, 18, 1–28.

Chang, F., Bock, K., & Goldberg, A. (2003). Can thematic roles leave traces of their places? *Cognition*, 90, 29–49.

Church, B., & Fisher, C. (1998). Long-term auditory word priming in preschoolers: Implicit memory support for language acquisition. *Journal of Memory and Language*, 39, 523–42.

Church, B., & Schacter, D. L. (1994). Perceptual specificity of auditory priming: Implicit memory for voice information and fundamental frequency. *Journal of Experimental Psychology: Learning, Memory, and Cognition*, 20, 521–33.

Crain, S., & Thornton, R. (1998). *Investigations in universal grammar: A guide to experiments on the acquisition of syntax and semantics.* Cambridge, MA: MIT.

Daneman, M., & Carpenter, P. (1980). Individual differences in working memory and reading. *Journal of Verbal Learning and Verbal Behaviour*, 19, 450–66.

Deutsch, A., & Shlomo, B. (1994). Attention mechanisms mediate the syntactic priming effect in auditory word identification. *Journal of Experimental Psychology: Learning, Memory, and Cognition*, 20, 595–607.

Dong, Y., Gui, S., & MacWhinney, B. (2005). Shared and separate meanings in the bilingual mental lexicon. *Bilingualism: Language and Cognition*, 8, 221–38.

Elston-Güttler, K. E., & Friederici, A. (2005). Native and L2 processing of homonyms in sentential context. *Journal of Memory and Language*, 52, 256–83.

Felser, C., & Roberts, L. (2007). Processing wh-dependencies in a second language: a cross-modal priming study. *Second Language Research*, 23, 9–36.

Grainger, J., & Frenck-Mestre, C. (1998). Masked priming by translation equivalents in proficient bilinguals. *Language and Cognitive Processes*, 13, 601–23.

Gries, S., & Wulff, S. (2005). Do foreign language learners also have constructions? Evidence from priming, sorting and corpora, *Annual Review of Cognitive Linguistics*, 3, 182–200.

Harley, T. (2001). *The psychology of language: From data to theory* (2nd Ed.). Hove, UK: Psychology Press.

Hartsuiker, R., Pickering, M., & Veltkamp, E. (2004). Is syntax separate or shared between languages? *Psychological Science*, 15, 409–14.

Heredia, R., & McLaughlin, B. (1992). Bilingual memory revisited. In R. J. Harris (Ed.), *Cognitive processing in bilinguals* (pp. 91–103). Amsterdam: Elsevier.

Kim, Y., & McDonough, K. (2008). Learners' production of passives during syntactic priming activities. *Applied Linguistics*, 29, 1, 149–54.

Kotz, S. (2001). Neurolinguistic evidence for bilingual language representation: A comparison of reaction times and event-related brain potentials. Bilingualism: Language *and Cognition*, 4, 143–54.

Kotz, S., & Elston-Güttler, K. E. (2004). The role of proficiency on processing categorical and associative information in the L2 as revealed by reaction times and event-related brain potentials. *Journal of Neurolinguistics*, 17, 215–35.

Leeser, M. (2007). Learner-based factors in L2 reading comprehension and processing grammatical form: Topic familiarity and working memory. *Language Learning*, 57, 229–270.

Libben, G., & Jarema, G. (2002). Mental lexicon research in the new millennium. *Brain and Language*, 81, 2–11.

Marsden, E. (2006). Exploring input processing in the classroom: An experimental comparison of processing instruction and enriched input. *Language Learning*, 56, 507–66.

Marsden, E., Altmann, G. & St. Claire, M. (2005). Priming of French verb inflections: the role of communicative redundancy and sentential comprehension. Paper presented at the *Annual Conference of the European Association of Second Language Acquisition*, Dubrovnik, Croatia, Sept. 2005.

Marslen-Wilson, W. D. (2007). Morphological processes in language comprehension. In G. Gaskell (Ed.), *Oxford Handbook of Psycholinguistics* (pp. 175–93). Oxford: OUP.

Marslen-Wilson, W., Ford, M., Older, L., & Zhou, X. (1996). The combinatorial lexicon: priming derivational affixes. In G. Cottrell, (Ed.). *Proceedings of the 18th annual conference of the Cognitive Science Society* (pp. 223–27). Mahwah, NJ: Lawrence Erlbaum Associates.

McDonough, K. (2006). Interaction and syntactic priming: English L2 speakers' production of dative constructions. *Studies in Second Language Acquisition*, 28, 179–207.

McDonough, K., & Mackey, A. (2006). Responses to recasts: Repetitions, primed production and linguistic development. *Language Learning*, 54, 693–720.

McDonough, K., & Mackey, A. (2008). Syntactic priming and ESL question development. *Studies in Second Language Acquisition*, 30, 31–47.

McDonough, K., & Trofimovich, P. (2008). *Using priming methods in second language research*. Routledge/Taylor and Francis Publishing Group.

McNamara, T. (2005). *Semantic priming: Perspectives from memory and word recognition*. New York: Psychology Press.

Neely, J. (1991). Semantic priming effects in visual word recognition: A selective review of current findings and theories. In D. Besner, & G. Humphreys (Eds.), *Basic processes in reading: Visual word recognition* (264–336). Hillsdale, NJ: Erlbaum.

Priming. (2004). In *The Concise Corsini Encyclopedia of Psychology and Behavioral Science*. Hoboken, NJ: Wiley. Retrieved December 19, 2008 from http://www.credoreference.com/entry/4410668

Robinson, R. (2003). Attention and memory in SLA. In C. Doughty, & M. Long (Eds.), *Handbook of second language acquisition* (pp. 631–78). Oxford: Blackwell.

Savage, C., Lieven, E., Theakston, A., & Tomasello, M. (2006). Structural priming as implicit learning: The persistence of lexical and structural priming in 4-year-olds. *Language Learning and Development*, 2, 27–49.

Schoonbaert, S., Hartsuiker, R., & Pickering, M. (2007). The representation of lexical and syntactic information in bilinguals: Evidence from syntactic priming. *Journal of Memory and Language*, 56, 153–71.

Schwartz, A., & Area da Luz Fontes, A. (2008). Cross-language mediated priming: Effects of context and lexical relationship. *Bilingualism: Language and Cognition*, 11, 95–110.

Segalowitz, N. (2006). Review of processing instruction: Theory, research and commentary. *Studies in Second Language Acquisition*, 28, 135–7.

Silva, R., & Clahsen, H. (2008). Morphologically complex words in L1 and L2 processing: Evidence from masked priming experiments in English. *Bilingualism: Language and Cognition*, 11, 245–60.

Smith, M. C. (1991). On the recruitment of semantic information for word fragment completion: Evidence from bilingual priming. *Journal of Experimental Psychology: Learning, Memory, and Cognition*, 17, 234–44.

Trofimovich, P. (2005). Spoken-word processing in native and second languages: An investigation of auditory word priming. *Applied Psycholinguistics*, 26, 479–504.

Trofimovich, P. (2008). What do second language listeners know about spoken words? effects of experience and attention in spoken word processing. *Journal of Psycholinguistic Research*, 37, 309–29.

Trofimovich, P., & Gatbonton, E. (2006). Repetition and focus on form in L2 Spanish word processing: Implications for pronunciation instruction. *The Modern Language Journal*, 90, 519–35.

VanPatten, B. (2002). Processing instruction: An update. *Language Learning*, 52, 755–803.

VanPatten, B. (2004). Input processing in SLA. In B.VanPatten (Ed.), *Processing instruction: Theory, research, and commentary* (pp. 5–32). Mahwah NJ: Lawrence Erlbaum.

VanPatten, B. (2007). Input processing in adult SLA. In B. VanPatten, & Williams, J. (Eds.), *Theories in Second Language Acquisition* (pp. 115–35). Mahwah, NJ: Lawrence Erlbaum.

VanPatten, B., Williams, J., Rott, S., & Overstreet, M. (Eds.). (2004). *Form Meaning Connections in Second Language Acquisition* (pp. 203–18). Mahwah, NJ: Lawrence Erlbaum Associates.

Walter, C. (2004). Transfer of reading comprehension skills to L2 is linked to mental representations of text and to L2 working memory. *Applied Linguistics*, 25, 315–39.

Wulff, S., & Gries S., (in press). *To-* vs. *ing-*complementation of advanced foreign language learners: corpus- and psycholinguistic evidence. To appear in *Annual Review of Cognitive Linguistics*.

Chapter 3

Cross-Linguistic Influence in L2 Verb Frames: The Effects of Word Familiarity and Language Proficiency[1]

Christopher J. Hall
York St John University, United Kingdom

Areli Reyes Durán
Universidad Autónoma de Tlaxcala, Mexico

Abstract

This study assesses the effects of word familiarity and general proficiency on cross-linguistic influence (CLI) at the level of verbal frames. English as a Foreign Language (EFL) learners at three proficiency levels chose between two versions of a sentence differing only in verbal frame (the target L2 frame or the frame of the L1 equivalent). Choice of L1 frame was taken as an instance of CLI. Verbs were known to learners, but varied in familiarity. Comparisons of CLI rates across word groups and proficiency levels show an independent effect of proficiency, suggesting that as proficiency increases, learners become less reliant on L1 for frame information.

Introduction

Vocabulary knowledge is an important component of language proficiency, and is often assessed as part of classroom-internal, institutional, and standardized tests. Scholars and practitioners in second language pedagogy and testing have for some time now recognized that mere *breadth* or *quantity* of lexical knowledge, reflected in number of memorized translation pairs, is a coarser-grained measure of communicative competence than *depth* or *quality* of vocabulary knowledge (Nation, 2001; Read, 2000). Depth of lexical knowledge embraces often very complex patterns of context-dependent form-meaning mapping. But one aspect of native-like vocabulary knowledge that in a sense falls between form-based breadth and meaning-based depth, is knowledge of how individual words are deployed morphosyntactically. This knowledge brings together a disparate range of linguistic features, which for learners can be relatively straightforward or highly arcane, depending on their degree of abstractness and the particular L1-L2 combination involved. Their significance for L2 proficiency is an underexplored topic, but one that has the potential to shed light on both proficiency development and the organization of the L2 mental lexicon, as we hope this study demonstrates.

What links these features together is their fundamentally grammatical but distinctly lexical nature. They serve grammatical (morphosyntactic) functions, and are unpredictable or at least underdetermined by form or meaning, but must be mentally represented in individual lexical entries because they are also unpredictable by grammatical rule. This idiosyncrasy means there is considerable cross-linguistic diversity in the ways that concepts are conventionally mapped onto morphosyntax, even in typologically related languages. Verbs are especially rich in grammatical information (cf. Levin, 1993 for English), and so constitute particularly significant challenges for learners than other word classes (Lennon, 1996). Examples of grammatical features of this type for the major lexical word classes across languages include:

- syntactic category (word class) (e.g. Eng. (*have*) *fun*, N. vs. Sp. *divertirse*, V.; Eng. *need*, V. vs. Fr. (*avoir*) *besoin* (*de*), N.);
- gender or declension class on nouns (e.g. Eng. *shop* = Sp. *tienda*, fem. vs. Fr. *magasin*, masc. vs. Ger. *Geschäft*, neuter);
- count/non-count on nouns (e.g. Sp. *muebles* vs. Eng. *furnitures);
- complement type (subcategorization frame) for verbs and adjectives (e.g. Eng. *wait for* vs. Ger. *warten auf*; Eng. *near to* vs. Sp. *cerca de*);
- thematic grid for verbs (e.g. Eng. *X likes Y* vs. Sp. *Y gusta a X*);

Some of these features can, of course, *correlate* with elements of phonological form and/or meaning. For instance, many animate nouns in Spanish exhibit a correlation between grammatical gender and both form and meaning: masculine and feminine gender covarying with –*o* and –*a* suffixes (form), and male and female sex (meaning), as in *niño*, "boy" vs. *niña*, "girl" (cf. inanimate *tienda*, "shop," where meaning is not involved, and *hombre*, "man" vs. *mujer*, "woman," where form is not involved).

More broadly, syntactic category correlates strongly (but not absolutely) with semantic categories. For example, there is a strong tendency for predicated actions to be expressed cross-linguistically through verbs, and for object reference to use nouns (cf. Croft, 1990, pp. 141–143). Similarly, languages which have adjectives and adpositions tend to use the former to express properties, and the latter, paths and places (cf. Jackendoff, 1983, p. 68). Correlations with phonological form tend to be language-specific, and therefore arbitrary, but correlations with meaning are *ipso facto* language-independent, and thus present fewer challenges to the additional language learner because they are less likely to differ from L1 patterns.

Idiosyncratic lexicogrammatical features can be easier for L2 learners when they resemble or coincide with L1 features due to significant contact or typological proximity (i.e. cognates arising from borrowing or a common ancestor language). Nation, for example, notes (2001, p. 56) that

> the grammatical learning burden of items depends on parallels between the second language and the first language, [. . .]. If a second language word takes the same grammatical patterns as its rough equivalent in the first language, then the learning burden will be light.

The phenomenon of *cross-linguistic influence* (Kellerman & Sharwood Smith, 1986) thus plays a particularly significant role in the learning of such features. This is especially so when the learner encounters a large number of cognates with words they already know in the L1 or another familiar language.

In previous studies (e.g. Ecke & Hall, 1998, 2000; Hall, 1996, 2002; Hall & Ecke, 2003; Hall & Schultz, 1994; Hall et al. 2009), we have investigated the role of cross-linguistic influence (henceforth CLI) as a default cognitive process in vocabulary development, essentially equivalent to Piagetian processes of assimilation and eventual accommodation (Piaget, 2001 [1951]). We have proposed that early word learning is characterized by "parasitic" connections from short-term memory representations of L2 word forms to lexical entries in the L1 activated on the basis of similarity detection (equivalent to the "subordinate"-type configuration of Weinreich, (1974 [1953]). Hence, novel L2 words which resemble known L1 words in phonological and/or orthographic *form* are automatically connected and therefore assumed to be translation equivalents (the cognate effect: cf. Hall, 2002). Where form similarity is lacking, we have proposed that the assumption of exact translation equivalence is maintained (at least by less proficient learners: see below). In such cases (the vast majority), we argue that novel forms are still connected at the lexical level, but this time with representations of the assumed translation's grammatical properties, that is the word's syntactic *frame*.[2]

* * *

In our work so far, we have assumed that CLI is primarily a function of word familiarity, that is that the parasitic process is triggered by a novel form coupled with a perceived meaning for which the learner knows an L1 word, independently of proficiency in, or exposure to, the language as a whole. According to the Parasitic Model (Hall, 1996, p. 237), it is subsequent encounters with individual items in context that lead to the gradual undoing of parasitic connections for those items. From this perspective, proficiency level is irrelevant: a word encountered for the first time is new to the beginning learner and the near-native speaker alike.

But as we acknowledged in Hall and Ecke (2003, pp. 72–73), there is often a degree of strategic competence deployed in vocabulary development, such that more proficient learners come to deal with new words in less "naïve" ways than less proficient learners. Research on vocabulary learning (e.g. Henning, 1973) and the bilingual mental lexicon (cf. Kroll & De Groot, 1997) has suggested that with increased proficiency, learners tend to rely less on lexical links (i.e. between L2 forms and perceived translation equivalents in L1) overall, and move towards direct semantic mapping (or *conceptual mediation*), effectively "bypassing" L1 lexical entries or "freeing" the L2 word from dependence on L1 (De Groot & Van Hell, 2005, pp. 20–21). What has not been adequately recognized in the literature is that for this to happen, and for the proficiency-related notion of accuracy to be a meaningful dimension in output (cf. Skehan, 1998), L2 entries must be furnished with their own frame representations.

This transition to greater autonomy and elaboration of L2 lexical entries can be visualized as an ongoing reconfiguration and expansion of networks of lexical "triads" of form, frame, and concept (Hall, 2005, pp. 79–83). Figure 3.1 uses this diagrammatic convention to depict two stages of the word learning process, here for the verb *like* being learned by a Spanish native speaker. In the first configuration (a) the English form is parasitic on the frame of its perceived translation equivalent *gustar*, where the thematic grid <T__E> indicates that the verb is used canonically with a preceding theme (T) and a following experiencer (E). When activated in performance, this configuration will result in non-nativelike usage, such as **Acapulco likes me* for *I like Acapulco* (from error data reported in Hall & Schultz, 1994). In a subsequent stage (b) the L2 lexical entry has achieved independence and now features its own thematic grid, the native-like <E__T>.

The evidence for CLI at the level of grammatical properties in lexical entries is abundant (cf. Adjémian, 1983; Hall et al., 2009; Helms-Park, 2003; Juffs, 1996, 1998; Montrul, 2001; Van Hout, Hulk, Kuiken, & Towell, 2003; Wei, 2003; White, 1996). But we are not aware of any research on whether lexical CLI of this type can be overcome, as learners "wise up" to the lack of complete isomorphism in cross-linguistic grammatical and semantic mapping. Is the cognitive default of lexical assimilation into L1 overridable by the accumulating experience of L1-L2 mismatches and/or increasing automaticity and fluency in L2 performance? More concretely: Does increased overall language proficiency result in a reduction of, or reduced life of, frame CLI for newly encountered (unfamiliar) words? And to what extent does overall language proficiency correlate with the use of a conscious translation strategy to determine L2 syntactic frames?

By asking such questions we are not necessarily presupposing that "language proficiency" is a conceptually coherent and ontologically sound construct.

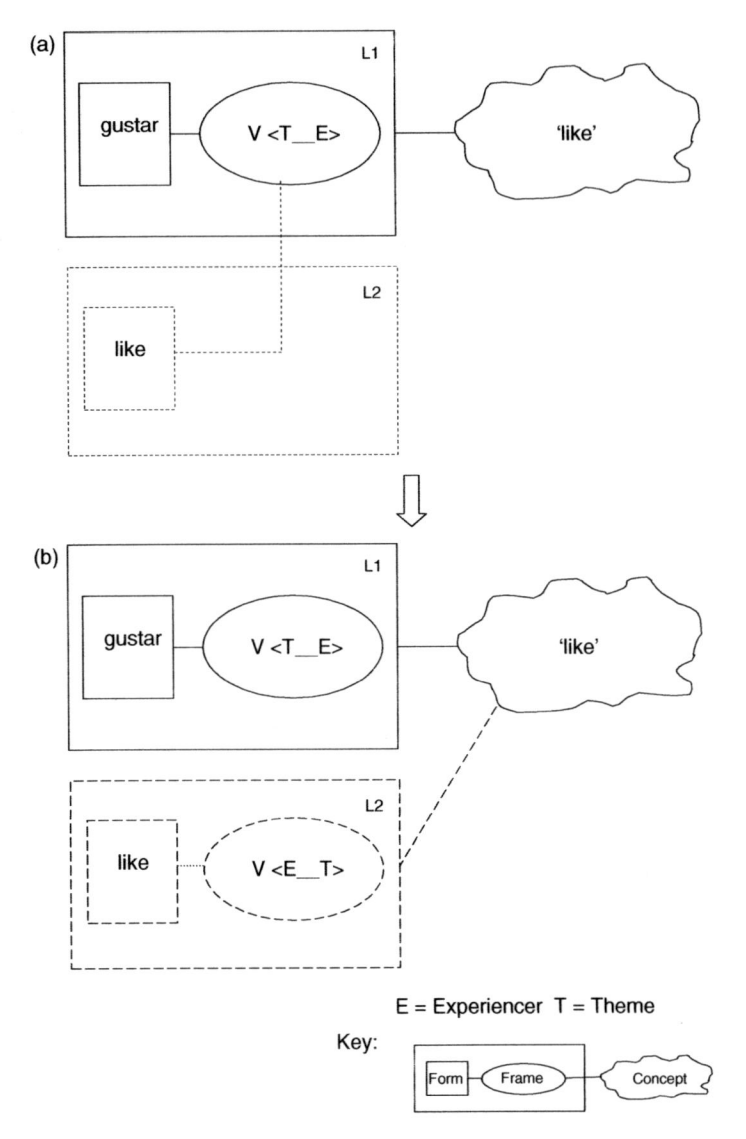

FIGURE 3.1 Changing frames in the transition from (a) parasitic to (b) autonomous lexical representations, as proficiency increases

Furthermore, by attempting to *answer* such questions we are not assuming that language proficiency—if it exists—can be entirely adequately *measured*. Elsewhere (in this volume and a large body of earlier literature) these vexed issues are explored in depth; it is not our intention to pursue them here. Rather, we hope to contribute primarily to our understanding of CLI, by trying to tease apart familiarity with individual words from familiarity with the L2 as a whole. We will not, therefore, attempt to define the construct "language proficiency," investigate its ontological status or argue for any particular formulation of it. Instead, we take placement in courses on the basis of standardized proficiency tests as an imprecise but usable and useful measure of experience/ability with L2.

We reasoned that as learners' proficiency increases on this measure, they will become less likely to build parasitic L1 frame connections for novel L2 forms. A number of proficiency-related factors would seem to point to this outcome, including the following: (a) more sophisticated L2 grammatical knowledge overall; (b) broader and deeper knowledge of L2 vocabulary; (c) lower expectations of isomorphic mapping between meaning and L1/L2 expressions; (d) more highly automatized L2 processing routines; but at the same time (e) more sophisticated strategic competence.

We predicted then, that we would find an independent effect of proficiency if we measured frame CLI empirically as the dependent variable and varied proficiency and word familiarity as the independent variables. Specifically, we formulated the following set of hypotheses:

1. Rates of frame CLI will decrease as item familiarity increases, because (a) learners are exposed to each item in a greater range of grammatical contexts and (b) repeated access in reception and production leads to reconfiguration of the lexical entry to exploit shortcuts which bypass L1.
2. Rates of frame CLI will also decrease as general proficiency increases, independently of familiarity, because of the rationale expounded above.
3. Overall confidence in frame knowledge will decrease as proficiency increases, because learners become increasingly aware of exceptions to isomorphic lexical mapping.
4. Use of translation as a basis for establishing L2 frames will decrease as proficiency increases, because more proficient learners (a) are more aware of exceptions to isomorphic mapping; (b) have greater depth of lexical knowledge overall; and (c) have more automatized access routines to more autonomous lexical entries.

In order to test these hypotheses, we elicited frame CLI in a group of EFL students of different proficiency levels, using a forced-choice grammaticality judgment task adapted from Hall et al. (2009), as described in the following section.

The Study

Participants were given a grammaticality judgment test requiring a choice between two versions of simple sentences differing only in the frame of the verb: the native-like frame and a nonnative-like frame based on that of the closest L1 translation equivalent. Participants were drawn from three institutionally defined proficiency levels, henceforth termed P1, P2 and P3 (see below). Each proficiency group judged a different number of sentence pairs:

- P3 ("advanced") learners judged 30 sentence pairs: 10 with verbs of high familiarity from the P1 level, 10 with verbs of medium familiarity from the P2 level, and 10 with verbs of low familiarity from their current level.
- P2 ("intermediate") learners judged 20 sentence pairs: 10 with medium familiarity verbs from the P1 level (the high familiarity verbs of the P3 learners) and 10 with verbs of low familiarity from their current level (the medium familiarity verbs of the P3 learners).
- P1 ("basic") learners judged only 10 sentence pairs with low familiarity verbs (the medium familiarity verbs of the P2 level and high familiarity verbs of the P3 learners).

Choice of the non-nativelike L1 frame as the grammatical option was taken as a manifestation of CLI.

Forty-five native Spanish-speaking learners of EFL, studying various academic subjects at a Mexican university, performed the grammaticality judgment task. They were pseudo-randomly selected from concurrently offered classes, as follows:

- P1: 15 students from "Basic Level" General English classes, using Book 1 of the textbook series *Skyline* (Brewer, Davies, & Rogers, 2001).
- P2: 15 students from "Intermediate Level" General English classes, using Book 4 of the *Skyline* series.
- P3: 15 students from "Advanced Level" Business English and Academic Speaking classes, having completed the *Skyline* series.

Students in the Basic Level classes were placed there on the basis of a (paper-based) TOEFL score of 320 or less or an equivalent score on the institution's internally TOEFL-calibrated placement examination. Students in the Intermediate Level classes had placed there by (a) passing the exit examination for the Basic Level, with a score equivalent to min. 400 on the TOEFL; (b) passing the TOEFL at between 400 and 500; or (c) passing the institutional placement exam with a score equivalent to between 400 and 500 on the TOEFL. Students in the Advanced Level classes had placed there by: (a) passing the exit examination for the Intermediate Level, with a score equivalent to min. 500 on the TOEFL; (b) passing the TOEFL at min. 500; or (c) passing the institutional placement exam with a score equivalent to min. 500 on the TOEFL. At the time of study, all participants had completed between 30 and 33 hours of instruction in their current level.[3]

Table 3.1 Stimuli design

Proficiency	Familiarity			Items
	Low	Mid	High	
P1	I			10 items
P2	II	I		20 items
P3	III	II	I	30 items

The stimuli were all verbs introduced in the *Skyline* series and at an equivalent level in at least one of two other comparable textbooks sampled (McCarthy & O'Dell, 2004; Soars & Soars, 2002). The earliest-introduced items (henceforth Group I) were taken from Book 1 of *Skyline* and at the time of study had already been introduced to the P1 students, the next-introduced set (henceforth Group II) were taken from Book 3, and the latest-introduced set (henceforth Group III) were taken from Book 5 (the last in the series). The stimuli design is shown in Table 3.1.

Each verb group comprised ten verbs which differed from their closest Spanish translation equivalent in syntactic frame. Frame differences all involved complement selection, drawn from the following three types:

a. preposition heading PP complement (same or distinct), e.g. Eng. *depend on* NP vs. Sp. *depender de* NP; or PP complement (present or absent), e.g. Eng. *listen to* NP vs. Sp. *escuchar* NP;
b. non-finite verb complement (gerundive or infinitive), e.g. Eng. *consider* V+*ing* vs. Sp. *considerar* V$_{[\text{inf}]}$;
c. reflexive pronoun complement (present or absent), e.g. Eng. *fight* (*with* NP) vs. Sp. *pelear* + *se* (*con* NP).

A full list of stimuli is given in Appendix A.

We devised short carrier sentences of between six and nine words for each verb and then constructed two versions, using the English frame in one and the frame of the Spanish equivalent in the other. Examples are given in (1) to (3), matching the three frame types (a) to (c) respectively. In each pair, the first sentence uses the English frame, and the second uses an English version of the Spanish frame.

(1) Your future **depends on** the decisions you make
    Your future **depends of** the decisions you make
(2) Teresa is considering **changing** her job
    Teresa is considering **to change** her job
(3) I always **fight** with my sister
    I always **fight me** with my sister

The full set of verbs and sentences is given in Appendix B.

In addition to the grammaticality judgment task, each participant completed a posttest to check: (a) their prior knowledge of the verbs and other words used in the carrier sentences and (b) their (awareness of) deployment of strategies during the task.

Results and Discussion

Vocabulary Knowledge

Before presenting the data directly addressing our hypotheses, we briefly summarize the posttest results on vocabulary knowledge to assess whether participants did indeed know the forms and meanings of the words whose usage they were to judge. In general, participants were very confident that they knew all the words in the sentences they saw. Figure 3.2 shows the breakdown of self-assessed receptive knowledge by proficiency level.

Furthermore, knowledge of verbs was generally high, with differences in line with proficiency levels and familiarity: see Figure 3.3.

We may be reasonably confident, then, that the majority of verb forms and meanings were known to the majority of participants and that the carrier sentences in which they appeared were unproblematic, even for the P1 participants.

Grammaticality Judgments

As expected, the overall rates of frame CLI diminished as proficiency and familiarity increased. Table 3.2 shows the frequency of CLI by word group for each proficiency level.

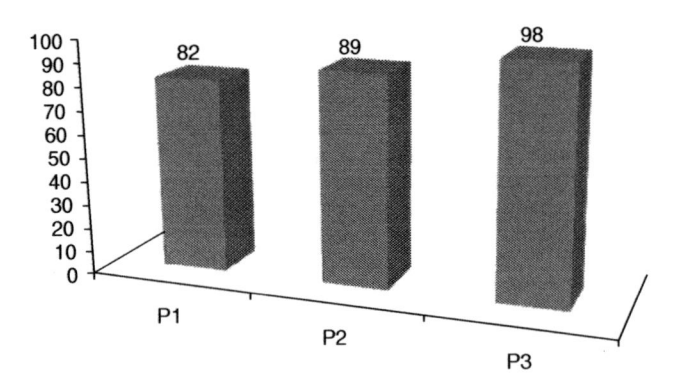

FIGURE 3.2 Receptive vocabulary knowledge, expressed as percentage of participants reporting all words used as known, by proficiency level

If we pool scores across word groups for P2 and P3, and compare overall percentage rates of CLI, we find a very significant main effect of proficiency level (F(2,42) = 8.155, $p < 0.001$). Table 3.3 shows the descriptive statistics.

A Tukey-Kramer *post hoc* test reveals that the P1 and P2 rates are not statistically different from each other, but that the P3 scores are significantly lower than the P1 rates ($p < 0.01$) and the P2 rates ($p < 0.05$).

The decline in CLI rates with increased familiarity can be observed in Figure 3.4 by comparing word group scores for P2 and P3 participants, in line with Hypothesis 1. Similarly, the decline in CLI rates with increased proficiency can be observed by comparing scores along the proficiency dimension for Group I and Group II words.

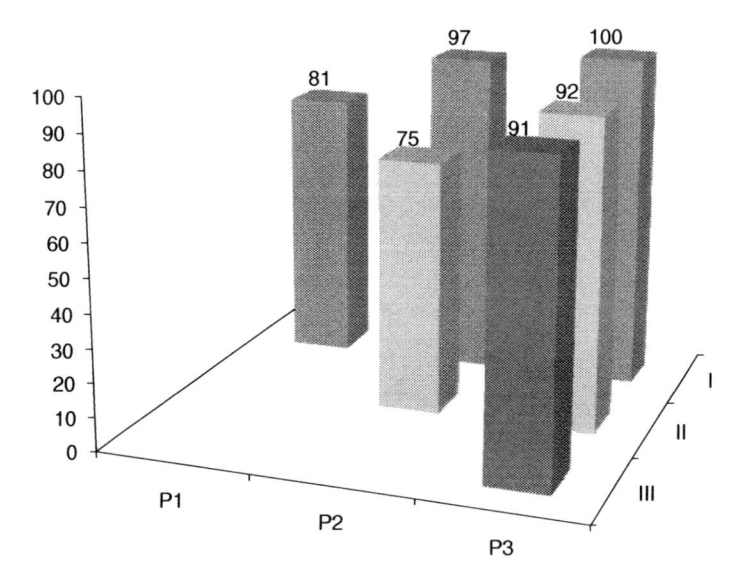

FIGURE 3.3 Knowledge of verb stimuli, expressed as mean percentage of participants giving correct translation, by proficiency level and word group

Table 3.2 Frequency of CLI across proficiency groups ($n = 45$)

Proficiency	Familiarity			Items
	Low	Mid	High	
P1	75			10 items
P2	78	57		20 items
P3	55	49	28	30 items

Table 3.3 Mean rates of CLI collapsed across word groups ($n = 45$)

Proficiency	Items	CLI (%)	S.D.
P1	10	50.00	16.04
P2	20	45.00	11.02
P3	30	29.33	16.23

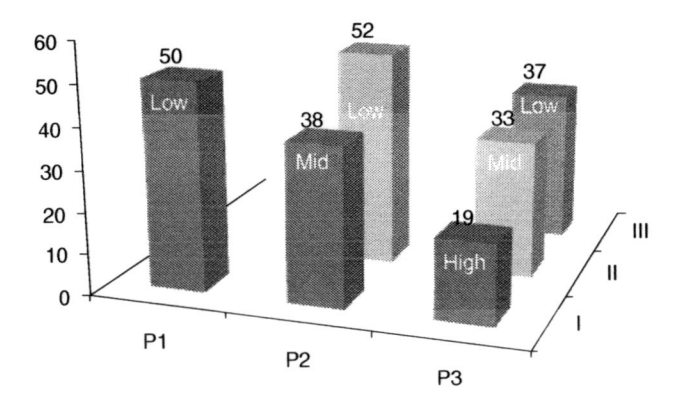

FIGURE 3.4 Mean rates of CLI, expressed as percentages, by proficiency level and word group

ANOVA results show a highly significant main effect of word group for P3 participants ($F(2,42) = 12.849$, $p < 0.0001$). Tukey-Kramer results reveal that the difference between Group II and Group III means was not significant, but that Group I is significantly lower than Group II ($p < 0.05$) and Group III ($p < 0.001$). For P2, comparing Groups I and II only, the difference is again significant ($t(14) = 2.303$, $p < 0.05$). There was also a highly significant main effect of proficiency level on Group I words ($F(2,42) = 12.684$, $p < 0.0001$). Although the difference between P1 and P2 again fails to reach significance on the Tukey-Kramer test, P3 is significantly lower than P2 ($p < 0.05$) and P1 ($p < 0.001$). For Group II words (P2 and P3 only), the difference is again significant ($t(28) = 2.378$, $p < 0.05$).

However, holding word familiarity steady while comparing across proficiency levels, as in Figure 3.5, obliges us to question the extent to which proficiency makes an independent contribution to the pattern of results, as Hypothesis 2 predicted. That is, in the crucial four-way comparison space between scores at the P2 and P3 levels, the differences for familiarity are not as striking as those for word group.

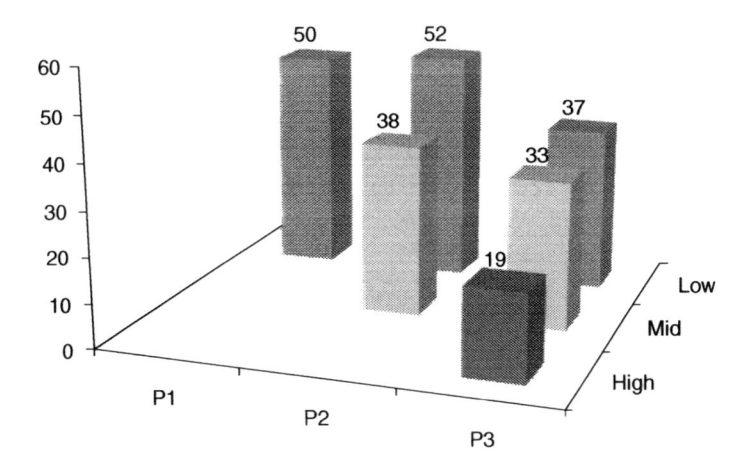

FIGURE 3.5 Mean rates of CLI, expressed as percentages, by proficiency and familiarity levels

Table 3.4 Hierarchical multiple regression assessing the independent contribution of proficiency to rates of CLI

		B	Std. Error	β
Step 1	Constant	4.433	0.321	
	Familiarity	−0.900	0.453	−0.252
Step 2	Constant	4.950	0.378	
	Familiarity	−0.900	0.436	−0.252*
	Proficiency	−1.033	0.436	−0.290*

Note: R^2 = .064 for Step 1; R^2 = .147 for Step 2; * $p < .01$.

To assess whether familiarity and proficiency make independent contributions to the persistence of CLI (Hypothesis 2), we performed a hierarchical multiple regression analysis on the P2 and P3, mid and low familiarity, subset of the data. We entered familiarity as the assumed predictor in step 1 (on the basis of Parasitic Model's predictions), and added proficiency in step 2. The resulting model, summarized in Table 3.4, does indeed reveal an independent contribution of proficiency.

The analysis demonstrates that, on its own, the contribution of familiarity to the variance in CLI rates for the items shared by P2 and P3 is, at 6.4 percent, not significant. But when proficiency is added, the combined contribution of the two variables amounts to almost 15 percent of the variance in CLI, and is significant ($p < 0.05$). The large portion of unexplained variance in the model means that, on their own, familiarity and proficiency are poor predictors of CLI for this subset of the data. However, if we evaluate the model within the context of the entire dataset across all three proficiency and familiarity levels, a more compelling view of the relationship emerges. The tilting plane along the axes of proficiency and word group visible in Figure 3.4 may well be attenuated in Figure 3.5 for the subset we can test, but the larger pattern is still evident and the model is entirely consistent with it.

Strategy Use

Apart from vocabulary knowledge, the posttest investigated learners' awareness of strategy use through self-report of confidence levels and conscious translation use. Participants were remarkably confident that they had chosen the correct option for the sentence pairs they saw. Indeed, as Figure 3.6 shows, none of the P1 participants reported guessing, and a clear majority felt completely sure of their responses (62.7 percent), with only 37.3 percent reporting that their response was the one that sounded best ("*sonaba mejor*"). The P2 and P3 participants were only slightly less confident that they had selected the correct response (57 percent and 57.3 percent) respectively, with only one or two participants reporting guessing. We therefore have no substantial evidence to support Hypothesis 3, which stated that confidence would decline as proficiency increased.

Participants' reported use of translation was entirely in line with Hypothesis 4, which stated that use of translation would decline as proficiency increased. As Figure 3.7 shows, a majority of P1 participants (64.7 percent) reported translating the sentences from English to Spanish. For P2, translators and non-translators

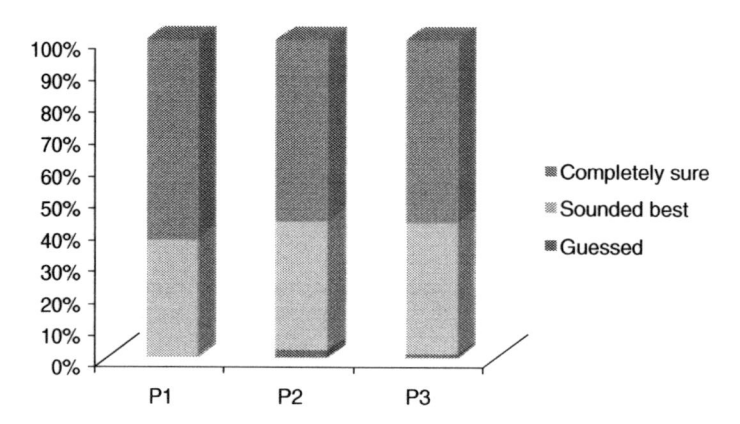

FIGURE 3.6 Reported confidence in correct response, by proficiency level

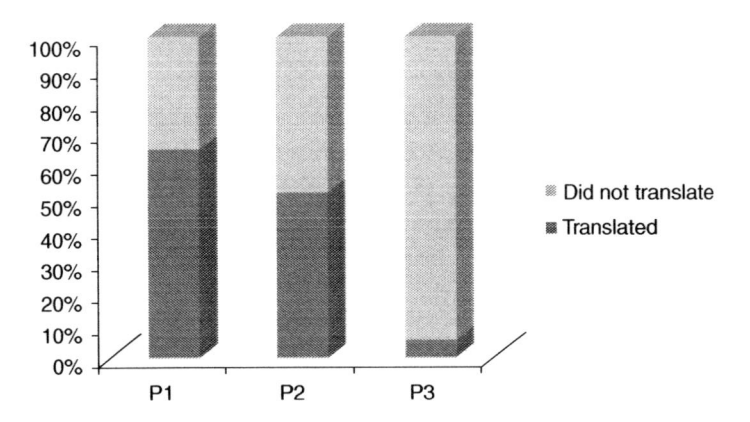

FIGURE 3.7 Reported use of translation, by proficiency level

were balanced, at 51.4 percent vs. 48.6 percent respectively. At the highest proficiency level, only a few P3 participants (5.1 percent) reported translating.

This pattern of strategy use mirrors the pattern of CLI, where the P3 participants' scores are significantly different from those from P1 and P2 (and these, recall, did not differ significantly from each other).

Limitations and Implications

Before reaching final conclusions, we should acknowledge and address potential limitations of the study. First, the sample size is relatively small, rendering our ultimate conclusions only tentative. Future studies could easily replicate this work with a larger number of participants, though the lack of stimuli exhibiting the relevant grammatical and semantic characteristics would remain. Second, as we recognized earlier, the operationalization of variables is not unproblematic. Starting with the dependent variable (frame CLI), it is true that a number of researchers have questioned the use of grammaticality judgment data to test hypotheses about interlanguage configurations. Their concern is based largely on evidence that second language learners use a different number and kind of strategies than native speakers (e.g. Davies & Kaplan, 1998). But in this study we constrained strategy use by requiring forced choices between paired options, and then followed up on strategy use in the posttest. In this regard, the translation strategy posttest results are informative, especially for the P3 participants: they reported close to zero use of overt translation, plus unexpectedly high confidence in their decisions, and yet their scores were significantly lower for the two less familiar groups of verbs. This suggests that the test was tapping into interlanguage lexical representations—with problems of indeterminacy (Sorace, 1996) unlikely—and that test scores gave a credible estimation of the extent to which participants' lexical entries are subject to CLI.

Of the independent variables, familiarity was the hardest to operationalize, since each learner's experience of the target language is different, especially the subjective frequency of individual words in meaningful and grammatical contexts. The decision to select stimuli verbs from textbook vocabulary lists was an attempt to minimize this diversity of experience, but of course it cannot be guaranteed that experience was homogeneous within proficiency levels and across word groups. Nevertheless, the vocabulary knowledge posttest results and ultimate pattern of CLI across stimuli encourage us to believe that the item groups reflected clearly distinguishable bands of familiarity with form-meaning pairings.

Our assessment is similar with regard to the issue of proficiency. Although we cannot claim to have sampled three homogenous groups at three identifiable and equidistant points on a continuum of proficiency, the use of bands of results from a standardized test battery assessing multiple components of L2 ability and knowledge provides a reasonable basis for comparison. It also has the dual benefits of (a) permitting alignment with vocabulary experience (through selection of items from level-associated course textbooks) and (b) facilitating application of the results to the practical realm of pedagogy (through the use of participants from authentic TOEFL-streamed classes), as we suggest in our concluding remarks.

Conclusion

Taken together, the results of this study suggest a pattern of syntactic frame learning in which the role of CLI from L1 equivalents decreases as learners gain more experience and ability with L2 across the board. Put another way: parasitic connections to L1 frames are more likely not only early in the process of learning a word, but also early in the process of learning a language. This finding will perhaps allow us to develop more nuanced views of both proficiency attainment/measurement and vocabulary learning/teaching. For example, we saw that those learners with TOEFL scores above 500 (*viz.* P3) behaved in quantitatively and qualitatively different ways from those with scores below 500. Although they still exhibit frame CLI with highly familiar words (and therefore have fossilized lexical entries), they also translate less, show less frame CLI across the board, and are less prone to exhibit frame CLI with unfamiliar verbs. These findings thus support theories positing a proficiency-correlated move towards a more autonomous L2 lexicon. They contribute to such theories in at least two ways: (a) by singling out the syntactic frame as the tentative lexical hub around which revolves the transition from parasitic word association to autonomous conceptual mediation and (b) by suggesting that the transition may not be completed until advanced levels of proficiency, and that even here it may not occur across the board, for either familiar or unfamiliar words.

In advance of further testing using larger samples, we might want to speculate that an important component of proficiency in a typologically related L2 is frame development, and that it might be measured through the testing or observation of sets of verb pairs which differ in syntactic frame. This possibility must, of course, be clearly distinguished from any call for CLI to be used as a general criterion for proficiency assessment: in our development of the Parasitic Model we have always stressed that CLI is a sign of effective learning, with "interference" phenomena the visible but negligible negative effect of the deployment of efficient lexical development strategies.

For vocabulary learning and teaching, the finding that unfamiliar words still provoke CLI for P3 participants suggests that the traditional use of paired, decontextualized translation equivalents (Nation, 2001, p. 351; De Groot and Van Hell, 2005, pp. 13–15) still has merit, even at advanced levels of proficiency. Additionally, teachers might use data like these to assure learners that the more they learn, the better they learn, even if they are not aware of it and so-called errors persist.

Finally, we hope that this study will encourage students of both proficiency and vocabulary to pay greater attention in their research to syntactic frame information. Currently, it is all too often neglected in the gap between form and meaning in the lexicon, and between vocabulary and grammar in the language system as a whole, and yet it is a key aspect of the contribution of vocabulary to overall language proficiency.

Notes

[1] This research was funded, in part, by a grant from the Mexican National Council for Science and Technology (CONACYT, grant number 39704). The data were first reported in Reyes' MA thesis, submitted to the Universidad de las Americas, Puebla, Mexico in 2005. We would like to acknowledge very useful input from Pavel Trofimovich and Rachel Wicaksono.

[2] This is essentially equivalent to the notion of lemma in Levelt's later work (cf. Levelt, Roelofs, & Meyer, 1999). Jiang, (2000) and Wei (2003) have made similar proposals for lexical CLI in L2 and L3 acquisition, using Levelt's earlier formulation of the lemma notion, in which semantic information was also included (Levelt, 1989).

[3] No members of P1 or P2 reported knowledge of a third or subsequent language. Eight P3 participants reported knowledge of additional languages. Participants were aged between 18 and 23 (P1) and 18 and 27 (P2 and P3).

References

Adjémian, C. (1983). The transferability of lexical properties. In S. Gass, & L. Selinker (Eds.). *Language Transfer in Language Learning* (pp. 250–68). Rowley, MA: Newbury House.

Brewer, S., Davies, P., & Rogers, M. (2001). *Skyline*, Books 1–5. London: Macmillan.

Croft, W. (1990). *Typology and Universals.* Cambridge: Cambridge University Press.

Davies, W. D., & Kaplan, T. I. (1998). Native speaker vs. L2 learner grammaticality judgements. *Applied Linguistics*, 19 (2), 183–203.

De Groot, A. M. B., & Van Hell, J. G. (2005). The learning of foreign language vocabulary. In J. F. Kroll, & A. M. B. De Groot (Eds.). *Handbook of Bilingualism. Psycholinguistic Approaches.* Oxford: Oxford University Press.

Ecke, P., & Hall, C. J. (1998). Tres niveles de la representación mental: Evidencia de errores léxicos en estudiantes de un tercer idioma. *Estudios de Lingüística Aplicada*, 28, 15–26.

Ecke, P., & Hall, C. J. (2000). Lexikalische Fehler in Deutsch als Drittsprache: Translexikalischer Einfluss auf drei Ebenen der mentalen Repräsentation. *Deutsch als Fremdsprache*, 37, 30–6.

Hall, C. J. (1996). La estrategia parasítica: Un modelo psicolingüístico del aprendizaje de vocabulario. In S. Cuevas, & J. Haidar (Eds.). *La Imaginación y la Intelegencia en el Lenguaje: Homenaje a Roman Jakobson* (pp. 229–38). Mexico City: INAH.

Hall, C. J. (2002). The automatic cognate form assumption: Evidence for the Parasitic Model of vocabulary development. *International Review of Applied Linguistics*, 40, 69–87.

Hall, C. J. (2005). *An Introduction to Language and Linguistics. Breaking the Language Spell.* London: Continuum.

Hall, C. J., & Ecke, P. (2003). Parasitism as a default mechanism in vocabulary acquisition. In J. Cenoz, B. Hufeisen, & U. Jessner (Eds.). *The Multilingual Lexicon* (pp. 71–85). Dordrecht: Kluwer.

Hall, C. J., Newbrand, D., Ecke, P., Sperr, U., Marchand, V., & Hayes, L. (2009). Learners' implicit assumptions about syntactic frames in new L3 words: The role of cognates, typological proximity and L2 status. *Language Learning*, 59, 1, 153–202.

Hall, C. J., & Schultz, M. (1994). Los errores de marco sintáctico: Evidencia del Modelo Parasitario del léxico mental en un segundo idioma. *Estudios de Lingüística Aplicada*, 12, 376–89.

Helms-Park, R. (2003). Transfer in SLA and creoles: The implications of causative serial verb constructions in the interlanguage of Vietnamese ESL learners. *Studies in Second Language Acquisition*, 25, 211–44.

Henning, G. H. (1973). Remembering foreign language vocabulary: Acoustic and semantic parameters. *Language Learning*, 23, 185–96.

Jiang, N. (2000). Lexical representation and development in a second language. *Applied Linguistics*, 21, 47–77.

Juffs, A. (1996). *Learnability and the Lexicon: Theories and second language acquisition research.* Philadelphia, PA: John Benjamins.

Juffs, A. (1998). Some effects of first language argument structure and morphosyntax on second language sentence processing. *Second Language Research*, 14, 406–24.

Kellerman, E., & Sharwood Smith, M. (1986). *Crosslinguistic influence in second language acquisition.* Oxford: Pergamon.

Kroll J. F., & De Groot, A. M. B. (1997). Lexical and conceptual memory in the bilingual: Mapping form to meaning in two languages. In De A. M. B. Groot, & J. F. Kroll (Eds.). *Tutorials in bilingualism: Psycholinguistic perspectives* (pp. 169–99). Mahwah, NJ: Lawrence Erlbaum.

Lennon, P. (1996). Getting "easy" verbs wrong at the advanced level. *International Review of Applied Linguistics,* 34, 23–36.

Levelt, W. J. M. (1989). *Speaking. From intention to articulation.* Cambridge, MA: MIT Press.

Levelt, W. J. M., Roelofs, A., & Meyer, A. S. (1999). A theory of lexical access in speech production. *Behavioral and Brain Sciences,* 22, 1–75.

Levin, B. (1993). *English verb classes and alternations: A preliminary investigation.* Chicago: University of Chicago Press.

McCarthy, M., & O'Dell, F. (2004). *English vocabulary in use.* Cambridge: Cambridge University Press.

Montrul, S. (Ed.) (2001). Representational and developmental issues in the lexico-syntactic interface: Acquiring verb meaning in a second language. Special issue of *Studies in Second Language Acquisition,* 23 (2), 145–313.

Nation, I. S. P. (2001). *Learning vocabulary in another language.* Cambridge: Cambridge University Press.

Piaget, J. (2001 [1951]). *The psychology of intelligence.* London: Routledge.

Read, J. (2000). *Assessing vocabulary.* Cambridge: Cambridge University Press.

Skehan, P. (1998). *A cognitive approach to language learning.* Oxford: Oxford University Press.

Soars, J., & Soars, L. (2002). *New headway English course.* Oxford: Oxford University Press.

Sorace, A. (1996). The use of acceptability judgments in second language acquisition research. In W. C. Ritchie, & T. K. Bhatia (Eds.). *Handbook of Second Language Acquisition* (pp. 375–409). San Diego, CA: Academic Press.

Van Hout, R., Hulk, A., Kuiken, F., & Towell, R. (Eds.) (2003). *The lexicon-syntax interface in second language acquisition.* Amsterdam: John Benjamins.

Wei, L. (2003). Activation of lemmas in the multilingual lexicon and transfer in third language learning. In J. Cenoz, B. Hufeisen, & U. Jessner, (Eds.). *The multilingual lexicon* (pp. 57–70). Dordrecht: Kluwer.

Weinreich, U. (1974 [1953]). *Languages in contact: findings and problems.* The Hague: Mouton.

White, L. (1996). Universal Grammar and second language acquisition: Current trends and new directions. In W. C. Ritchie, & T. K. Bhatia (Eds.). *Handbook of second language acquisition* (pp. 85–120). New York: Academic Press.

Appendices

Appendix A: Verb Stimuli and Spanish Translation Equivalents

Group I		
	English	**Spanish**
I-1	ask for	pedir
I-2	depend on	depender de
I-3	listen to	escuchar
I-4	look at	mirar
I-5	consider	considerar
I-6	enjoy	disfrutar
I-7	finish	terminar
I-8	fight	pelearse
I-9	marry	casarse
I-10	relax	relajarse

Group II		
	English	**Spanish**
II-1	provide with	proporcionar
II-2	think about	pensar en
II-3	wait for	esperar
II-4	worry about	preocupar por
II-5	avoid	evitar
II-6	miss	extrañar
II-7	mind	importar
II-8	suggest	sugerir
II-9	stay	quedarse
II-10	feel	sentirse

	Group III	
	English	**Spanish**
III-1	congratulate on	felicitar por
III-2	count on	contar con
III-3	remind of	recordar a
III-4	blame for	culpar de
III-5	admit	admitir
III-6	delay	retrasar
III-7	deny	negar
III-8	regret	lamentar
III-9	oppose	oponerse
III-10	confess	confesarse

Appendix B: Stimuli Verbs in Carrier Sentences Using (a) the Native-Like Frame and (b) the Nonnative-Like Frame

I-1 (a) He will not ask for money.
    (b) He will not ask money.
I-2 (a) Your future depends on the decisions you make.
    (b) Your future depends of the decisions you make.
I-3 (a) My father never listens to me.
    (b) My father never listens me.
I-4 (a) Fred was looking at the map.
    (b) Fred was looking the map.
I-5 (a) Teresa is considering changing her job.
    (b) Teresa is considering to change her job.
I-6 (a) Robert doesn't enjoy going to school.
    (b) Robert doesn't enjoy to go to school.
I-7 (a) They finished painting their new house last month.
    (b) They finished to paint their new house last month.
I-8 (a) I always fight with my sister.
    (b) I always fight me with my sister.
I-9 (a) Sue wants to marry a rich man.
    (b) Sue wants to marry her a rich man.
I-10 (a) We relax when we walk.
    (b) We relax us when we walk.
II-1 (a) Their boss provided them with the appropriate material.
    (b) Their boss provided them the appropriate material.
II-2 (a) He'll be too busy to think about you.
    (b) He'll be too busy to think in you.
II-3 (a) I have been waiting for him for about two hours.
    (b) I have been waiting him for about two hours.

II-4 (a) She never worries about her children.
   (b) She never worries for her children.
II-5 (a) Teachers avoid having problems with their principal.
   (b) Teachers avoid to have problems with their principal.
II-6 (a) Famous people often miss living a normal life.
   (b) Famous people often miss to live a normal life.
II-7 (a) Would you mind opening the door?
   (b) Would you mind to open the door
II-8 (a) Martha has suggested going to the cinema.
   (b) Martha has suggested to go to the cinema.
II-9 (a) Martin asked me to stay at home.
   (b) Martin asked me to stay me at home.
II-10 (a) Susan often feels sad and depressed.
   (b) Susan often feels her sad and depressed.
III-1 (a) Their teacher congratulated them on their excellent grades.
   (b) Their teacher congratulated them for their excellent grades.
III-2 (a) You can count on me to help you any time.
   (b) You can count with me to help you any time.
III-3 (a) She reminds me of her sister.
   (b) She reminds me to her sister.
III-4 (a) Nobody blamed them for the accident.
   (b) Nobody blamed them of the accident.
III-5 (a) The young boy admitted taking part in the robbery.
   (b) The young boy admitted to take part in the robbery.
III-6 (a) He has delayed sending the papers again.
   (b) He has delayed to send the papers again.
III-7 (a) The secretary denies having taken the documents.
   (b) The secretary denies to have taken the documents.
III-8 (a) Anne regrets not being able to visit him on his birthday.
   (b) Anne regrets not to be able to visit him on his birthday.
III-9 (a) I have always opposed the war.
   (b) I have always opposed me the war.
III-10 (a) Has she ever confessed to a priest?
   (b) Has she ever confessed her to a priest?

Chapter 4

The Role of Working Memory in the Development of L2 Grammatical Proficiency

Clare Wright
Newcastle University, United Kingdom

Abstract

This study investigates the correlation between Working Memory (WM) capacity and individual differences in the development of L2 grammatical proficiency in an immersion setting. Adult Chinese speakers of English were tested over a ten-month period for acquisition of English question forms using timed oral and written tasks, and a battery of WM tasks. Significant differences were found between individuals' linguistic development, and between task mode (oral vs. written), and question type (subject vs. object). Positive (though non-significant) correlations were found between linguistic and WM scores, supporting the claim (Miyake & Friedman, 1998) that WM plays a role in L2 development.

Introduction

The study discussed here examines the potential interaction between WM capacity and individual variation in adult acquisition of a second language (L2), with specific reference to acquisition of English wh-questions (wh-movement) by instructed Chinese speakers of English.

Wh-movement has been long identified as an area of individual variation in morpho-syntactic proficiency in adult L2 acquisition (Johnson & Newport, 1991). WM (Baddeley, 1986, 2000) has been claimed to be 'key' to understanding such L2 variation (Miyake & Friedman, 1998), following previous investigations into connections between memory, processing and L2 acquisition (see, for example, Brown & Hulme, 1992; Lado, 1965). Robust correlations have been found between WM capacity and acquisition of L2 vocabulary, oral fluency and reading skills (Fortkamp, 1999; Harrington & Sawyer, 1992; Service, 1992). However, longitudinal research to test this claim for morphosyntactic acquisition, especially when tested orally, remains sparse, with virtually none from a generative perspective (Juffs, 2004).

This study explores some of the assumptions and methodology in current research by investigating if WM capacity is a significant factor in individual variation in rate of acquisition for CSE in an immersion environment. Two semi-longitudinal studies were carried out assessing acquisition of wh-question formation by advanced Chinese speakers of English (CSE) during study-abroad periods in the United Kingdom. Eleven participants took part in a preliminary exploratory study, presented in detail here, using a battery of innovative linguistic tests (oral and written) and WM tests. Individuals' rates of acquisition differed significantly, and patterns of asymmetry were also found between task mode (oral vs. written), and question type (subject vs. object). Positive (though non-significant) correlations between rates of L2 acquisition and WM provided some support for the research hypotheses tested here, although a number of methodological issues arose, which are being addressed in a second larger study currently being undertaken.

Theoretical and Empirical Background

English wh-question formation was identified as a source of wide individual variation in acquisition, particularly for CSE, even at advanced levels and after immersion in English (Han, 2004; Johnson & Newport, 1991; Schachter & Yip, 1990; Wright, 2006). Wh-questions require syntactic movement while Chinese lacks overt wh-movement; acquisition of the L2 linguistic knowledge to produce accurate wh-questions is seen as late acquired (Pienemann, 1998), especially for long-distance movement such as 'What did John say Mary wanted?' or constrained by subjacency, such as *'What did the book about please Mary?'

Standard generative accounts of whether CSE acquire wh-movement remain inconclusive (see, e.g. White & Genesee, 1996; Hawkins & Chan, 1997; White, 2003; Schwartz, Ma & Kim, 2008), while other accounts of wh-movement suggest that general cognitive processes explain such individual variation (Clahsen & Felser, 2006; Johnson & Newport, 1991; McDonald, 2006). The question of how input triggers acquisition of the L2 (Carroll, 2001; Sakas & Fodor, 2001; Schwartz, 1993) also remains debated. CSE have commonly been taught in an input-poor learning environment, where a traditional emphasis on explicit and written linguistic knowledge can result in wide variation between oral and written proficiency (Gu, 2003; R. Ellis, 1994), although research suggests that CSE can reach native-like competence even without exposure to native language immersion (White & Juffs, 1998). Focusing on acquisition of wh-movement should therefore provide insight into how instructed L2ers access explicitly learned structures (short-distance wh-movement, long-distance wh-movement), and structures assumed to be implicitly learned (subjacency).

The 'coalitionist' model proposed by Herschensohn (2000) is used here as a construct which allows some interface between the generative and non-generative research paradigms referred to above. In this model, Herschensohn argues 'that the L2er uses a coalition of resources' including a UG template, L1 transfer, primary linguistic data and 'instructional bootstrapping' (ibid: 220). She discusses how the language user is able to draw on both implicit and explicit knowledge about language 'presumably located outside the language module in the knowledge base' (ibid: 184–85), and accessible either, in simplified terms, via implicit procedural memory, or explicit declarative memory (Paradis, 2004; Ullman, 2001).

The assumption drawn here is that L2 users with little naturalistic L2 input, but using 'instructional bootstrapping', will initially store L2 linguistic knowledge of morphology and syntax primarily as consciously accessible or explicit knowledge. After sufficient exposure to primary linguistic data, implicit knowledge develops, subject to the UG template. Until the L2 user can utilize the quicker, more efficient but non-accessible implicit system, it is assumed that conscious access of explicit knowledge is key for the L2 user. Therefore WM, the temporary 'workspace' for conscious attention to complex tasks, will also be key to efficiently retrieving or inhibiting existing explicit knowledge and processing novel information (Smith & Kosslyn, 2007, 247).

Much of the research on WM in native language and L2 acquisition has been based on versions of Baddeley and Hitch's (1974) multi-component model. The latest model (Baddeley, 2000, 2003) posits domain-specific temporary storage via the phonological loop and the visuo-spatial sketch-pad. Domain-general attentional control and processing efficiency is through a central executive, with an episodic buffer allowing domain-general storage for more than the standard 1-2 seconds (see Figure 4.1). The episodic buffer, a new element (Baddeley, 2000), is designed to explain how novel and retrieved information can be combined and maintained, for example allowing a prose passage of around 90 seconds to be retained and repeated accurately.

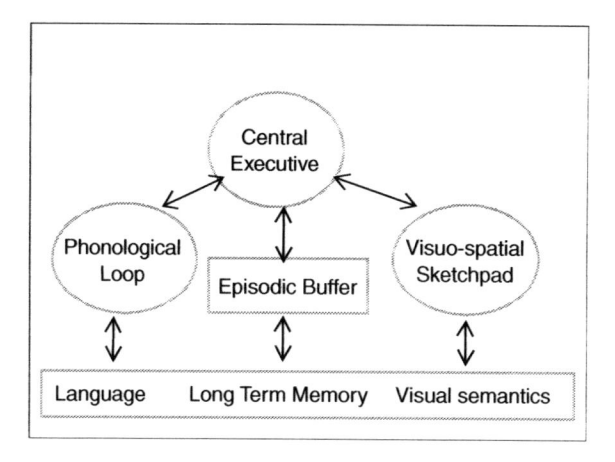

FIGURE 4.1 Baddeley's (2000) Multicomponent Model of Working Memory

WM is seen as capacity-constrained: as storage capacity reaches or exceeds its limit, processing efficiency is reduced, so greater storage capacity allows greater processing efficiency. Initial research findings using WM tests for phonological loop storage and central executive efficiency have found a robust correlation between WM and native-language (L1) proficiency (Gathercole, 2006; Gathercole & Baddeley, 1993). This robustness extends to certain aspects of L2 proficiency: for vocabulary acquisition, reading comprehension, resolving syntactic ambiguities and oral fluency (Baddeley, Gathercole & Papagno, 1998; Ellis & Sinclair, 1996; Fortkamp, 1999; Harrington & Sawyer, 1992; Miyake & Friedman, 1998; Osaka & Osaka, 1992; Service, 1992).

The evidence leads to three assumptions underpinning the current study of ways in which WM may be key to L2 acquisition even at an advanced level. The first relates to the role of WM in attentional control, where WM acts as a kind of 'bottle-neck' (Emerson, Miyake & Rettinger, 1999) through which L2 linguistic operations have to pass – the more novel the sound, or the more complex the task, the more significant the capacity of the 'bottle-neck'. For L2 users, producing target-like (or accurate) morphosyntax under pressure, such as in spontaneous speech or timed grammaticality tasks, requires conscious control over accessing explicit L2 knowledge and inhibiting L1 language patterns.

The second assumption is that the more difficult the morphosyntax (such as for long-distance wh-movement), the greater the effort in processing accurate forms. This assumption is supported by research into the role of WM in native-language complex syntax, such as assigning relative-clause reference (Miyake, Carpenter & Just, 1994) and subordination and adverbial use (Fry, 2002). Furthermore, processing difficulties are hypothesized as an explanation for individual variation in L2 (Cook, 1997; Service et al., Simola, Metsanheimo & Maury, 2002) even in generative accounts such as White and Juffs (1998), who explained evidence of variation in native-like L2 acquisition as 'implicit competence processed more slowly' (ibid: 127).

The third assumption concerns linguistic development in an immersion setting: that WM may be hypothesised to play a part in the processing of primary linguistic input, through processing novel acoustic information via the phonological loop, which may be particularly important when the amount and type of input changes in an immersion setting. For example, following this assumption, greater WM capacity would be predicted to facilitate quicker transition through developmental stages, or facilitate greater accuracy. This assumption follows psycholinguistic research into the major role played by noticing in converting input to intake (Carroll, 2001; Sagarra, 2007; Schmidt, 1990; VanPatten, 1996; VanPatten, 2005).

There is however increasing concern about the reliability and validity of commonly used WM tasks (Juffs & Rodriguez, 2006; Yoshimura, 2001), which casts doubt on the role WM can play across general L2 proficiency. The most common tasks consist of storage-only measurements (such as digit span, word span, non-word repetition) or storage plus processing measurements (such as reading span, speaking span, elicited imitation). Non-word repetition has been one of the most robust tools for correlations with L1 and L2 vocabulary learning (see Gathercole, 2006 for a recent overview). Daneman and Carpenter's (1980) Reading Span Measure (RSM) and Daneman and Green's (1986) Speaking Span Measure (SSM) have also been widely used (Harrington & Sawyer, 1992; Osaka & Osaka, 1992; Sagarra, 2000; Yoshimura, 2001 for RSM, Fortkamp, 1999; Mizera, 2006 for SSM). However, early suggestions that these storage plus processing tasks would yield strong correlations with general L2 proficiency have not been borne out in further research, and current thinking is that WM is highly task-specific: for instance, RSM may only correlate with L2 reading proficiency (Yoshimura, 2001). Other research even contradicts some of the findings suggested above (Mizera, 2006 found no relation between oral fluency and WM, unlike Fortkamp, 1999).

There is also some debate over Baddeley's multi-component model used in the L2 studies cited above (Andrade, 2001; Caplan & Waters, 1999; Cowan, 1999; Miyake & Shah, 1999). Some models of language learning (Clahsen & Felser, 2006; Craik & Lockhart, 1972) identify 'depth of processing' as the key to successful transfer of linguistic knowledge between long-term and short-term memory. Finally conceptual issues remain unresolved such as how WM might interface with different memory models for language acquisition (N. Ellis, 2005; Jackendoff, 1997; Schmidt, 1994; Skehan, 1998), and how WM is separable from general processing constraints in L2 (Clahsen & Felser, 2006; Cook, 1997; Juffs, 2004; Sagarra, 2007). Nevertheless, Baddeley's model remains the most widely used for researching WM in language acquisition and is thus the basis for this study.

Methodology

Study Design and Participants

To investigate the conceptual and methodological issues raised above, a semi-longitudinal study was designed to test for positive correlations between WM and L2 variation in acquisition by adult Chinese speakers of English during a study-abroad period. Two research hypotheses were addressed:

i. Immersion facilitates acquisition of wh-movement
ii. WM correlates with development of wh-movement in an immersion environment.

Linguistic data was collected at Time 1 (within two months of arrival) and at Time 2 (after nine to ten months' immersion). WM data was collected at Time

1 and at Time 2. Since a directional correlation was assumed between WM and linguistic development, only WM scores from Time 1 were used in the analysis reported here.

Eleven advanced adult speakers of English, with Mandarin Chinese as L1, were recruited from a cohort of newly arrived postgraduates at UK universities[1]. All were instructed learners with no previous immersion exposure, with a minimum IELTS score of 5.5 in the previous four months. The group consisted of three participants from Taiwan, and eight from Mainland China; there were four males and seven females. Bio-data on learning background and exposure to input were gathered, to test for inter-learner variation in exposure to English prior to immersion (Dornyei, 2003), and no significant differences were found.

Linguistic Data Collection

Linguistic data were collected using two time-constrained tests of oral and written proficiency in question formation: a guided oral question and answer 2-way gap fill task (Task 1), and a written grammaticality judgement task (Task 2), adapted from White and Juffs (1998).

Task 1: Oral Production (OP)

Task 1 measured question forms produced in a seven-minute dialogue to complete a picture of a party scene. Following a commonly accepted hierarchy of acquisition (e.g., Pienemann, 1998), question forms produced by the participants were divided into two groups: Group 1 (formulaic chunks, intonation only, question word fronting without head movement and copula fronting), and Group 2 (head movement and 'do'-support, cancelling inversion in embedded clauses), such as 'Will he come later?', 'What did the girl eat?', 'Can you tell me when the boy arrived?'.

Target-like (native-like) production of questions from Group 2 were taken to imply acquisition of wh-movement. The total number of utterances was also measured for evidence of task avoidance (Schachter, 1974). The total number of Group 2 questions was then divided by the total number of utterances during the seven-minute test to produce an OP score.

Task 2: Grammaticality Judgement (GJ)

A written task (Task 2) was also used in view of the difficulty in analysing oral data of untangling 'performance noise' from underlying competence (Murphy, 1997). Task 2, based on White and Juffs (1998), asked for graded judgements (using a Likert scale of −3 to +3) of grammatical acceptability on complex question forms, derived from the party scene used in the first task. Scoring was calculated for native-like accuracy on 22 tokens of subject and object long-distance movement questions and subjacency violations (10 ungrammatical and 12 grammatical tokens). Examples of ungrammatical tokens are given below:

(1) *Who did Tom expect give the present?   *Subject*
(2) *What did John know did Ann like?   *Object*
(3) *What did Tom bring a present after he sent?   *Subjacency* *

Working Memory Data Collection

In line with current best practice in testing WM (see, e.g., Conway et al. 2005), a battery of tasks was used: a non-verbal task (Digits Back), and two innovative verbal tasks, designed for this study (Story Recall, and a combined Word Span and Sentence Span task).

Task A: Digits Back (DB L1, DB L2)

The first task, Digits Back, was chosen as being widely used (Waters & Caplan, 2003), and therefore providing a reliable benchmark, easy to administer, and unrelated to linguistic proficiency (since advanced learners would all be familiar with the English digit names). It would also provide a cross-linguistic comparison between individuals' scores in Mandarin and English, in the light of research showing differences between Digit Span scores in Mandarin and other languages (e.g. Chincotta & Underwood, 1997).[2] This would shed further light into investigations as to how far WM is language-independent (Osaka & Osaka, 1992) or affected by differences in L2 processing (Cook, 1997; Service et al., 2002). Participants heard sets of numbers, increasing in length from four to seven, read out at a rate of one digit per second (two strings per set) first in English and later in Mandarin. After each string, participants repeated the numbers in reverse order. Scoring was calculated following an 'all or nothing' score, using the length of the set where two strings were last recalled correctly (Conway et al. 2005: 774).

Task B: Story Recall (SR L1, SR L2)

Task B was created to address the issue of how to test newer models of the WM construct, in particular Baddeley's episodic buffer for which virtually no research on L2 WM has yet been published.[3]

The Story Recall task devised for this study was based on standard psychology tests (see, e.g., Coughlan & Hollows, 1985), which measures the accuracy in recalling prose passages of over 30 seconds in length. This test had been identified as correlating with use of complex syntax such as subordinate clauses and adverbial phrases in native language research (Fry, 2002). The purpose of using the task in this study was to assess whether it was also a reliable, valid means of testing WM in L2, and if WM as measured by such a test correlated with the use of complex question formation.

The original Coughlan and Hollows test was adapted and translated into Mandarin (lasting 54 seconds). A different story in English (with similar schematic structure) was devised by the researcher (lasting 33 seconds). The length of the L2 was shortened to avoid possible 'floor effects' due to task difficulty (Harrington & Sawyer, 1992: 28). Two bilingual raters worked with the researcher in scoring the Mandarin data to ensure scoring reliability. Scoring for the task (SR) was out of 50 for accurate recall of morpho-syntactic and semantic elements.

Task C: Word Span and Sentence Span (WS, SS)

Task C was adapted from Daneman and Carpenter's (1980) Listening Span task. It was devised to examine the offset between storage and processing through the combined testing of phonological short-term storage (Word Span) and central executive capacity (Sentence Span), using a direction-based task.

Pairs of directions using the words 'left', 'right', 'up' or 'down' were created, increasing by one in each pair from five to twelve words. An example pair of sentences is given in (4) below.

(4) (i) Walk **up** the street until the lights. (length: 7 words)
 (ii) Take the second turn on the **left**.

Participants heard, then repeated, both strings; the repetition provided a secondary processing task. Scoring, like the Digits Back test, was a 'quasi-absolute' score given here in percentage form, indexing two measures. The score for Sentence Span (SS) was the longest sentence length (measured in number of words out of 12) when direction words were correctly recalled. The score for Word Span (WS) was the longest sentence length when all the words in the sentence were correctly recalled. Due to limitations of time, this task was only done in English (L2).

Results

All the scores for linguistic and WM data were encoded using SPSS, and converted to percentage scores shown here, for ease of comparison across all tasks. Non-parametric statistical tests were used, given the small sample size ($n = 11$).

The minimum, maximum and mean scores on linguistic and WM tasks at Time 1 and linguistic tasks at Time 2 are shown in Tables 4.1 and 4.2. Wilcoxon signed rank tests of difference were performed to check for significant differences between the linguistic scores at the two different test times, and for inter-language differences in the WM tasks in Mandarin and English. Tests of difference on the linguistic tasks showed that the two OP scores were not significantly different ($p > .05$), but that the GJ scores were significantly different ($p = .007$). Tests of difference for the WM tasks comparing L1 and L2 showed that the DB scores were not significantly different ($p > .01$) but the SR scores were significantly different ($p = .005$).

Individuals' linguistic scores at Time 2 were then correlated with WM across all tasks, using Spearman's rho to test for evidence of positive correlation in line with the second research hypothesis that WM would affect linguistic development during immersion. The correlations were not significant for any of the tests, although there were moderate positive correlations between SS and OP ($r = .32$) and GJ ($r = .28$). The results are shown in Table 4.3.

The lack of significant findings initially appear to provide poor support for the research hypotheses tested here. However, on closer examination of the results, it was clear that using a simple group mean score at Time 2 obscured unexpected and more interesting individual variation in patterns of linguistic development between Time 1 and Time 2. The data were therefore assessed to show individuals' linguistic development over the time of the study, that is, how much individuals' linguistic scores showed a change (either negative or positive). Individuals' changes in GJ scores (Task 2) were further analysed

Table 4.1 Linguistic data scores

Linguistic Scores by Task	Minimum	Maximum	Mean
OP Time 1	0	27	9
OP Time 2	8	31	19
GJ Time 1	18	46	37
GJ Time 2	36	68	50

Table 4.2 WM data scores

Working Memory Scores	Minimum	Maximum	Mean
DB L1	77	100	91
DB L2	57	86	79
SR L1	64	96	81
SR L2	14	62	44
Word Span	42	83	61
Sentence Span	42	100	75

Table 4.3 Correlation of linguistic and WM scores

	DBL1	DBL2	SRL1	SRL2	WS	SS
OP Time 2	−0.02	−0.09	0.13	0.04	0.14	0.32
Sig.	0.96	0.80	0.72	0.91	0.68	0.34
GJ Time 2	0.28	0.23	0.12	0.19	0.25	0.28
Sig.	0.41	0.53	0.73	0.59	0.46	0.41

Table 4.4 Variation in linguistic development

	Minimum	Maximum	Mean
Change in OP	−25	22	4
Change in GJ	−1	23	10
Change in objects (GJ)	−10	50	17
Change in subjects (GJ)	−30	50	5

Table 4.5 Correlation of variation in linguistic development and WM scores

	DB L1	SR L1	SR L2	WS	SS
Change OP	0.43	0.33	0.14	−0.01	0.27
Sig.	0.19	0.35	0.69	0.98	0.42
Change obj	0.01	−0.13	−0.06	−0.37	−0.38
Sig.	0.97	0.71	0.87	0.26	0.25
Change sub	0.30	0.45	**0.60**	0.13	−0.05
Sig.	0.38	0.20	**0.05**	0.69	0.87

by question type, yielding a significant subject-object asymmetry ($p = .003$). Results are shown shown in Table 4.4 (in percentage terms, as for the earlier results).

These scores were then correlated with WM scores to see more precisely if WM scores at Time 1 showed a positive correlation with the degree of change in both tasks, and by question type in Task 2. No significant results were found for the change in grammaticality judgements (GJ, Task 2): all correlations were negative except for Digits Back in L1 ($r = .23$, $p > .005$); in addition, no significant results were found for Digits Back in L2. Therefore, results for changes in GJ and DB L2 are not shown here, However, positive correlations were found for change in oral production (OP, Task 1), and asymmetric correlations were found with changes in subject and object grammaticality judgements (GJ, Task 2. These results are shown in Table 4.5.

There was one significant correlation between the change in subject accuracy and Story Recall in L2 (p = .05), shown in Table 4.5 in bold.

Discussion

There were no clear patterns of either linguistic development or of significant correlation between linguistic and WM tasks, so there is no robust support for the research hypotheses that immersion would facilitate acquisition and that WM would correlate with linguistic development during immersion.

The first general conclusion is that immersion for nine months was not long enough to trigger significant development across the whole group, as evident from the unexpected wide range of individual variation; indeed four out of eleven participants showed negative scores for their linguistic development in both oral and written tasks. However, the evidence of significant subject-object asymmetry (found also by Schachter & Yip, 1990 and White & Juffs, 1998) indicates that linguistic development may occur at different rates, not just by individual but by linguistic phenomenon. Further research using more fine-grained measures of linguistic development would be able to test this suggestion.

Second, the different WM task scores revealed little consistency; DB and SR did not correlate across language, suggesting they may be language-dependent (contrary to Osaka & Osaka, 1992) and there were no significant correlations between the tasks, suggesting that WM tasks are also task-dependent (as found by Yoshimura, 2001). However, the innovative nature of the verbal WM tasks (SR, WS and SS) may have made them difficult to compare with other WM studies using the standard Daneman and Carpenter (1980) test.

Third, the different WM tasks showed no consistent pattern of correlation with either oral or written linguistic data. The strongest positive correlations (although not significant) were found between the oral data (OP) and WM, ranging from r = –0.01 to r = .43. Given that OP was tested in an online task, and WM is hypothesised to relate to managing complex online or pressured tasks (Baddeley, 2003, Sagarra, 2007), this finding was as expected. The strongest correlations were for WM tested in L1, thought to be a 'purer' measure of WM, not confounded by issues of L2 language proficiency (Service et al. 2002) and thus supporting the general assumption that WM capacity plays a role in L2. There was a significant strong correlation between SR L2 and change in subject question accuracy (r = .60, p = 0.05) in the offline written grammaticality judgement task (GJ), offering some evidence that WM capacity affects L2 even in less pressured tasks. However, another, linguistic, explanation could be that L2 proficiency at the GJ task may help L2 performance in the SR task. The subject-object asymmetry could be explained by differences in processing subject extraction compared with objects, as suggested by White and Juffs (1998). Further more fine-grained data collection to include processing information (such as using a reaction time test) would allow this suggestion to be tested.

In addition to the points identified above, the study was also affected by a number of methodological issues. First, the small group size reduced the likelihood of significant findings; in addition, the drop out of participants meant that the original interview pairings for the oral task (Task 1) at Time 1 were not exactly replicated at Time 2; furthermore, limiting the scoring from Task 1 to only full lexical wh-questions produced very small numbers of raw data. Second, the design of the Word Span and Sentence Span, trying to measure both phonological storage and executive control in a single test, could have undermined the reliability of the test design. Additionally, the 'quasi-absolute' scoring system is no longer seen as the optimal scoring system (Conway et al. 2005), particularly for such small groups, whereas a 'partial' scoring system which takes account of more individual variation in results, is seen as more valid.

In order to address these issues, a second larger study has been devised, with more participants ($n = 30$). The GJ task has been redesigned as a computer-based RT task (DMDX) to allow for greater precision on patterns of processing of different types of wh-movement, including subject and object extraction. The WM listening span task and scoring have been redesigned to fit more closely with existing WM methodology. The study is still ongoing, although initial analysis of the reaction time data from the first point of collection (Time 1) replicates the significant difference in accuracy on subject-object judgements ($p = .004$) found in the first study. Data from Time 2 is anticipated to show how far WM may play a role in individual variation in improvements in oral output, and in faster and more accurate RT scores.

Conclusion

The exploratory nature of the preliminary study discussed here revealed evidence of patterns of individual variation in acquisition of English wh-questions, but also evidence of different patterns of processing in different modes (oral vs. written) and for different types (subject vs. object extraction). The unexpectedly wide range of individual variation in development during immersion and the cross-task variation in WM scores did not provide a robust basis for the hypotheses tested here that WM would correlate with linguistic development during immersion. The theoretical and methodological limitations of the preliminary study are being addressed in a second study, in order to contribute further to our understanding of the L2 user's 'coalition of resources' (Herschensohn, 2000), of the complex interface between input and memory and how WM is involved in the process of second language acquisition.

Notes

[1] Thirty participants were originally recruited, but only eleven remained throughout the length of the study, so I only refer to their data here.

[2] Referring to the greater speed with which Chinese single syllable digits can be spoken in comparison to, say, English.

[3] Fehringer and Fry (2007) tested story recall on bilingual and near-native L2 speakers of German and English; I am grateful to the authors for permission to adapt their story recall test for this study. However, I am unaware of any research using such a task for Mandarin L1.

References

Andrade, J. (Ed.) (2001). *Working memory in perspective.* Hove: Psychology Press.

Baddeley, A. (1986). *Working memory.* Oxford: Clarendon Press.

Baddeley, A. (2000). The episodic buffer: A new component of working memory? *Trends in Cognitive Sciences,* 4, 417–23.

Baddeley, A. (2003). Working memory and language: An overview. *Journal of Communications Disorders,* 36, 189–208.

Baddeley, A., Gathercole, S., & Papagno, C. (1998). The phonological loop as a language learning device. *Psychological Review,* 105, 158–73.

Baddeley, A., & Hitch, G. (1974). Working memory. In G. Bower (Ed.). *The psychology of learning and motivation* (pp. 47–89). New York: Academic Press.

Brown, G., & Hulme, C. (1992). Cognitive processing and second language processing: The role of short term memory. In R. Harris (Ed.). *Cognitive processing in bilinguals* (pp. 105–21). Amsterdam: Elsevier.

Caplan, D., & Waters, G. (1999). Verbal working memory and sentence comprehension. *Behavioral and Brain Sciences,* 22(1), 77–94.

Carroll, S. (2001). *Input and Evidence.* Amsterdam: John Benjamins.

Chincotta, D., & Underwood, G. (1997). Digit span and articulatory suppression: a cross-linguistic comparison. *European Journal of Cognitive Psychology,* 9, 89–96.

Clahsen, H., & Felser, C. (2006). Grammatical processing in language learners. *Applied Psycholinguistics,* 27, 3–42.

Conway, A., Kane, M., Bunting, M., Hambrick, D., Wilhelm, O., & Engle, R. (2005). Working memory span tasks: A methodological review and user's guide. *Psychonomic Bulletin and Review,* 12, 769–86.

Cook, V. (1997). The consequences of bilingualism for cognitive processing. In A. de Groot, & J. Kroll (Eds.). *Tutorials in bilingualism: psycholinguistic perspectives* (pp. 279–300). Mahwah, NJ: Lawrence Erlbaum.

Coughlan, A., & Hollows, S. (1985). *The Adult Memory and Information Processing Battery (AMIPB) Test Manual.* Leeds: A K Coughlan.

Cowan, N. (1999). An embedded-processes model of working memory. In A. Mikaye, & P. Shah (Eds.). *Models of working memory* (pp. 62–101). Cambridge: Cambridge University Press.

Craik, F., & Lockhart, R. (1972). Levels of processing: A framework for memory research. *Journal of Verbal Learning and Verbal Behavior*, 11, 671–84.
Daneman, M., & Carpenter, P. (1980). Individual differences in working memory and reading. *Journal of Verbal Learning and Verbal Behavior*, 19, 450–66.
Daneman, M., & Green, I. (1986). Individual differences in comprehending and producing words in context. *Journal of Memory and Language*, 25, 1–18.
Dornyei, Z. (2003). *Questionnaires in second language research*. Mahwah, NJ: Lawrence Erlbaum.
Ellis, N. (1994). *Implicit and explicit learning of languages*. London: Academic Press.
Ellis, N. (2005). At the interface: Dynamic interactions of explicit and implicit language knowledge. *Studies in Second Language Acquisition*, 27, 305–52.
Ellis, N., & Sinclair, S. (1996). Working memory in the acquisition of vocabulary and syntax: putting language in good order. *Quarterly Journal of Experimental Psychology*, 49A, 234–50.
Ellis, R. (1994). *The Study of Second Language Acquisition*. Oxford, Oxford University Press.
Emerson, M., Miyake, A., & Rettinger, D. (1999). Individual differences in integrating and coordinating multiple sources of information. *Journal of Experimental Psychology: Learning, Memory and Cognition*, 25, 1300–21.
Fehringer, C., & Fry, C. (2007). Frills, furbelows and activated memory: Syntactically optional elements in the spontaneous language production of bilingual speakers. *Language Sciences*, 29, 497–574.
Fortkamp, M. (1999). Working memory capacity and aspects of L2 speech production. *Communication and Cognition*, 32, 259–95.
Fry, C. (2002). Language complexity, working memory and social intelligence. Unpublished PhD thesis, Newcastle University, Newcastle, UK.
Gathercole, S. (2006). Nonword repetition and word learning: The nature of the relationship. *Applied Psycholinguistics*, 27, 513–43.
Gathercole, S., & Baddeley, A. (1993). *Working memory and language*. Hillsdale, NJ: Lawrence Erlbaum.
Gu, Y. (2003). Fine brush and freehand: The vocabulary-learning art of two successful Chinese EFL learners. *TESOL Quarterly*, 37, 73–10.
Han, Z. (2004). *Fossilisation in adult second language acquisition*. Clevedon: Multilingual Matters.
Harrington, M., & Sawyer, M. (1992). L2 working memory and L2 reading skill. *Studies in Second Language Acquisition*, 14, 25–38.
Hawkins, R. (2001). *Second language syntax*. Oxford: Blackwell.
Hawkins, R., & Chan, C. (1997). The partial availability of Universal Grammar in second language acquisition. *Second Language Research*, 13, 187–226.
Herschensohn, J. (2000). *The second time around: minimalism and L2 Acquisition*. Amsterdam: John Benjamins.
Jackendoff, R. (1997). *The architecture of the language faculty*. Cambridge, MA: MIT Press.
Johnson, J., & Newport, E. (1991). Critical period effects on universal properties of language: The status of subjacency in the acquisition of a second language. *Cognition*, 39, 215–58.
Juffs, A. (2004). Representation, processing and working memory in a second language. *Transactions of the Philological Society*, 102, 199–225.

Juffs, A., & Rodriguez, G. (2006). Second language sentence processing and working memory in college-educated and low-educated learners of English as a second language. *EuroSLA Conference*, Antalya, Turkey.

Lado, R. (1965). Memory span as a factor in second language learning. *International Review of Applied Linguistics*, 3, 123–9.

McDonald, J. (2006). Beyond the critical period: Processing-based explanations for poor grammaticality judgment performance by late second language learners. *Journal of Memory and Language*, 55, 381–401.

Miyake, A., Carpenter, P., & Just, M. (1994). Working memory constraints on the resolution of lexical ambiguity. *Journal of Memory and Language*, 33, 175–202.

Miyake, A., & Friedman, N. (1998). Individual differences in second language proficiency: Working memory as language aptitude. In A. Healy, & L. Bourne (Eds.). *Foreign language learning* (pp. 339–64). Mahwah, NJ: Lawrence Erlbaum.

Miyake, A., & Shah, P. (Eds.). (1999). *Models of working memory*. Cambridge: Cambridge University Press.

Mizera, G. (2006). Working memory and L2 oral fluency. (Unpublished PhD thesis), University of Pittsburgh.

Murphy, V. (1997). The effect of modality on a grammaticality judgement task. *Second Language Research*, 13, 34–65.

Osaka, M., & Osaka, N. (1992). Language-independent working memory as measured by Japanese and English reading span tests. *Bulletin of the Psychonomic Society*, 30, 287–9.

Paradis, M. (2004). *A neurolinguistic theory of bilingualism*. Amsterdam/Philadelphia: John Benjamins.

Pienemann, M. (1998). *Language processing and second-language development: processability theory*. Amsterdam, John Benjamins.

Sagarra, N. (2000). The longitudinal role of working memory on adult acquisition of L2 grammar. *Dissertation Abstracts International*, A (Humanities and Social Sciences), 61 (5).

Sagarra, N. (2007). Working Memory and L2 processing of redundant grammatical forms. In Z. Han, E. S. Park, A. Revesz, C. Combs, & J. H. Kim (Eds.). *Understanding second language process* (pp. 133–47). Clevedon: Multilingual Matters.

Sakas, W., & Fodor, J. (2001). The structural triggers learner. In S. Bertolo (Ed.). *Language acquisition and learnability* (pp. 172–233). Cambridge: Cambridge University Press.

Schachter, J. (1974). An error in error analysis. *Language Learning*, 24, 205–14.

Schachter, J., & Yip, V. (1990). Why does anyone object to subject extraction? *Studies in Second Language Acquisition*, 12, 379–92.

Schmidt, R. (1990). The role of consciousness in second language learning. *Applied Linguistics*, 11, 129–58.

Schmidt, R. (1994). Implicit learning and the cognitive unconscious: Of artificial grammars and SLA. In N. Ellis (Ed.). *Implicit and explicit learning of languages* (pp. 165–210). London, Academic Press.

Schwartz, B. (1993). On explicit and negative data effecting and affecting competence and linguistic behaviour. *Studies in Second Language Acquisition*, 15, 147–63.

Schwartz, B., Ma, J., & Kim, J. (2008). Island sensitivity in development: L2 adults, L2 children and L2 youths. Third Newcastle University Postgraduate Conference in Theoretical and Applied Linguistics, Newcastle upon Tyne, UK.

Service, E. (1992). Phonology, working memory, and foreign language learning. *Quarterly Journal of Experimental Psychology A*, 45 (1), 21–50.

Service, E., Simola, M., Metsanheimo, O., & Maury, S. (2002). Bilingual working memory span is affected by language skill. *European Journal of Cognitive Psychology*, 14 (3), 383–408.

Skehan, P. (1998). *A cognitive approach to learning language*. Oxford: Oxford University Press.

Smith, E., & Kosslyn, S. (2007). *Cognitive Psychology: Mind and Brain*. New York: Prentice Hall.

Ullman, M. (2001). The neural basis of lexicon and grammar in first and second language: The declarative/procedural model. *Bilingualism: Language and Cognition*, 4, 105–22.

VanPatten, B. (1996). *Input processing and grammar instruction: Theory and research*. Norwood, NJ: Ablex.

VanPatten, B. (2005). Processing instruction. In C. Sanz (Ed.), *Mind and Context in Adult Second Language Acquisition* (pp. 267–81). Washington, DC: Georgetown University Press.

Waters, G., & Caplan, D. (2003). The reliability and stability of verbal working memory measures. *Behavior Research Methods, Instruments and Computers*, 35(4), 550–64.

White, L. (2003). *Second language acquisition and universal grammar*. Cambridge: Cambridge University Press.

White, L., & Genesee, F. (1996). How native is near native? The issue of ultimate attainment in adult second language acquisition. *Second Language Research*, 11, 233–65.

White, L., & Juffs, A. (1998). Constraints on wh-movement in two different contexts of nonnative language acquisition: Competence and processing. In S. Flynn, G. Martohardjono, & W. O'Neil (Eds.). *The generative study of second language acquisition* (pp. 111–29). Mahwah, NJ: Lawrence Erlbaum.

Wright, C. (2006). Is interlanguage variation in complex CP structures predictable? *Proceedings of the Fourth University of Cambridge–Postgraduate Conference in Language Research*, 277284.

Yoshimura, Y. (2001). The role of working memory in language aptitude. In X. Bonch-Bruevich, W. Crawford, J. Hellerman, C. Higgins, & H. Nguyen (Eds.). *Second Language Research Forum* (pp. 144–63). Somerville, MA: Cascadilla Press.

Part Two

Factors Contributing to the Attainment of L2 Proficiency

Chapter 5

Statistical Learning and Innate Knowledge in the Development of Second Language Proficiency: Evidence From the Acquisition of Gender Concord

Roger Hawkins
University of Essex, United Kingdom

Abstract

Empirical studies show that adult second language (L2) learners are unconsciously sensitive to statistical properties of input, such as frequency of forms. Such properties have typically not figured in 'nativist' accounts of L2 proficiency. One potential challenge for nativist accounts is explaining pervasive optionality in the use by L2 speakers of morphological variants of the same form (e.g. the *le* vs *la* definite article contrast in French, or the *rojo* vs *roja* 'red' adjective contrast in Spanish). This chapter considers two accounts of such optionality. On the basis of evidence from a study of the L2 acquisition of Dutch noun-adjective gender concord by Blom, Polišenská and Weerman (2008), it is argued that statistical properties of input do play a role.

Introduction: The Standard View of the Role of Input in Generative Theories of Second Language Development

A number of empirical studies have shown that adults who learn new languages are sensitive, at an unconscious level, to statistical properties of new linguistic input such as the 'transitional probabilities' that hold between syllables, and the frequency with which discrete units recur. Here are two examples illustrating these findings. Saffran, Newport and Aslin (1996) played English-speaking adult informants a continuous stream of syllables from an artificial mini-language that they had not encountered before, for example:

(1) bi-da-ku-pa-do-ti-go-la-bu

The stream of syllables was produced by a speech synthesizer, imitating a female voice. Unknown to participants, the stream consisted of random combinations of four, three-syllable 'words' that had been established in advance: *bidaku, padoti, tupiro* and *golabu*. After 21 minutes, participants were presented with a randomized set of these words mixed up with 'non-word' sequences of syllables such as *da-ku-pa and *ku-pa-do, and were asked to decide which sequences were 'words' from the language they had just heard. Participants showed a significant preference for the 'words' over the non-words. Saffran et al. (1996) interpret these results to indicate that adults are sensitive to the probability with which one syllable will follow another in the linguistic experience they encounter. For example, in the stream of syllables they heard, only *da* can follow *bi*, and only *ku* can follow *da* (because *da* is the central syllable in *bidaku*), whereas *bi* can be preceded by any of *ti, ro, bu* and *ku* can be followed by any of *pa, tu, go*. Adults are sensitive to the probability of one syllable following or preceding another, and compute these probabilities very rapidly to identify recurring discrete units ('words') in the input they encounter. The ability to compute such statistical properties in input may well be an important element in the identification of morphemes in continuous speech in newly encountered 'real' languages, and appears to be an ability that persists beyond childhood.

A second example, this time of adults' sensitivity to the frequency of forms in input, is provided in a study by Hudson Kam and Newport (1999). These researchers asked four groups of native speakers of English each to learn an artificial mini language. These languages contained article-like elements that were attached as suffixes to nouns. For one group of participants, every noun was marked with an article, but for the other three groups articles attached to nouns in different proportions: 45 per cent of nouns were marked for one group, 60 per cent for the second group and 75 per cent for the third. Crucially, there were no detectable semantic, morphological or phonological cues to the distribution of these articles; that is, the only cue to distribution was frequency. Hudson Kam and Newport found that in a post-treatment production task, most of the participants supplied articles in the same proportion that they had encountered them, suggesting that adult language learners unconsciously 'tally' the frequency of forms that they encounter in input.

The sensitivity of adult learners to the statistical properties of linguistic input plays a central role in some theories of second language acquisition (SLA). 'Emergentist' or 'usage-based' approaches see the ability of language learners to identify and extract patterns from the input they are exposed to as the key element of learning:

> Acquisition of grammar is the piecemeal learning of many thousands of constructions and the frequency-biased abstraction of regularities that emerge from learners' lifetime analysis of the distributional characteristics of the language input. (Ellis, 2002: 144)

By contrast, in generative ('nativist') approaches to SLA, the statistical properties of input have typically not been considered of much interest. Generative approaches assume that learners have pre-existing knowledge of possible properties that human languages encode. This is Universal Grammar (UG). UG guides language learners' interpretation of raw linguistic experience. The role that input plays in language development from this perspective is in providing key data (or even a single datum) that triggers the activation of an innately determined linguistic category to which those data (and all similar subsequent data) are assigned. To illustrate the triggering function of input, consider the example of the second language (L2) acquisition of English articles.

Ionin and colleagues (Ionin, Ko & Wexler, 2004; Ionin, Zubizarreta & Bautista Maldonado, 2008) argue that UG provides just two options for article interpretation: definiteness (a value realized by articles in English, French, Spanish, for example) and specificity (a value realized in Samoan). They then investigate knowledge of English articles by two groups of speakers of first languages (L1s) that lack articles, Russian and Korean, using a multiple choice selection task where participants had to decide which of *a*, *the* or Ø was appropriate in sentences like (2):

(2) a. Beth is having dinner with – *girl* from her class. Her name is Angie.
    b. Peter played with – *little friend* yesterday. I don't know who it was.

For native speakers, *a* is the expected choice in both these contexts because the references to *girl* and *little friend* are the first mention of the people in question, and are unknown to the interlocutor to whom the sentences are addressed. In other words, the meaning of the nominal constituent in each case is indefinite. However, (2a) differs from (2b) in specificity: *girl* in (2a) is specific because the speaker of the sentence identifies her as a specific member of Beth's class; *little friend* in (2b) is non-specific because the speaker does not identify a particular member of the set of Peter's friends. Ionin et al. (2008) found that intermediate proficiency English speakers in their sample had constructed grammars for the English articles that were sensitive to both definiteness and specificity (unlike the grammars of native speakers, where articles only encode definiteness). Consider the choices made by 10 L1 Russian speakers on items like those in (2), illustrated in Table 5.1.

Table 5.1 Russian L1 intermediate proficiency L2 speakers of English ($N = 10$); article choice in sentences like (2a) and (2b)

	a(%)	the(%)
Sentence 2a	72	27
Sentence 2b	95	3

These results show that the Russian speakers are more likely to choose *the* in indefinite specific contexts than in indefinite non-specific contexts (and this difference was statistically significant). In other words, they are allowing *the* to have both a definite and an indefinite specific meaning.

These findings suggest that L2 learners of English who lack articles in their L1s are not simply creating a grammar for English articles that is based on input, because input should tell them that only definiteness is relevant for English article interpretation, not specificity. Rather, they appear to have created grammars that reflect the two linguistic categories provided by UG: definiteness and specificity. The function of input has been to activate these two categories.

This example shows that from a generative perspective input is essential for activating properties of UG which are then linked to and categorize that input. Statistical properties of input have not been regarded as playing any role in this process. In this case, the fact that *the* may be more frequent than *a* has typically been considered irrelevant for understanding how learners establish the interpretation to be assigned to *the/a*.

An Explanatory Problem for Generative Theories of Second Language Development: Pervasive Optionality

In an ideal world, the input-triggering perspective of generative theories of SLA predicts that once a category of UG has been activated by input, the link between the two will be stable. For example, once English input has triggered the requirement in L2 grammars for count singular nouns to have an overt determiner, then whenever a count singular noun is used, some form of determiner should be supplied. Once L2 learners are producing sentences like (3a–b), they should not produce sentences like (3c):

(3) a. Beth is having dinner with **a girl** from her class
    b. Beth is having dinner with **the girl** from her class
    c. *Beth is having dinner with **girl** from her class

However, a robust and often-repeated observation about L2 speech and writing is that speakers use forms optionally where they are categorical for native speakers, and where there appears to be triggering evidence in input for the obligatoriness of the property. In the case of English articles, White (2003) has shown that a Turkish speaker (Turkish lacks articles) with ten years of immersion in English always uses articles to mark definiteness and not specificity (hence has gone beyond the stage of 'fluctuating' shown by the intermediate proficiency Russian speakers in Table 5.1), but omits definite articles in obligatory contexts in 26.5 per cent of cases, and indefinite articles in 40.25 per cent of cases (based on Table 8 in White, 2003: 136). Such cases are a challenge for explanation within a generative theory of L2 development. If input has triggered the selection of a Determiner category in an L2 speaker's mental grammar, and the appropriate semantic value for the meaning of articles has also been triggered (definiteness rather than specificity), then why does that speaker fail to supply articles where they are categorically required in the grammars of native speakers?

Two possible approaches to answering this question will be described below, in relation to the specific case of optionality in the marking of *gender concord between determiners, adjectives and nouns* in languages that mark a grammatical gender distinction (French, Spanish and Dutch). First, consider an illustration of optionality in the production of gender concord from an L2 speaker of Canadian French (with L1 English). French has a grammatical gender system with two categories: masculine and feminine. Nouns are necessarily assigned to one category or the other. Determiners and adjectives generally take different forms depending on whether they co-occur with a masculine or feminine noun. The example is from a transcript of the speech of one of the informants in a study by Bazergui, Connors, Lenoble and Majkrak (1990) of a group of informants who had been learning French for 12 years, and as part of that had undergone a 'late-immersion' programme where half of the high school curriculum was taught in French. The informants were therefore of relatively advanced proficiency. They were asked to watch and then describe (in conversation with a Francophone interviewer) an animated film. The film showed a war between geometric shapes (squares, spheres and triangles) which resulted in the squares and spheres merging into octagons.

(4) *Sample of speech from Anglophone participant 4 describing an animated film (Bazergui et al. 1990).*

il y a **une** balle qui vient . . . **la** balle il comprend pas . . . et on fait **une** guerre . . . [maintenant ils ont] **la** même forme . . . **une** carré qui a tombé sur son tête – sur **sa** tête . . . il est **le** même forme . . . et lui faire **la** même forme . . . les carrés sont comme **une** mur . . . **le** même chose que dans **le** film, je pense . . . je veux faire **la** même chose, je pense . . . **le** carré a réalisé que . . . les deux équipes pensent **le** même chose . . . [1]

The dots . . . indicate material from the transcript that has been omitted for expository purposes.

In terms of concord between the gender of the nouns and the form of the determiner in this brief transcript, there are three kinds of patterns:

Target concord: *une balle-la balle* (f) 'a ball-the ball', *une guerre* (f) 'a war', *sa tête* (f) 'his head', *le film* (m) 'the film'.

Non-target concord: *une mur* 'a wall' (*mur* is masculine, but co-occurs with a feminine determiner).

Optional concord: *la même forme-le même forme* 'the same shape' (*forme* is feminine), *une carré-le carré* 'a square-the square' (*carré* is masculine), *le même chose-la même chose* 'the same thing' (*chose* is feminine).

Optionality in the marking of gender concord between nouns and determiners/adjectives by L2 speakers appears not to be random, however. Typically they use one form of determiner/adjective in a target-like way, restricting it only to nouns that have that gender. The other form, however, is overgeneralized. For example, a typical pattern in L2 French is a speaker who uses *la* (the feminine form of the definite article) only with feminine nouns, but uses *le* (the masculine form of the definite article) both with masculine and feminine nouns. This would produce the pattern in (5a), rather than the random pattern of (5b) (using nouns from the transcript (4) to illustrate).

(5) a. la balle (f), la chose (f), le carré (m), le mur (m), *le balle (f), *le chose (f)
    b. la balle (f), la chose (f), *la carré (m), le mur (m), *le balle (f), le carré (m)

The problem posed for generative theories of SLA by non-random optionality of this kind in the speech or writing of L2 speakers is that French input appears to provide categorical triggering evidence for stable concord, of the kind illustrated in (6), where a noun of gender [α] selects a determiner of morphological form [α], and a noun of gender [β] selects a determiner of morphological form [β]:

(6) N[α] → determiner of morphological form [α]
    N[β] → determiner of morphological form [β]

Given such input, if concord between nouns and determiners/adjectives is a property provided by UG, and L2 speakers' grammars are UG-derived, optionality in their production of the language should not arise. There are at least two ways in which this kind of optionality could be explained from a generative perspective. These are discussed in the following section.

Two Approaches to Explaining Optionality in Gender Concord Marking within Generative Theories of Second Language Acquisition

Optionality as a Function of the Organization of the Grammar: The Missing Surface Inflection Hypothesis

One approach to explaining optionality in the marking of gender concord proposes that the grammatical representations of L2 speakers are fully target-like, but that L2 speakers diverge from native speakers in the way they compute those representations for real-time use. It is this that leads to optionality in production. This is an approach adopted by Prévost and White (2000) under a hypothesis known as the *Missing Surface Inflection Hypothesis*. The approach assumes that where there is a paradigm of morphological forms, as is the case for masculine and feminine determiners and adjectives, one form is fully specified for the contexts in which it can appear, while the other form is underspecified, as illustrated for the case of the French definite articles in (7):

(7) la ↔ [D, +definite, +feminine]
    le ↔ [D, +definite]

Here, although *la* is specified both for definiteness and for co-occurrence with feminine nouns, *le* is only specified for definiteness. The justification for this kind of representation is that it captures the generalization that *le* not only co-occurs with masculine nouns, but also with expressions that appear to lack a gender specification, as in the example of (8). *La* cannot occur in such contexts.

(8) (*A proof-reader, amending typographical errors:*) Dans 'il y avait une femme femme qui est venue', rayez le/*la deuxième 'femme'.
    'In 'there was a woman woman who came', delete the second 'woman'.

However, given the representation for *le* in (7), it is potentially consistent with any context where a determiner is definite, including (wrongly) feminine nouns. Both *la* and *le* are potentially insertable in a context like (9):

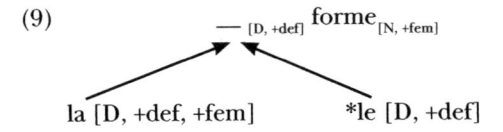

(9) ___ [D, +def] forme [N, +fem]

    la [D, +def, +fem]   *le [D, +def]

To eliminate this possibility, it is assumed that there is a constraint on selecting morphological forms from a paradigm that I will refer to here as a 'Competition Condition' (referred to in Halle (1997) as a 'Subset Principle'):

(10) *Competition Condition*

Where two forms in a morphological paradigm compete for insertion, choose the more specified form.

The Competition Condition ensures that *la*, but not *le*, is chosen to co-occur with *forme* in the grammars of native speakers, and more generally, that native speakers will rarely show optionality in marking gender concord.

It is the Competition Condition that is the basis for an account of L2 optionality under the Missing Surface Inflection Hypothesis. This proposes that L2 learners have target-like grammatical representations, but lack the Competition Condition. The effect in the case of gender concord is that L2 learners will always use the feminine form of the determiner with feminine gender nouns because *la* is specified for [+feminine], but will use the masculine form of the determiner with nouns of both masculine and feminine gender (because *le* is underspecified for gender). This is exactly the pattern that is typically found in the speech/writing of L2 speakers.[2]

The crucial point about the Missing Surface Inflection Hypothesis is that it assumes that the ability of L2 learners to acquire grammatical representations is unimpaired, and that optionality results from the relaxation of a constraint on computing representations.

Optionality as the Result of a Representational Deficit: The Compensatory Role of Statistical Learning

A second approach to explaining optionality in the marking of gender concord, in contrast to the Missing Surface Inflection Hypothesis, proposes that there is indeed a representational deficit. The mechanism provided by UG that implements gender concord between nouns and determiners/adjectives becomes inaccessible to older L2 learners (at least where such a property has not been activated in those learners' L1, as in the case of monolingual English speakers). Although L2 learners will encounter categorical evidence for gender concord in the input they get from languages like French, their knowledge of concord will be like that in (11):

(11) $N[\alpha]$ → determiner of morphological form [?]
$N[\beta]$ → determiner of morphological form [?]

In other words, such L2 speakers have no idea which determiner form to select in the context of masculine and feminine nouns.

If this were the whole story, however, random selection of articles would be expected (as in (5b)). But as the illustrative transcript in (4) shows, proficient L2 speakers of French produce many cases of determiner-noun concord in a target-like way. Also, where optionality occurs, it is not random (as already discussed), but involves overgeneralization of one of the forms in a paradigm. Furthermore, as learners gain in proficiency, optionality decreases. Low proficiency learners can be highly optional, but advanced proficiency speakers are less so. This can be illustrated from a study by McCarthy (2008) of noun-adjective gender concord in the speech of L1 English speakers of L2 Spanish. The study involved 15 participants of intermediate proficiency, 9 participants of advanced proficiency, and a control group of 10 native speakers. The task was an elicited production task where an interviewer asked individual participants questions about a series of photographs. The form that the questioning took elicited first the naming of an object with an indefinite determiner (to identify whether participants assign target gender in a simple naming task), followed by two further questions, the second of which produced an answer involving a predicative adjective where gender concord had to be realized with the item depicted in the photograph. The form that test items take is illustrated in (12):

(12) Photograph of a boy holding an apple
    Qu 1: What is the boy holding?   Expected answer: *una manzana*
                                                                                                      'an apple'
    Qu 2: What is he going to do with it? Expected answer: *va a comerla*
                                                                                                       'He's going to eat it'
    Qu 3: What colour is the apple?   Expected answer: *la manzana es roja*
                                                                                                         'The apple is red'

In one of her analyses of the data, McCarthy counted the tokens of correct noun-adjective concord. The native speaker controls produced 100 per cent expected responses. The L2 participants produced the responses shown in Table 5.2.

These results show two things clearly. First, asymmetry in the optionality of concord marking by the intermediate proficiency speakers, who overgeneralize the masculine forms of adjectives (e.g. using *rojo* 'red (masc)' with feminine nouns) in 34/93 cases (37 per cent), but not the feminine forms with masculine nouns (only 2/73 (3 per cent) of cases). Second, that this optionality decreases with proficiency. The advanced proficiency speakers are overgeneralizing the masculine forms of adjectives in only 8/61 (13 per cent) of cases.

To account for these observations within a representational deficit account, appeal can be made to L2 learners' unconscious ability to calculate the statistical properties of input described in the introduction. Specifically, I will claim that there is a principle that underlies all language learning that I will refer to as the *Input Analysis Imperative*.

(13) *Input Analysis Imperative*

Input contrasts must receive a representation.

Table 5.2 Token use of masculine and feminine forms of predictive Spanish adjectives (*rojo/roja*)

	Masculine		Feminine	
	Intermediate	Advanced	Intermediate	Advanced
Accurate	71	44	59	53
Inaccurate	2	2	34	8

Based on McCarthy (2008) table 6.

This principle requires that when learners identify a contrast between related word-forms in the input they are exposed to, such as that between *le-la, rojo-roja,* that contrast must receive a grammatical representation. In the case of L1 learners, such contrasts activate properties of UG, which then categorizes the relevant data. This is the standard generative view of the 'triggering' role that input plays in the development of grammatical knowledge. Under a representational deficit view of second language development, L2 learners do not have this 'internal grammatical advice' available for some properties (gender concord for monolingual English-speaking learners of French and Spanish), and yet they are still subject to the Input Analysis Imperative. In these circumstances they resort to using statistical information about the input they encounter to compensate for the lack of UG-derived categories. For example, English-speaking L2 learners of Spanish keep (unconscious) track of the frequency of *Adj+o* (e.g. *rojo*) and *Adj+a* (e.g. *roja*) in their contexts of use; English-speaking L2 learners of French keep track of the frequency of *le* and *la* in their contexts of use. The most frequent form becomes a 'default': the form of preference in adjective or definite article contexts. The other, less frequent, form is listed in memory with the nouns with which it co-occurs as a set of exceptions. To illustrate, an English-speaking L2 speaker of French might have a representation of the French singular definite articles along the lines of (14):

(14) le ↔ [D, +definite]
     la ↔ ___ $_{[D, +def]}$ cravatte, ___ $_{[D, +def]}$ tartine, ___ $_{[D, +def]}$ forme, . . .

A grammar of this kind would lead a learner generally to produce *le* with all definite nouns, except for those where that learner has established that *la* is required (with the nouns *cravatte, tartine, forme,* . . .). Optionality arises where the activation level in memory of the exceptions is weak, so that a learner cannot recall the exception on every occasion, but does recall it on some occasions. This leads to the optional use of both forms in cases like *la même forme-le même forme* 'the same shape', *le même chose-la même chose* 'the same thing'. Optionality decreases as learners become more proficient, because the activation levels of the exceptions strengthen through frequent encounter/repetition of those forms. This is exactly the pattern found in the transition from intermediate to advanced proficiency L2 Spanish in McCarthy's study of noun and predicative adjective concord.

The Nature of L2 Proficiency, and Deciding between the Two Approaches to Optionality

Interestingly, the two approaches described above to explaining observed optionality in the speech/writing of L2 speakers – the Missing Surface Inflection

Hypothesis and the Representational Deficit Hypothesis – make two quite different claims about the nature of L2 proficiency. The Missing Surface Inflection Hypothesis claims that where L2 learners diverge from native speakers, they may be grammatically proficient but have a problem computing the link between grammatical representations and the morphological forms that express those representations. The Representational Deficit Hypothesis claims that learners may be morphologically proficient, and do not have a problem computing the link to grammatical representations, but lack key elements of those representations (such as the property that determines gender concord). It would be of considerable interest if data could be found to tease the two accounts apart, and determine which of them offers the correct account of the nature of L2 proficiency in older L2 learners.

Unfortunately, production data from L2 speakers of French and Spanish relating to gender concord appears unable to offer the appropriate evidence. This is because the underspecified forms in the morphological paradigms (definite article *le*, and masculine adjective form *–o*) are also the most frequent forms in input. A scenario is needed where the morphologically underspecified form is not the most frequent form in input. If such a case could be found, it is predicted that if the Missing Surface Inflection Hypothesis is correct, then L2 learners will overgeneralize the morphologically underspecified form (even though it is not the most frequent form), whereas if the Representational Deficit Hypothesis is correct, then L2 learners will overgeneralize the most frequent form (even though this form is more highly specified morphologically than the other form).

Dutch noun-adjective gender concord appears to offer just this kind of scenario, according to Blom et al. (2008). Modern Dutch has a two-gender system, common and neuter, that is reflected in the choice of definite articles, although the indefinite article does not vary in form, as illustrated in (15).

(15) a. de hond 'the dog'   een hond 'a dog'   (common)
     b. het paard 'the horse'   een paard 'a horse'   (neuter)

Adjectives take two forms, a bare form and a form inflected with –e, as illustrated in (16).

(16) groen ~ groene 'green'

The choice of adjective form is gender- and context-sensitive. In attributive position (preceding the noun) the bare form of the adjective only co-occurs with indefinite, neuter singular nouns (for example *een groen huis* 'a green house'). In all other attributive positions the inflected form of the adjective is used (*het groene huis* 'the green house', *een groene hond* 'a green dog', and so on). By contrast, in predicative position only the bare form of the adjective is possible, whether the noun with which it agrees is of common or neuter gender, definite or indefinite (for example, *de deur is groen* 'the door is green', *het huis is groen* 'the house is green').

By looking at samples of child-directed speech from adult speakers of Dutch in the CHILDES database (MacWhinney, 2000), Blom et al. (2008) established that, counting across both attributive and predicative adjective contexts, the frequency of bare adjectives was 77 per cent in comparison to 23 per cent for adjectives inflected with –e. At the same time, to explain the distribution of adjectives in attributive position in the grammars of native speakers, a morphological representation like that in (17) appears to be necessary:

(17) –Ø ↔ [Adj, +attributive, –definite, +neuter, +singular]+___
    –e ↔ [Adj, +attributive]+___

Example (17) determines that for native speakers a bare attributive adjective will be inserted only in cases where the noun is indefinite, singular and of neuter gender; in every other attributive case an adjective inflected with –e will be inserted. Although an inflected adjective is also consistent with indefinite, singular, neuter nouns, the Competition Condition will exclude its insertion in these contexts.

It is now possible to see that the Missing Surface Inflection Hypothesis and the Representational Deficit Hypothesis make different predictions in this case. The former predicts that L2 learners will overgeneralize Adj+e to attributive positions where Adj+Ø is required, because L2 learners lack the Competition Condition. The latter predicts that L2 learners will overgeneralize Adj+Ø to attributive positions where Adj+e is required because they cannot access the gender concord property offered by UG and resort to frequency information in input to compensate. The bare adjective form is more frequent than the form inflected with –e, and will therefore become the 'default', with the inflected adjective listed with specific nouns as exceptions to this default.

To test the production of attributive adjective forms, Blom et al. (2008) used an elicited oral production task based on pairs of pictures. For example, in one pair of pictures, the first one depicts two glasses, a large one and a small one. The second one depicts a hand picking up the large glass. Participants were interviewed individually, with the experimenter prompting particular responses, as illustrated in (18).

(18) Experimenter   Expected participant response
     Kijk, twee glazen
     'Look, two glasses'

     Dit is een ...   groot glas (neuter)
     'This is a ...'   'big glass'

| En dat is een … | klein glas |
| 'And that is a …' | 'small glass' |

| Ik pak … | Het grote glas |
| 'I take …' | 'the big glass' |

Participants were three- to seven-year-old L1 child learners of Dutch, and 53 L2 learners of Dutch divided into two child L2 groups (aged 4–7) of different proficiency levels and two adult L2 groups (similarly divided into two proficiency levels). The first languages of the L2 groups were Moroccan Arabic and Berber. Results from the study comparing the different groups are presented in Table 5.3. (Only the results from the three-year-old L1 learners are shown in the table. Among the L2 learners, group II is more proficient than group I).

Table 5.3 shows that all the child learners (L1 and L2) overgeneralize Adj+e to the contexts where a bare adjective is required. By contrast, the adult learners show the opposite pattern, overgeneralizing bare adjectives to contexts where Adj+e is required. This suggests that the child learners have a grammatical representation like that of (17) for gender concord, but disobey the Competition Condition (consistent with the Missing Surface Inflection Hypothesis). By contrast the adult learners appear to have selected the most frequent adjective form in input – Adj+Ø – as the default form, consistent with them not having the grammatical representation (17), and using frequency information as a way of compensating for this gap in their knowledge. At the same time, the more proficient adult L2 speakers are also overgeneralizing Adj+e to a noteworthy extent. Perhaps this is again an effect of frequency of Adj+e in the attributive position (where the frequency ratio is 60 per cent Adj+e to 40 per cent Adj+Ø according to Blom et al. 2008). Where less proficient speakers are sensitive to overall frequency of forms, more proficient speakers are beginning to

Table 5.3 Overgeneralization of Adj+Ø and Adj+e in attributive position by L1 and L2 speakers of Dutch in a production task, shown as % and tokens in parentheses

| | Adjective misuse | |
Group	Adj+Ø for Adj+e	Adj+e for Adj+Ø
L1 (3-yr-olds)	0 (0/16)	84 (16/19)
Child L2 I	8 (14/171)	81 (134/165)
Child L2 II	6 (10/169)	81 (127/151)
Adult L2 I	77 (34/44)	20 (9/44)
Adult L2 II	71 (49/69)	44 (34/77)

Blom, Polišenká and Weerman (2008).

distinguish attributive and predicative position, but still have representations that are sensitive to input frequency rather than features of grammatical gender concord.

The results from the study by Blom et al. (2008) are highly suggestive that where gender concord is concerned, adult L2 learners have a representational deficit, and satisfy the Input Analysis Imperative by using statistical properties of the input to determine a default form. By contrast, child language learners, whether L1 or L2, appear to have appropriate grammatical representations for gender concord phenomena, but have not invoked the Competition Condition.

Discussion

This chapter has considered the possible role that the learning of statistical properties of input might play in the development of L2 proficiency in generative ('nativist') theories of SLA. It was suggested that the standard generative view of the role of input does not consider statistical properties (such as transitional probabilities between syllables or frequency) of much interest, because the key role of input is to trigger internally-derived linguistic knowledge (from Universal Grammar). However, given such a view, an explanatory challenge for generative theories of SLA is the pervasive optionality in the use of morphological competitors observed in the speech/writing of L2 speakers where native speakers are categorical, and input provides evidence for the categorical use of forms.

Two kinds of explanation of L2 optionality were described. One, the Missing Surface Inflection Hypothesis, does not require appeal to the statistical properties of input, but rather attributes optionality to a malfunctioning of a constraint that is part of the grammar: the Competition Condition. For native speakers, this constrains the selection of competing morphological forms in cases like the gender-distinguished definite articles in French and adjectives in Spanish. For L2 speakers, the Competition Condition is relaxed, with the consequence that the morphologically underspecified form in the paradigm appears in contexts where a more specified form should appear. The second proposed explanation, the Representational Deficit Hypothesis, claims that optionality of the kind described results from L2 learners having non-target grammatical representations where the property that determines gender concord between nouns and determiners/adjectives is absent. Learners compensate for this absence by using frequency information in the input to establish a mental representation. The most frequent form of a morphological paradigm is established as the default, while the other form is listed with the nouns with which it co-occurs as a set of exceptions. The level of activation of each member of the listed exceptions will vary. Where the activation level is low, a particular exception to the default may only be accessed on some occasions, but not others, giving rise to the observed asymmetrical optionality in the speech/writing of L2 speakers.

It was suggested that evidence of optional production of noun-determiner and noun-adjective gender concord by L2 speakers of French and Spanish was consistent with both of the proposed explanations because in French and Spanish morphologically underspecified forms are also the most frequent forms in input. However, Dutch noun-adjective concord appears to offer a scenario where the morphologically underspecified form in attributive position is not the most frequent form. It was argued that this dissociation of morphological underspecification from input frequency offered a domain in which the Missing Surface Inflection Hypothesis and Representational Deficit Hypothesis accounts might be distinguished.

A study by Blom et al. (2008) shows that child learners of Dutch (both early L1 and L2 learners), in an oral elicited production task, perform in a way that is consistent with the Missing Surface Inflection Hypothesis. The adult L2 learners in the sample, however, performed in a way consistent with the Representational Deficit Hypothesis, overgeneralizing the most frequent form in input, rather than the morphologically underspecified form. Such evidence suggests that adult L2 proficiency might be characterized by grammatical deficits in some areas of knowledge, which are compensated for by adults' ability to draw on unconscious sensitivity to statistical properties of input.

Notes

[1] 'A ball comes . . . the ball doesn't understand . . . and they have a war . . . [now they are] the same shape . . . a square that has fallen on its head . . . it is the same shape . . . and make it the same shape . . . the squares are like a wall . . . the same thing as in the film, I suppose . . . the square has realized that . . . the two camps think the same thing . . .'

[2] The name 'Missing Surface Inflection Hypothesis' arises from morphological paradigms where the under-specified form is phonologically null, as in those cases of English verbal inflection where third person singular present tense –s is specified for person, number and tense, past tense –ed is specified for tense, and the least specified form is the phonologically null –Ø, used in all other cases with finite verbs. L2 speakers of English typically use –s and –ed in appropriate contexts, but overgeneralize verbs with the –Ø inflection (see Ionin and Wexler, 2002, Lardiere, 2007 for examples).

References

Bazergui, N., Connors, K., Lenoble, M., & Majkrak, B. (1990). *Acquisition du français (L2) chez des adultes à Montréal*. Québec: Office de la langue française.

Blom, E., Polišenská, D., & Weerman, F. (2008). Articles, adjectives and age of onset: The acquisition of Dutch grammatical gender. *Second Language Research*, 24, 297–331.

Ellis, N. C. (2002). Frequency effects in language processing: A review with implications for theories of implicit and explicit language acquisition. *Studies in Second Language Acquisition*, 24, 143–88.

Halle, M. (1997). Distributed morphology: Impoverishment and fission. *MIT Working Papers in Linguistics*, 30, 425–49.

Hudson Kam, C., & Newport, E. (1999). Creolization: Could adults really have done it all? In A. Greenhill, H. Littlefield, & C. Tano (Eds.). *Proceedings of the 23rd Annual Boston University Conference on Language Development* (pp. 265–76). Somerville MA: Cascadilla Press.

Ionin, T., & Wexler, K. (2002). Why is 'is' easier than '-s'?: Acquisition of tense/agreement morphology by child second language learners of English. *Second Language Research*, 18, 95–136.

Ionin, T., Ko, H., & Wexler, K. (2004). Article semantics in L2 acquisition: the role of specificity. *Language Acquisition*, 12, 3–69.

Ionin, T., Zubizarreta, M-L., & Bautista Maldonado, S. (2008). Sources of linguistic knowledge in the second language acquisition of English *articles*. *Lingua*, 118, 554–76.

Lardiere, D. (2007). *Ultimate attainment in second language acquisition: A Case Study*. Mahwah, NJ: Lawrence Erlbaum Associates.

MacWhinney, B. (2000). *The CHILDES project: Tools for analyzing talk* (3rd ed.). Mahwah, NJ: Lawrence Erlbaum.

McCarthy, C. (2008). Morphological variability in the comprehension of agreement: An argument for representation over computation. *Second Language Research*, 24, 459–86.

Prévost, P., & White, L. (2000). Missing surface inflection or impairment in second language acquisition? Evidence from tense and agreement. *Second Language Research*, 16, 103–33.

Saffran, J., Newport, E., & Aslin, R. (1996). Word segmentation: The role of distributional cues. *Journal of Memory and Language*, 35, 606–21.

White, L. (2003). Fossilization in steady state L2 grammars: persistent problems with inflectional morphology. *Bilingualism: Language and Cognition*, 6, 129–41.

Chapter 6

Metalinguistic Knowledge: A Stepping Stone Towards L2 Proficiency?

Karen Roehr
University of Essex, United Kingdom

Gabriela Adela Gánem-Gutiérrez
University of Essex, United Kingdom

Abstract

We present a study involving 16 English-speaking university learners of L2 German and L2 Spanish. Through test-based measurement and analyses of learners' reported use of metalinguistic knowledge during performance on a form-focused task, we identified L2 aspects which showed correlations between learners' more accurate and sophisticated use of metalinguistic knowledge on the one hand and successful task completion on the other hand. These L2 aspects were profiled for their implicit and explicit learning difficulty in order to identify the characteristics of linguistic constructions and metalinguistic descriptions that may be particularly suitable for explicit teaching and learning drawing on metalinguistic knowledge.

Introduction

For at least three decades, researchers have been trying to gain an understanding of the role of explicit knowledge in adult second language (L2) learning (e.g. Alderson, Clapham & Steel, 1997; Bialystok, 1979; Sorace, 1985; for recent reviews, see DeKeyser, 2003; Ellis, 2004). This chapter reports a small-scale empirical study which was aimed at contributing to the ongoing quest. The key variable under discussion is metalinguistic knowledge, defined as explicit knowledge about language (Ellis, 2004; Roehr, 2008).

In what follows, we consider the potential contribution of metalinguistic knowledge to the development of L2 proficiency in a small group of English-speaking university-level learners of L2 German and L2 Spanish ($N = 16$). Drawing on our empirical findings as well as existing research in the field, we put forward specific hypotheses about the implicit and explicit learning difficulty of particular linguistic constructions and their associated metalinguistic descriptions. These hypotheses are intended to serve as a basis for future empirical enquiry.

Four notions are of relevance to the study at hand: metalinguistic knowledge, L2 proficiency, implicit learning difficulty and explicit learning difficulty. Metalinguistic knowledge refers to a person's explicit knowledge about language (Alderson et al., 1997; Bialystok, 1979; Elder, Warren, Hajek, Manwaring, & Davies, 1999; Ellis, 2004). Explicit knowledge is represented declaratively, can be brought into awareness, and is potentially available for verbal report. Explicit knowledge can be contrasted with implicit knowledge, which cannot be brought into awareness or articulated (Anderson, 2005; Hulstijn, 2005). In simple terms, explicit knowledge is potentially conscious knowledge; by extension, metalinguistic knowledge is potentially conscious knowledge about language.

The notion of L2 proficiency refers to a learner's language ability, which consists of language knowledge and strategic competence. Together, language knowledge and strategic competence allow the language user to create and interpret discourse, that is to express, comprehend or negotiate intended meanings (Bachman & Palmer, 1996).

Following Ellis (2006: 432), implicit learning difficulty refers to what is easy or difficult to acquire as implicit L2 knowledge, while explicit learning difficulty refers to what is easy or difficult to acquire as explicit L2 knowledge.

Background

One way of identifying the potential usefulness of metalinguistic knowledge to the learner in their quest for L2 proficiency is to consider the implicit and explicit learning difficulty of the L2 aspects that are being acquired. In view of our construct definitions, linguistic constructions may be described in terms of implicit learning difficulty, while metalinguistic descriptions that constitute a person's explicit knowledge about linguistic constructions may be described in terms of explicit learning difficulty.

Existing research has considered metalinguistic knowledge with regard to the nature of the categories and rules that make up this kind of knowledge, as well as the nature of the L2 aspects described and explained by such explicit categories and rules. More often than not, this type of research has conceptualized metalinguistic knowledge as knowledge of pedagogical grammar in the broadest sense, that is knowledge that explicitly describes and explains selected L2 constructions in order to promote and guide instructed language acquisition (Chalker, 1994; Westney, 1994). Such explicit descriptions may vary along several parameters, including complexity, scope and reliability (DeKeyser, 1994; Hulstijn & de Graaff, 1994).

For instance, explicit descriptions may refer to prototypical or peripheral uses of a particular L2 construction (Hu, 2002). Moreover, the L2 construction described may itself vary in terms of complexity, perceptual salience or communicative redundancy (Hulstijn & de Graaff, 1994). In view of this multifaceted interaction between the type of explicit description and the type of L2 construction described, it is notoriously difficult to predict which aspects of metalinguistic knowledge are likely to be helpful to the L2 learner. Accordingly, positions have shifted somewhat over the years, with earlier work advocating fairly categorically either the teaching of more complex descriptions (Hulstijn & de Graaff, 1994) or the teaching of simpler rules (DeKeyser, 1994).

In recent years, researchers have tried to unravel the threads. DeKeyser (2003) has highlighted the fact that the difficulty – and hence the potential usefulness – of metalinguistic descriptions is a complex function of a number of variables, including the characteristics of the description itself, the characteristics of the L2 construction being described (see also DeKeyser, 2005) and individual learner differences in aptitude. In consonance with this position, findings reported by Ellis (2006) suggest that the difficulty of specific L2 aspects may depend on whether these aspects are learned implicitly or explicitly. Furthermore, these two researchers have proposed a list of characteristics which appear to determine the relative learning difficulty of L2 morphosyntactic constructions. Before taking a closer look at these characteristics, let us consider the empirical study which has informed our views on this issue.

Research Design

The empirical study presented here is part of a more comprehensive project concerned with metalinguistic knowledge in adult L2 learning (Gánem-Gutiérrez & Roehr, under review; Roehr & Gánem-Gutiérrez, 2008). We only report the component of the project that is directly relevant to the issue at hand, that is how the notions of implicit and explicit learning difficulty may aid our understanding of the potential contribution of metalinguistic knowledge to the attainment of L2 proficiency. This component of the study involved 16 English-speaking university-level learners of L2 German ($N=7$) and L2 Spanish ($N=9$). In view of the small sample size, it is worth bearing in mind that any findings we report must be regarded as preliminary and provisional.

The participants were students of L2 German or L2 Spanish at the same British university. On average, learners of German and Spanish receive three to four hours of language tuition per week during term time. Language tutors use either a mixed-skills approach which addresses speaking, listening, reading, writing and grammar practice in a balanced way within individual sessions, or a skills-based approach which focuses on specific abilities in each session. In the latter case, learners attend two hours of oral and aural practice, one hour of reading and writing practice, and one hour of grammar-focused practice per week. All participants were volunteers who were prepared to put aside some of their own time to take part in the study; all participants were compensated for their time. Prior written consent was obtained from all learners.

The L2 German group consisted of six females and one male and ranged in age from 18 to 44 years (mean = 24.0; median = 20.0). Six learners were undergraduate students and one learner was also a member of university staff. On average, the participants had studied the L2 for 4.1 years at school and/or college and for 0.9 years at university. The learners had spent a mean of 2.7 weeks in an L2 immersion setting. Moreover, the participants had studied up to two other languages apart from the L2 under investigation. These languages were all Romance languages and included French, Italian, Portuguese and Spanish.

The L2 Spanish group consisted of six females and three males and ranged in age from 18 to 46 years (mean = 23.0; median = 21.0). Eight learners were undergraduate students and one learner was also a member of university staff. On average, the participants had studied the L2 for 3.3 years at school and/or college and for 1.4 years at university. Length of L2 immersion varied considerably between learners, ranging from 2 to 60 weeks (mean = 15.8). Moreover, the participants had studied up to three other languages apart from the L2 under investigation. These languages included Dutch, French, German, Italian, Portuguese, Latin and Ancient Greek.

The participants completed a three-part instrument consisting of a biodata questionnaire, a test of L2 metalinguistic knowledge, and a form-focused sentence-level task during which think-aloud protocols were recorded.

The biodata questionnaire contained a total of 12 questions about demographic variables (age, gender), the participants' current status at the university where the study was conducted (e.g. undergraduate student, postgraduate student, year of study, etc.) and their language learning history.

The tests of German and Spanish metalinguistic knowledge measured learners' ability to explicitly describe and explain aspects of the L2, operationalized as the ability to correct, describe and explain 20 highlighted sentence-level errors involving selected L2 aspects. The description/explanation task effectively tested learners' ability to implement pedagogical grammar rules, since each targeted error could be described and explained by means of a statement of the type 'As form X occurs/function X is being expressed, form Y needs to be used.' Essentially, the targeted metalinguistic description answered the question 'What form?', while the targeted metalinguistic explanation answered the question 'Why this form?'. Items targeting syntactic, morphological, lexico-semantic and pragmatic aspects of the L2 were included. Targeted L2 aspects were selected on the basis of the participants' language course syllabuses.

The form-focused task consisted of a suite of twenty discrete items at sentence level, ten in gap-fill format and ten in four-way multiple-choice format.

Syntactic, morphological, lexico-semantic and pragmatic features of the L2 were included, with items matched as closely as possible with the items targeted by the test of L2 metalinguistic knowledge. In some instances, direct matching was not possible, for example when specific collocations which could not be repeated verbatim were tested. Examples of targeted aspects of L2 German are adjectival inflection, perfect tense with *haben* vs. *sein*, the idiomatic use of voice in modal verbs (*sollen* vs. *sollte*) and formal vs. informal form of address. Examples of targeted aspects of L2 Spanish are use of reflexive pronouns, radical changing verbs, the collocation *hacer frío/calor* and formal vs. informal form of address.

During the completion of the form-focused task, participants verbalized what they were thinking, that is they 'thought aloud'. This introspective method can be employed to gain insight into the controlled thought processes an individual goes through while resolving a cognitive task (Ericsson & Simon, 1993; Green, 1998; Young, 2005). The rationale behind this approach was to see whether participants would use any metalinguistic knowledge while resolving the task, how accurate and sophisticated their metalinguistic knowledge would be if they used any, and whether reported use of metalinguistic knowledge would be related to successful performance on the task.

Three specific research questions were addressed:

RQ1: What is the relationship between learners' L2 metalinguistic knowledge, reported use of metalinguistic knowledge during completion of a form-focused task and correctness of response on the form-focused task?

RQ2: Which L2 German items yield significant correlations between reported use of metalinguistic knowledge and correctness of response on the form-focused task?

RQ3: Which L2 Spanish items yield significant correlations between reported use of metalinguistic knowledge and correctness of response on the form-focused task?

Participants' answers to the items on the test of L2 metalinguistic knowledge were scored in accordance with prepared answer keys. For each fully appropriate error correction one point was awarded. For each adequate description and for each adequate explanation one point was awarded, respectively. Adequate descriptions and explanations were defined as any descriptions and explanations that were not incorrect and that showed at least some evidence of meaningful generalization beyond the instances provided in the test items themselves. As scoring learners' descriptions and explanations involved qualitative judgements, answers were first scored by one of the researchers and then scored blind by a second marker. In the case of the German test, interrater agreement was 95.6 per cent; in the case of the Spanish test, interrater agreement was 92.7 per cent. Disagreements were resolved through discussion between the two markers.

Participants' performance on the form-focused task was scored dichotomously in accordance with prepared answer keys. The think-aloud protocols were audio-recorded and transcribed in full. The transcripts from the 16 learners comprised a total of 21,178 words. The transcripts were coded for reported use of metalinguistic knowledge on the basis of a hierarchical coding scheme ranging from 0 to 3 points, with 0 indicating no use of metalinguistic knowledge and increasing scores (from 1 up to 3) per item indicating both increased accuracy and increased sophistication in the use of metalinguistic knowledge.

As coding the transcripts for reported use of metalinguistic knowledge involved qualitative judgements, two markers were involved. Based on a detailed coding scheme, the transcripts were first coded by one of the researchers and then coded blind by a second marker. In the case of the German transcripts, interrater agreement was 92.0per cent; in the case of the Spanish transcripts, interrater agreement was 87.0 per cent. Disagreements were resolved through discussion between the markers.

All statistical analyses were carried out with SPSS version 14.0.

Results

In order to answer RQ1, we calculated bivariate correlations between participants scores on the test of L2 metalinguistic knowledge, their scores on the form-focused task and reported use of metalinguistic knowledge during completion of the form-focused task. Results are shown in Table 6.1.

Table 6.1 shows significant positive correlations throughout, although the relationships differ somewhat in strength. First and foremost, there is a strong positive relationship between participants' performance on the test of L2 metalinguistic knowledge and their performance on the form-focused task. This is perhaps unsurprising because the two measures were matched in terms of targeted L2 aspects; moreover, the form-focused nature of the sentence-level task may well have encouraged the use of any available metalinguistic knowledge, especially as performance was not timed.

Table 6.1 Correlations (Pearson's r) between L2 metalinguistic knowledge, correctness of response on the form-focused task and reported use of metalinguistic knowledge (MLK) on the form-focused task

	Use of MLK on form-focused task	Correctness of response on form-focused task
Test of metalinguistic knowledge	.54*	.85**
Use of MLK on form-focused task	1	.51*

* significant at the .05 level (two-tailed); ** significant at the .01 level (two-tailed).

By the same token, Table 6.1 reveals a positive relationship of medium strength between reported use of metalinguistic knowledge during completion of the form-focused task and performance on the test of L2 metalinguistic knowledge. A possible interpretation of this result is that metalinguistic knowledge is reasonably stable, as suggested in the previous paragraph. Put differently, if participants were able to produce metalinguistic knowledge in the context of the dedicated test, they were often also able to draw on this knowledge and thus reported using it during the completion of the form-focused task.

More interestingly perhaps, Table 6.1 also shows a positive relationship, though again only of medium strength, between reported use of metalinguistic knowledge during task performance and correctness of response on the form-focused task. In other words, and most crucially, use of metalinguistic knowledge and successful performance were indeed associated in this instance.

In order to address RQ2, we calculated bivariate correlations between participants' scores on the form-focused task and their reported use of metalinguistic knowledge for all the individual aspects of L2 German targeted by the task. Significant results are shown in Table 6.2.

Table 6.2 reveals that items targeting five aspects of L2 German resulted in significant positive correlations between reported use of metalinguistic knowledge and correctness of response on the form-focused task. All correlations are strong.

In order to address RQ3, we calculated bivariate correlations between participants' scores on the form-focused task and their reported use of metalinguistic knowledge for all the individual aspects of L2 Spanish targeted by the task. Significant results are shown in Table 6.3.

Table 6.3 shows that items targeting two aspects of L2 Spanish resulted in significant positive correlations, both of which are quite strong.

The results in Table 6.2 and Table 6.3 suggest an association between reported use of metalinguistic knowledge during task performance and successful task

Table 6.2 Significant correlations between reported use of metalinguistic knowledge and correctness of response on the form-focused task (L2 German)

Targeted L2 aspect	Pearson's r
Use of case: Direct object in the accusative	.87*
Use of case: Prepositions with dative	.91**
Use of case: Genitive (possession)	.87*
Negation: *nicht* vs. *kein*	.80*
Perfect tense with *haben* vs. *sein*	.81*

* significant at the .05 level (two-tailed); ** significant at the .01 level (two-tailed)

Table 6.3 Significant correlations between reported use of metalinguistic knowledge and correctness of response on the form-focused task (L2 Spanish)

Targeted L2 aspect	Pearson's r
Formal vs. informal form of address/register	.76*
Agreement: Present tense verb endings	.67*

* significant at the .05 level (two-tailed)

completion in the case of items targeting a total of seven L2 aspects, that is, five German constructions and two Spanish constructions. While correlation coefficients cannot uncover the directionality of a possible cause-effect relationship, it is nonetheless plausible to hypothesize that the association identified is indicative of potential benefits of metalinguistic knowledge during performance on these items and in the context of this particular type of task.

Discussion

The results reported in the preceding section raise a pertinent question: How can we account for the finding that certain aspects of L2 German and L2 Spanish show a positive association between reported use of metalinguistic knowledge and successful task completion, while others do not?

Scrutiny of the published literature yielded no studies of L2 Spanish with a comparable research design. However, two points of comparison are available for L2 German, that is, studies by Klapper and Rees (2003) and Roehr (2008). Unfortunately, the L2 aspects identified by Klapper and Rees as benefiting 'substantially from planned, formal and explicit instruction' for English-speaking learners of L2 German (2003: 308) are different from the constructions we identified, except for 'Adjectives', which presumably refers to adjectival inflection depending on case, number and gender. This aspect overlaps with the three 'Use of case' aspects in Table 6.2, which likewise involved inflection for case, number, and gender, though not of adjectives.

Roehr (2008) reports eight L2 German constructions displaying significant positive relationships between successful performance on a written form-focused L2 task and description/explanation ability as measured in the context of a test of L2 metalinguistic knowledge. Significant correlations in the study in question were generally much weaker than in the present study, but, interestingly, there is some convergence between the respective L2 aspects. 'Prepositions and cases', 'Adjectival inflection' and 'Genitive case' in particular stand out, since they overlap with the three 'Use of case' aspects in Table 6.2. Taken together, the available findings, though as yet few and far between, indicate that aspects of the L2 which involve inflection for case, number and gender may be used more successfully in the context of form-focused tasks if the learner draws on metalinguistic knowledge.

If we wish to arrive at a possible explanatory account for the pattern of results obtained as well as further specific hypotheses, it will be helpful to move beyond empirical findings and examine the implicit and explicit learning difficulty of the seven L2 aspects which yielded significant correlations in the present study. In order to specify the implicit and explicit learning difficulty of particular L2 aspects, the characteristics of both the L2 constructions in question and their associated metalinguistic descriptions need to be considered. This takes us back to existing research in the field which we briefly reviewed above.

DeKeyser (2005) proposed a list of characteristics believed to impact on the relative learning difficulty of aspects of L2 morphosyntax. DeKeyser argued that a lack of transparency in form-meaning mappings is a primary source of difficulty. According to DeKeyser, lack of transparency can be attributed to three factors, namely, communicative redundancy of form, optionality of form and opacity, which refers to the reliability of a form-meaning mapping. Opacity (and learning difficulty) is high when different forms denote the same meaning, or when the same form stands for different meanings. Additional factors responsible for the learning difficulty of L2 form-meaning mappings are frequency in the input, phonological salience of the form and regularity of the form-meaning relationship in the sense of scope, or the number of cases covered (DeKeyser, 2005).

The latter three characteristics, that is frequency, salience and regularity, are also listed by Ellis (2006), but, together with processability, they are presented as specifically contributing to implicit learning difficulty. Ellis (2006) posits a further set of characteristics as accounting for explicit learning difficulty, that is, systematicity, which refers to the rule-based vs. item-based nature of the form-meaning mapping described by a pedagogical grammar rule, the relative technicality of the metalanguage used in a pedagogical grammar rule and conceptual complexity of the form-meaning mapping described by a pedagogical grammar rule. Conceptual complexity is understood as a composite notion which includes formal and functional complexity. In sum, recent work offers a range of parameters according to which L2 aspects can be classified in order to identify their potential difficulty for the L2 learner.

Drawing on both DeKeyser (2005) and Ellis (2006), we developed a slightly adapted taxonomy for assessing the implicit and explicit learning difficulty of the L2 aspects included in the present study. While our taxonomy essentially covers the same criteria, we aimed to avoid, as far as possible, composite parameters such as DeKeyser's lack of transparency, which is a function of communicative redundancy of form, optionality of form, and opacity, or Ellis's regularity, which is a function of scope and reliability. Furthermore, we did not include parameters that depend on specific linguistic theories, such as Ellis's processability.

Table 6.4 Taxonomy of variables contributing to implicit and explicit learning difficulty

Variable	Operational definition	Learning difficulty
Frequency	How frequently an L2 construction occurs in the input.	High frequency decreases implicit learning difficulty.
Perceptual salience	How easily an L2 construction can be perceived auditorily in spoken input.	High perceptual salience decreases implicit learning difficulty.
Communicative redundancy	How much an L2 construction contributes to the communicative intent of a message.	High communicative redundancy increases implicit learning difficulty.
Opacity (lack of reliability) of form-meaning mapping: One form, x meanings	To what extent an L2 form maps onto a single or multiple meanings/functions.	High opacity increases implicit learning difficulty.
Opacity (lack of reliability) of meaning-form mapping: One meaning, x forms	To what extent an L2 meaning/function maps onto a single or multiple forms.	High opacity increases implicit learning difficulty.
Schematicity	The extent to which a linguistic construction is schematic or specific; and whether a metalinguistic description covers a schematic or a specific linguistic construction.	High schematicity decreases implicit and explicit learning difficulty.
Conceptual complexity	The number of elements that need to be taken into account in a metalinguistic description, i.e. the number of categories and relations between categories included in the description.	High conceptual complexity increases explicit learning difficulty.
Technicality of metalanguage	The relative familiarity and abstractness of the metalanguage used in the metalinguistic description.	High technicality of metalanguage increases explicit learning difficulty.
Truth value	The extent to which a metalinguistic description applies without exception.	High truth value decreases explicit learning difficulty.

In brief, we aimed to develop a practical taxonomy that would allow for straightforward profiling of both L2 constructions and their associated metalinguistic descriptions. The resulting taxonomy includes nine variables which are presented in Table 6.4, together with their operational definitions and their predicted impact on learning difficulty.

As Table 6.4 indicates, the variables frequency in the input, perceptual salience, communicative redundancy, opacity of form-meaning mapping (one form, x meanings), and opacity of meaning-form mapping (one meaning, x forms) refer to the characteristics of linguistic constructions and impact on implicit learning difficulty. The variable schematicity refers to the characteristics of both linguistic constructions and metalinguistic descriptions and affects both implicit and explicit learning difficulty. The variables conceptual complexity, technicality of metalanguage and truth value refer to the characteristics of metalinguistic descriptions and impact on explicit learning difficulty.

We used the taxonomy in Table 6.4 to profile the seven L2 aspects that had resulted in significant positive correlations in our study. Our reasoning was as follows: If any commonalities in learning difficulty could be identified, a basis for formulating hypotheses about which aspects of an L2 may generally be suitable for explicit learning and teaching drawing on metalinguistic knowledge might be established. When classifying the L2 aspects included in our study, we made impressionistic judgements. We considered each targeted L2 construction and its associated metalinguistic description, and we then assigned one of three values to each variable, that is low, medium or high. After applying this procedure, we found that the seven L2 aspects which had yielded significant correlations shared the profile shown in Table 6.5.

Table 6.5 reveals that with regard to explicit learning difficulty, all seven L2 aspects can be explained by means of metalinguistic descriptions showing

Table 6.5 Profile of L2 aspects resulting in significant correlations

Variable	Value	Learning difficulty
Frequency	High or medium	Low or medium
Perceptual salience	Low or medium	High or medium
Communicative redundancy	High or medium	High or medium
Opacity of form-meaning mapping: One form, x meanings	Low or medium	Low or medium
Opacity of meaning-form mapping: One meaning, x forms	Low or medium	Low or medium
Schematicity	High or medium	Low or medium
Conceptual complexity	Low or medium	Low or medium
Technicality of metalanguage	Low or medium	Low or medium
Truth value	High or medium	Low or medium

favourable or neutral values. In other words, the L2 aspects all pose relatively little explicit learning difficulty. With regard to schematicity, which is predicted to affect both explicit and implicit learning difficulty, values are also either favourable or neutral. In respect of implicit learning difficulty, favourable or neutral values are in evidence on two parameters, but values for the parameters of perceptual salience and communicative redundancy are either unfavourable or neutral; this should increase implicit learning difficulty.

In summary, the profile in Table 6.5 allows us to hypothesize that the negative effects of low or medium perceptual salience and high or medium communicative redundancy may be compensated for by a favourable combination of parameters leading to decreased explicit learning difficulty, in particular if these are coupled with high or medium input frequency and possibly also medium or low opacity of form-meaning and meaning-form mappings.

We then proceeded to assign values for implicit and explicit learning difficulty to all other L2 aspects included in the present study. Aspects underlying items on the form-focused task which did not yield significant correlations between reported use of metalinguistic knowledge and correctness of response as well as aspects included in the test of L2 metalinguistic knowledge which could not be matched directly with items on the form-focused task were taken into account. Our rationale for this step was that both our participant sample and the number of items targeting each construction were so small that we might have missed relationships that would be significant in a larger-scale study.

Based on our taxonomy, we identified six further constructions of L2 German and six further constructions of L2 Spanish which shared a similar profile with the constructions that had yielded significant correlations.

With regard to explicit learning difficulty, all targeted L2 German aspects had a profile similar to the seven aspects that had yielded significant results; in other words, the respective metalinguistic descriptions are of low or medium conceptual complexity, they involve metalanguage of low or medium technicality and descriptions are of high or medium truth value. Out of these aspects, a sub-set of eleven constructions additionally exhibited positive or neutral values for schematicity. Scrutiny of the parameters responsible for implicit learning difficulty revealed that out of these eleven aspects, four shared the same profile with the L2 aspects which had resulted in significant correlations, namely, form-meaning and meaning-form mappings are of medium or low opacity and input frequency is medium or high, while values for perceptual salience and communicative redundancy are negative or neutral. The aspects in question are 'Agreement: Present tense verb endings', 'Use of case: Prepositions with accusative or dative: *Wechselpräpositionen*', 'Adverbials of place and direction' and 'Use of tense/mood/voice: Passive with *werden*'.

If medium or low opacity of form-meaning/meaning-form mapping is not made a condition, that is if it is assumed that negative values on this implicit parameter may also be compensated for by decreased explicit learning difficulty, then two further aspects might equally benefit from use of metalinguistic knowledge: 'Use of case: Adjectival inflection' and 'Politeness: Use of modal particles'.

Taken together, no fewer than six out of the eleven L2 German aspects which either yielded significant correlations or which share a similar profile in terms of predicted learning difficulty involve inflection for case, number and gender, thus broadly mirroring the results obtained in existing research on L2 German acquired by English-speaking learners (Klapper & Rees, 2003; Roehr, 2008).

In relation to L2 Spanish, all targeted aspects had a profile similar to the aspects that had yielded significant results with regard to explicit learning difficulty; in other words, the respective metalinguistic descriptions are of low or medium conceptual complexity, they involve metalanguage of low or medium technicality and descriptions are of high or medium truth value. Out of these aspects, a sub-set of fourteen additionally exhibited positive or neutral values for schematicity.

Scrutiny of the parameters responsible for implicit learning difficulty revealed that out of these fourteen aspects, five shared the same profile with the L2 aspects which had resulted in significant correlations, namely, form-meaning and meaning-form mappings are of medium or low opacity and input frequency is medium or high, while values for perceptual salience and communicative redundancy are negative or neutral. The aspects in question are 'Use of personal pronouns', 'Use of reflexive pronouns', 'Adjectival inflection', 'Preterite tense', and 'Radical changing verbs'. If medium or low opacity of form-meaning/meaning-form mapping is not made a condition, then one further aspect might likewise benefit from use of metalinguistic knowledge: 'Subjunctive after statements of possibility/probability'.

In sum, we hypothesize that the following aspects of L2 German and L2 Spanish will yield significant correlations between English-speaking learners' reported use of metalinguistic knowledge during item resolution and correctness of response on a form-focused task in a study involving a larger number of participants and a larger set of items targeting each of these aspects:

L2 German:

- Use of case: Direct object in the accusative
- Use of case: Prepositions with dative
- Use of case: Prepositions with accusative or dative: *Wechselpräpositionen*
- Use of case: Genitive (possession)
- Use of case: Adjectival inflection
- Agreement: Present tense verb endings
- Use of tense/mood/voice: Passive with *werden*

- Perfect tense with *haben* vs. *sein*
- Negation: *nicht* vs. *kein*
- Adverbials of place and direction

Politeness: Use of modal particles

L2 Spanish:

- Use of personal pronouns
- Use of reflexive pronouns
- Adjectival inflection
- Agreement: Present tense verb endings
- Radical changing verbs
- Preterite tense
- Subjunctive after statements of possibility/probability
- Formal vs. informal form of address/register.

Conclusion

The small-scale study we have reported here was aimed at contributing to our understanding of the potential benefits of metalinguistic knowledge in instructed adult L2 learning. Drawing on a revised taxonomy strongly influenced by the work of DeKeyser (2005) and Ellis (2006), we profiled aspects of L2 German and L2 Spanish for their implicit and explicit learning difficulty. This led to specific hypotheses about which aspects of these two languages might be particularly amenable to the use of metalinguistic knowledge in the context of form-focused task performance. Thus, we hypothesize that if instructed adult L2 learners employ their metalinguistic knowledge in the context of the L2 aspects listed in the previous section, then this might function as a stepping stone towards L2 proficiency.

By the same token, it is of course also possible to use our taxonomy to identify L2 aspects with an opposing profile, that is L2 aspects which might be less amenable to the use of metalinguistic knowledge in the context of form-focused task performance. In the case of such L2 aspects, one could hypothesize that only learners who are highly adept at and comfortable with using metalinguistic knowledge may benefit from drawing on explicit knowledge and processes (see Roehr & Gánem-Gutiérrez, 2008).

Even though the findings presented here can only be regarded as tentative because of the small size of our data set, they have informed ongoing empirical research (Zietek, in preparation); they will also be a basis for our own future investigations into the role of metalinguistic knowledge in adult L2 learning.

Acknowledgement

The study was supported by the University of Essex Research Promotion Fund.

References

Alderson, J. C., Clapham, C., & Steel, D. (1997). Metalinguistic knowledge, language aptitude and language proficiency. *Language Teaching Research*, 1, 93–121.

Anderson, J. R. (2005). *Cognitive psychology and its implications* (6th ed.). New York: Worth Publishers.

Bachman, L. F., & Palmer, A. S. (1996). *Language testing in practice: Designing and developing useful language tests.* Oxford: Oxford University Press.

Bialystok, E. (1979). Explicit and implicit judgements of L2 grammaticality. *Language Learning*, 29, 81–103.

Chalker, S. (1994). Pedagogical grammar: Principles and problems. In M. Bygate, A. Tonkyn, & E. Williams (Eds.). *Grammar and the language teacher* (pp. 31–44). New York: Prentice Hall.

DeKeyser, R. M. (1994). How implicit can adult second language learning be? *AILA Review*, 11, 83–96.

DeKeyser, R. M. (2003). Implicit and explicit learning. In C. J. Doughty, & M. H. Long (Eds.). *The handbook of second language acquisition* (pp. 313–48). Malden, MA: Blackwell.

DeKeyser, R. M. (2005). What makes learning second-language grammar difficult? A review of issues. *Language Learning*, 55, 1–25.

Elder, C., Warren, J., Hajek, J., Manwaring, D., & Davies, A. (1999). Metalinguistic knowledge: How important is it in studying a language at university? *Australian Review of Applied Linguistics*, 22, 81–95.

Ellis, R. (2004). The definition and measurement of L2 explicit knowledge. *Language Learning*, 54, 227–75.

Ellis, R. (2006). Modelling learning difficulty and second language proficiency: The differential contributions of implicit and explicit knowledge. *Applied Linguistics*, 27, 431–63.

Ericsson, K. A., & Simon, H. A. (1993). *Protocol analysis: Verbal reports as data* (revised ed.). Cambridge, MA: MIT Press.

Gánem-Gutiérrez, G. A., & Roehr, K. (under review). Talking about language: L2 learners' use of metalinguistic knowledge on contrasting pedagogic tasks.

Green, A. (1998). *Verbal protocol analysis in language testing research: A handbook.* Cambridge: Cambridge University Press.

Hu, G. (2002). Psychological constraints on the utility of metalinguistic knowledge in second language production. *Studies in Second Language Acquisition*, 24, 347–86.

Hulstijn, J. H. (2005). Theoretical and empirical issues in the study of implicit and explicit second-language learning: Introduction. *Studies in Second Language Acquisition*, 27, 129–40.

Hulstijn, J. H., & de Graaff, R. (1994). Under what conditions does explicit knowledge of a second language facilitate the acquisition of implicit knowledge? A research proposal. *AILA Review*, 11, 97–112.

Klapper, J., & Rees, J. (2003). Reviewing the case for explicit grammar instruction in the university foreign language learning context. *Language Teaching Research*, 7, 285–314.

Roehr, K. (2008). Metalinguistic knowledge and language ability in university-level L2 learners. *Applied Linguistics*, 29, 173–99.

Roehr, K., & Gánem-Gutiérrez, G. A. (2008). Metalinguistic knowledge in instructed L2 learning: An individual difference variable? Essex Research Reports in Linguistics, 57.5.

Sorace, A. (1985). Metalinguistic knowledge and language use in acquisition-poor environments. *Applied Linguistics*, 6, 239–54.

Westney, P. (1994). Rules and pedagogical grammar. In T. Odlin (Ed.). *Perspectives on pedagogical grammar* (pp. 72–96). Cambridge: Cambridge University Press.

Young, K. A. (2005). Direct from the source: The value of 'think-aloud' data in understanding learning. *Journal of Educational Enquiry*, 6, 19–33.

Zietek, A. A. (in preparation). Metalinguistic knowledge and cognitive style in instructed Polish learners of L2 English. Unpublished MA dissertation, University of Essex.

Chapter 7

The Development of Vocabulary Proficiency in Relation to Learning Style

Paul Booth
Kingston University, United Kingdom

Abstract

Learners differ in vocabulary knowledge and these differences can be related to strengths and weaknesses in memory- and analysis-orientated learning (Milton, 2007 and Harley & Hart, 1997). This chapter shows that analysis-oriented learners tend to be more consistent in their lexical development than memory-orientated learners who tend to show greater fluctuations. Lexical diversity and rarity are measured from learners' written texts. Learners are categorized according to their strengths and weaknesses in visual memory of paired associates and grammatical sensitivity. Understanding how learners vary in their approaches to L2 learning can help us to understand differences in learners' lexical development.

Introduction

One way of assessing vocabulary proficiency is to examine the lexical richness of learners' output. This takes the form of analysing the lexical diversity and rarity of the vocabulary used in speech and writing. However, assessing lexical proficiency is by no means a straightforward task. Having direct access to learners' full lexical knowledge is not possible because learners do not produce all of their lexical knowledge at any one time. Moreover, the test or task invariably has a direct impact on the words learners actually demonstrate knowledge of. An indication of the dynamic nature of this knowledge is that learners also tend to regress and progress over time (see Larsen-Freeman, 2006). Lexical knowledge and lexical development appear not to be constant or linear.

One way of understanding learners' lexical proficiency is to examine how certain abilities and learning styles have an impact on the trajectory of lexical knowledge. There is evidence to suggest that learning style or aptitude strengths relate to vocabulary proficiency and that individuals do vary (see Harley and

Hart, 1997 and Milton, 2007). These studies suggest that memory- and analysis-orientated learners differ in terms of vocabulary acquisition. This study will focus on how learners differ over five points in time rather than at a single point, and how learners' lexical trajectories may be related to learning style.

Measures of Lexical Knowledge: Diversity and Rarity

Lexical diversity can be measured as the number of different types of words which a learner uses, that is type token ratio[1] (TTR). Problems with TTR have been well documented (e.g. Jarvis, 2002). One of the fundamental problems with this measurement, and other functions of TTR, is that the TTR falls as the number of words increases. A person only has a finite amount of words at their disposal and so as the text increases in tokens then the likelihood of repetition of tokens of the same type increases. This is why TTR is high to begin with when there is less repetition but then gradually decreases over a larger sample of words. Malvern and Richards tackle this phenomenon by producing a method of measuring lexical diversity that is a measurement made over a series of points in order to establish the pattern of fall of the curve rather than any particular value on it (Malvern, Richards, Chipere & Durán, 2004, p. 59). The statistic[2] is not any particular point on the curve, but it is the pattern of fall of the curve which is calculated. The parameter (D) is a mathematical ideal curve which is the closest fitting curve to the actual TTR curve from real language.

Lexical rarity uses frequency lists to determine the sophistication of the words used. *P-Lex* (Meara, 2007) is a computer program that calculates lexical richness by analysing ten word segments of a text and then counts the number of 'difficult' words in the text. It then calculates the number of blocks containing difficult words and the probability[3] of this happening. In this context though, the key factor is not the likelihood of rare events happening over time, but of the distribution of certain, that is 'diificult', words occurring in a length of text. The program calculates the closest fitting Poisson curve and reports this curve by means of a central parameter, (λ) lambda (Bell, 2002, p. 80). Learners not only differ in lexical knowledge but also in the manner in which they approach language leaning.

Learning Style

Skehan's model of learning style is informed by his own work with learners clustered by aptitude type (see Skehan, 1986) and the relationship between instruction and aptitude differences (Wesche, 1981). Skehan (1998, p. 250) identifies memory- and analysis-orientated learners. Analysis-orientated learners would favour rule-based representation and processing, whereas memory-orientated learners would favour exemplar-based representation and processing. The theory is that learners can be high or low in either or both dimensions. In terms of lexis, high analysis foreign language learners would have a parsimoniously organized, single representation lexical system but low analysis would mean a smaller, less differentiated system. High memory learners would have a wide range of lexicalized exemplars and multiple representations of lexical elements; however, low memory learners would have a smaller repertoire of lexical elements and might not have the multiple representations.

How learners are tested for this model of learning style comes not from a learning style test per se, but from Meara, Milton and Lorenzo-Duz's (2001) Language Aptitude Tests. LAT B for memory is a timed test of ability to remember pairs of words when they are displayed in writing. LAT C for analysis is a test of ability to find or infer rules from examples of a language unknown to the test taker. So learners can be differentiated and categorized in terms of strengths and weaknesses of these dimensions. In light of the above discussion, the following research questions are proposed:

1. Are any patterns in lexical diversity (parameter D) trajectories related to strengths and weaknesses in Memory and Analysis?
2. Are any patterns in lexical rarity (*P-Lex*) trajectories related to strengths and weaknesses in Memory and Analysis?
3. Is productive lexical development as measured by lexical diversity and lexical rarity a linear or nonlinear trajectory over time?

Method

The Participants

The participants were 12 second language learners of English who were enrolled in a private language school in London. All learners were post-Cambridge First Certificate level grade C or above (i.e. post upper-intermediate) and were enrolled on an intensive language course designed to help them pass the Cambridge Advanced Exam. They all worked for the same bank in Switzerland which had sponsored them for this exam course over a period of 12 weeks. Therefore there was extrinsic motivation for them to do well. Among the 12 learners, 9 of the learners' L1 was German or Swiss-German, one was French, one was bilingual in Bengali and German, and one was bilingual in Croatian and German. The mean age for this group was 22 years (oldest 31, youngest 19) and there were 5 males and 7 females. At the time of Memory and Analysis tests they had all lived in the UK for three months.

Data Processing

In this study Meara and Miralpeix's *D-Tools* (2007) which is based on Malvern and Richard's *vocd* program was used, but it is more user-friendly in that texts can be transcribed on Microsoft Notepad. Because lexical diversity is only one aspect of lexical richness, *P-Lex* was also used to measure lexical rarity to give a more complete picture of lexical richness.

The raw data which the *D-Tools* and *P-Lex* software used were participants' texts written at five different points in time, with two weeks between each point. The texts were written under exam conditions so no dictionaries were allowed and the learners had one hour to write each text. The learners had no advanced warning of the writing tasks but were familiar with the genre of the writing they were expected to produce:

Text 1: A character reference for a job
Text 2: A report (fund raising for a charity organization)
Text 3: A report (profit investment)
Text 4: A letter recommending changes for a friendship club
Text 5: A complaint letter to the editor

When learner texts were inputted, grammar errors were not corrected, wrong words were deleted, superficial spelling mistakes were corrected but words that were unclear because of spelling errors were deleted. Hyphenated words and phrasal verbs were treated as one word and contractions were treated as two. Numbers were included either as written words or as numerals. LAT B (Memory) and LAT C (Analysis) were completed by the participants towards the end of their language course.

Results

The participants were grouped according to Meara et al.'s (2001) categorization of scores (see Tables 7.1 and 7.2). The Memory and Analysis scores of all

Table 7.1 LAT B Memory scores and their interpretation

84–100	top 10% of all scores
74–83	next 20% of all scores
43–73	middle 40% of all scores
34–42	next 20% of all scores
0–33	bottom 10% of all scores

Table 7.2 LAT C Analysis scores and their interpretation

90–100	top 10% of all scores
70–89	next 20% of all scores
60–69	middle 40% of all scores
50–59	next 20% of all scores
0–49	bottom 10% of all scores

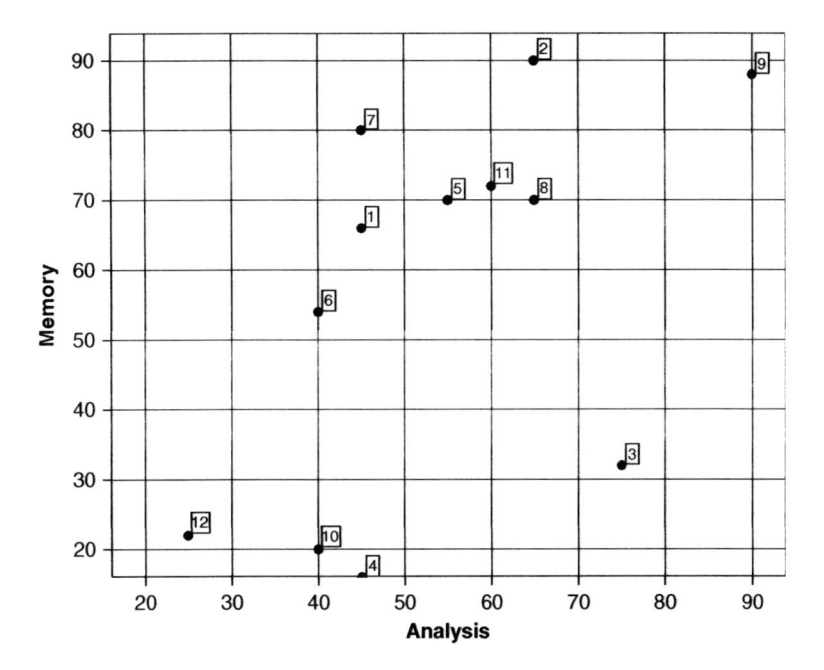

FIGURE 7.1 Memory and Analysis scores

learners can be seen in Figure 7.1, and the participants with strengths and weaknesses in Memory and Analysis scores can be seen in Tables 7.3, 7.4 and 7.5.

The trajectories of learners with extreme Memory and Analysis scores will be presented to ascertain whether there are any similarities or differences between these learners. The trajectories from participants whose Memory and Analysis scores fall into the middle bands are not presented because the effect of learning style on their lexical profiles may not be so strong. So I will only present learners with extreme scores (i.e. bottom and top 30 per cent) in Memory and/or Analysis to determine whether there are any relationships.

100 Issues in Second Language Proficiency

Table 7.3 Group 1: bottom 10 per cent Memory and Analysis

Participant	Memory	Analysis
4	16	45
10	20	40
12	22	25

Table 7.4 Group 2: top 30 per cent Memory

Participant	Memory	Analysis
2	90	65
7	80	45

Table 7.5 Group 3: top 30 per cent Analysis

Participant	Memory	Analysis
3	32	75
9	88	90

The groupings were as shown in Tables 7.3, 7.4 and 7.5.

In the top Analysis group I have included a participant who also has a high Memory score because there was only one participant with a high Analysis but low Memory score. The following section looks at the number of tokens produced by the group over five data collection points. There were occasions when not all learners participated.

We can see from Figure 7.2 that the number of words (tokens) which this group wrote during their timed essays increased. Correlations were made between the D statistic and number of words. There was no relationship between the number of words and the D statistic. This is encouraging because the texts were not standardized for word count (see Table 7.6).

Lexical Diversity

The group mean for lexical diversity shows a slight increase and then a steady decline in the last half of the 12-week intensive course. Figure 7.3 and Table 7.7

The Development of Vocabulary Proficiency

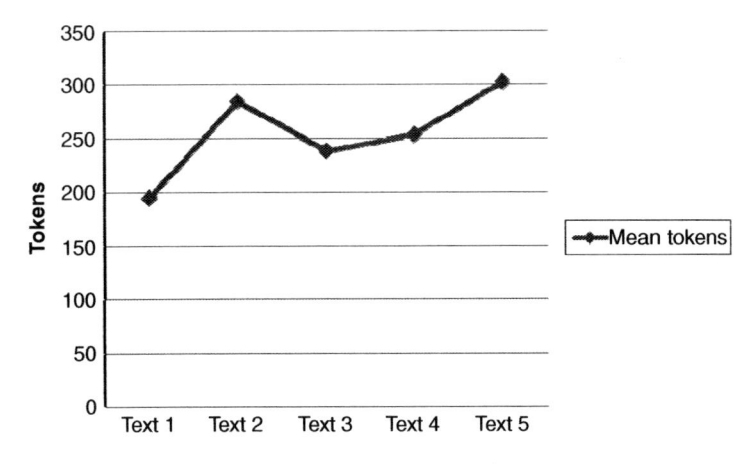

FIGURE 7.2 Mean number of tokens

Table 7.6 Mean numbers of words

	N	Minimum	Maximum	Mean	SD
Text 1	11	151.00	242.00	191.18	31.54
Text 2	11	213.00	350.00	286.91	34.82
Text 3	10	168.00	292.00	243.60	39.42
Text 4	12	189.00	314.00	256.33	34.83
Text 5	10	242.00	355.00	306.60	37.12

highlight that lexical diversity does not suddenly increase during the initial few days but, as a mean of the group, remains relatively stable and then declines. There may be various reasons for this trajectory which will be discussed later. Interestingly, the steady decline falls further than the starting point at the beginning of the course.

To determine whether the differences in diversity scores between the different points in time were significant or not, a non-parametric one-factor within subjects ANOVA was carried out. A non-parametric measure was used because of the small number of participants. Unsurprisingly, Table 7.8 shows the differences between the texts at different points in time were not significant.

The following section shows the individual lexical diversity trajectories in relation to top and bottom scores from the Memory and Analysis tests. Whereas the mean diversity trajectory is smooth, some individual trajectories show greater variation and others remain relatively smooth. Figure 7.4 is of individual lexical diversity profiles from learners with bottom Memory and Analysis scores and is plotted over five texts.

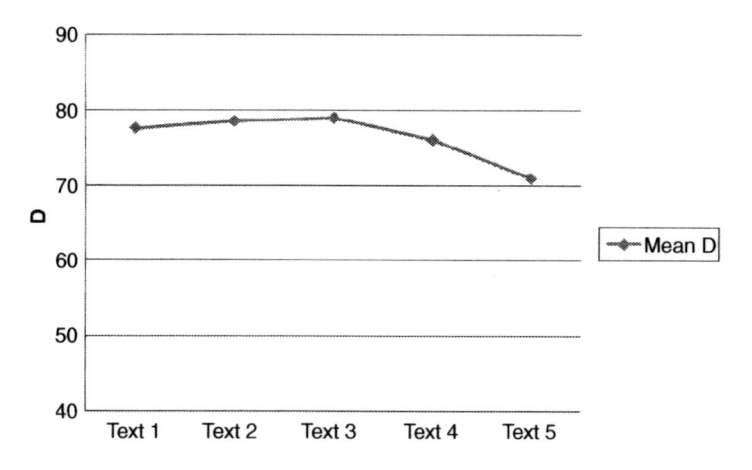

FIGURE 7.3 Mean lexical diversity (parameter D)

Table 7.7 Mean lexical diversity (D)

	Text 1	Text 2	Text 3	Text 4	Text 5
N	11	11	10	12	10
Mean	77.59	78.58	78.98	76.08	70.97
SD	9.66	13.07	13.87	15.16	8.48
Minimum	65.21	64.33	60.68	56.74	59.63
Maximum	93.39	100.6	101.42	113.13	84.51

Table 7.8 Friedman ANOVA lexical diversity

N	6
Chi-square	6.93
Df	4.00
Asymp. sig.	0.14
Exact sig.	0.14
Point probability	0.01

We can see in Figure 7.4 that these three learners who have low LAT B and C scores did not progress in terms of lexical diversity as the course wore on. There are peaks and troughs, however, which is expected considering all of the variables in writing texts over a short intensive course. Participant 4 has a particularly dramatic saw-tooth profile and the D statistic reflects this fluctuation

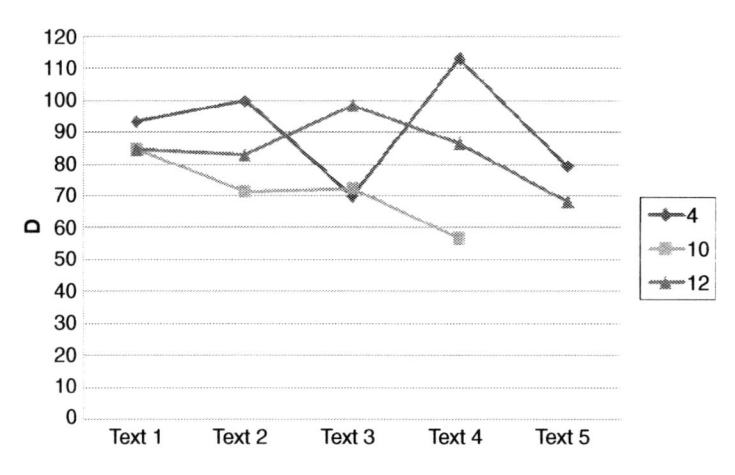

The Development of Vocabulary Proficiency 103

FIGURE 7.4 Lexical diversity plotted against texts at bottom Memory and Analysis level (participants 4, 10 and 12)

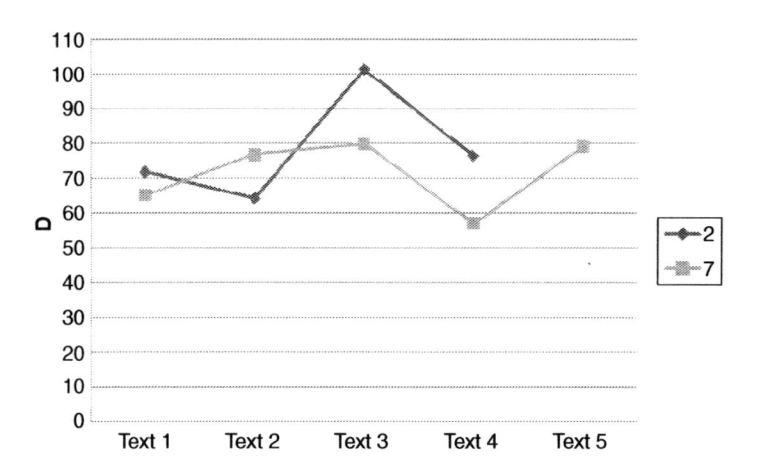

FIGURE 7.5 Lexical diversity plotted against texts at top Memory level (participants 2 and 7)

in diversity. The score for text 4 is the highest diversity score of any of the other participants. However, the overall lack of development, that is all of the participants ended with a lower *D* statistic than when they started, may indicate that it is difficult for learners to progress if they do not score beyond a certain threshold in Memory and Analysis.

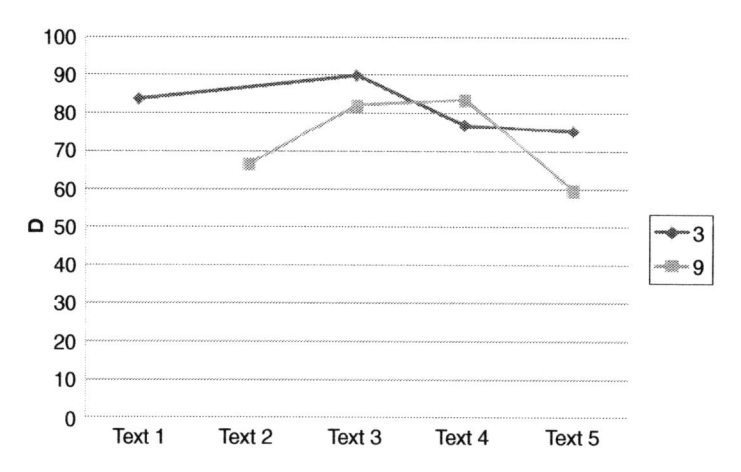

FIGURE 7.6 Lexical diversity plotted against texts at top Analysis level (participants 3 and 9)

In Figure 7.5 the two trajectories show a wide range of diversity scores, especially participant 2 who scored the highest on the Memory test out of the entire cohort. Although these two trajectories fluctuate, the overall trajectory is not down but relatively level compared to the previous group.

The two trajectories in Figure 7.6 tend to remain fairly close together and relatively smooth. They appear more consistent in relation to the other groups. Although they both fall towards the end of the course, they do not display the wide swings in diversity as some of the other trajectories. In fact Participant 3 with above middle Analysis but bottom Memory scores has remained fairly consistent in terms of diversity.

In order to examine lexical rarity, the next set of data used is the lambda statistic from the *P-Lex* software. First, the mean group statistic will be given and then the data will be analysed using a one-way ANOVA to determine whether there are any differences between the values taken at different points in time. Then individual word rarity trajectories using the same participants who scored high or low on the Memory and Analysis dimensions will be analysed.

Word Rarity

The *P-Lex* software was used to determine word rarity and the statistic given is the lambda values. The mean trajectory in Figure 7.7 differs from diversity in that there is a discernable peak in lexical rarity for text 3. Although the mean diversity was at its peak at this point as well, the trajectory was much smoother. The start and finish points highlight (Table 7.9) an improvement in terms

The Development of Vocabulary Proficiency

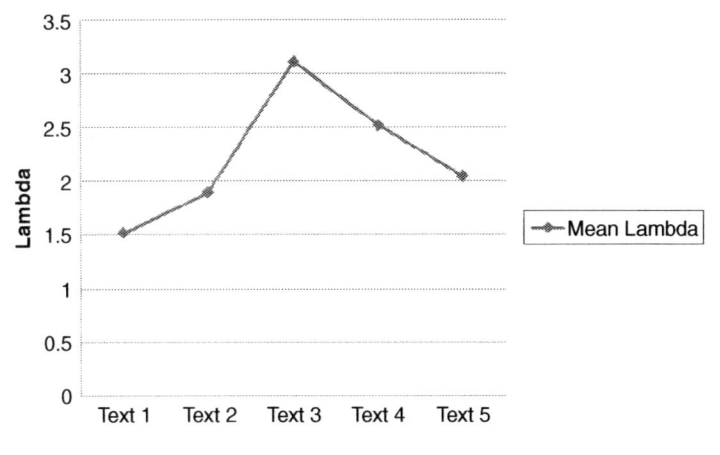

FIGURE 7.7 Mean word rarity

Table 7.9 Mean word rarity

	Text 1	Text 2	Text 3	Text 4	Text 5
N	11	11	10	12	10
Mean	1.51	1.89	3.12	2.51	2.04
SD	0.26	0.32	0.52	0.24	0.31
Minimum	1.13	1.37	2.06	2.16	1.49
Maximum	2.11	2.34	4.04	2.95	2.57

Table 7.10 Friedman ANOVA word rarity

N	6
Chi-square	19.529
Df	4.000
Asymp. sig.	0.001
Exact sig.	0.000
Point probability	0.000

of rarity at the end of the course while for diversity there was virtually no improvement.

In order to determine whether the differences were significant or not across the different texts, a Friedman one-way ANOVA test was conducted.

106   *Issues in Second Language Proficiency*

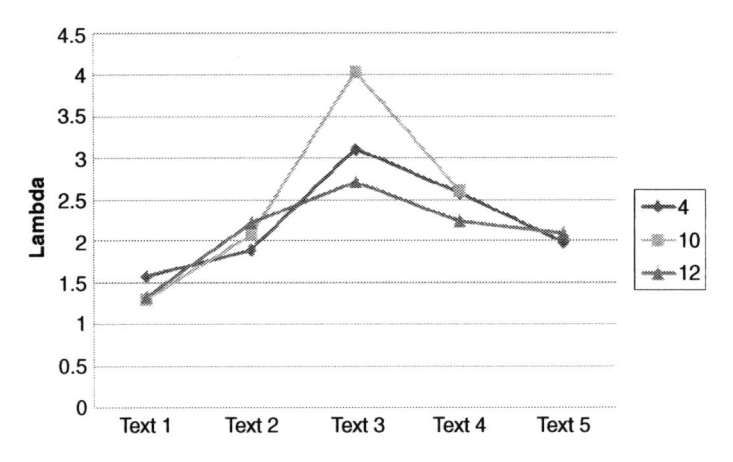

FIGURE 7.8 Word rarity plotted against texts at bottom Memory and Analysis level (participants 4, 10 and 12)

This test shows that the rankings for the texts differ significantly across the texts, as can be seen in Table 7.10: $X^2 (6) = 19.53$; $p < 0.01$. The following section examines the word rarity plotted against Memory and Analysis scores using the same groups as before and starts with the bottom scores.

Whereas the diversity trajectories for these three participants fell over five pieces of writing, the rarity scores (lambda) in Figure 7.8 rose and then fell which follow the pattern from the group average. The trajectory from participant 10 is particularly high for text 3. Recall that in the previous section, this participant's diversity trajectory fell rather steeply.

In Figure 7.9, although both participants began with practically identical scores, they both rose and fell without any apparent relationship between them. No coherent pattern emerges between top Memory learners and their word rarity trajectories.

The two participants who scored high on the Analysis dimension rise and fall in tandem (Figure 7.10). As with their lexical diversity scores, their lambda scores tend not to fluctuate as much as the scores from learners who are in the top Memory but low Analysis range.

The first research question asked whether there is a relationship between the lexical diversity (*D*) scores and learners' strengths and weaknesses in Memory and Analysis. The *D* trajectories tended to fluctuate more with learners who displayed low Memory and Analysis and those with high Memory only. Smoother, less dramatic trajectories were found with the two learners who were in the top Analysis group.

In answer to the second question, the lambda scores (*P-Lex*) from the three learners who scored low in both Memory and Analysis showed that their lexical

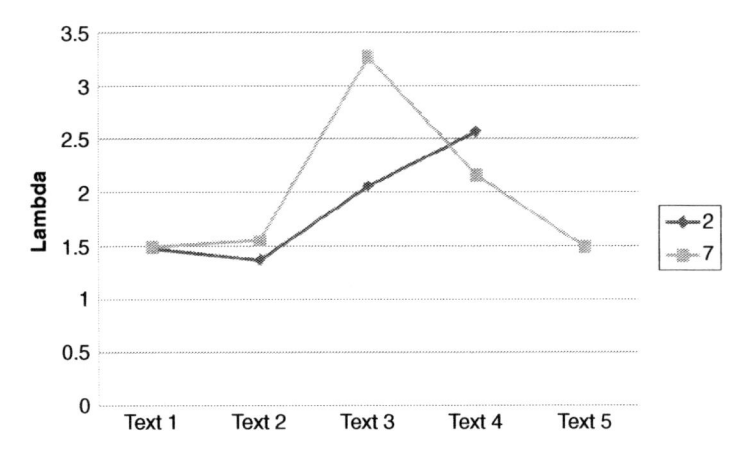

FIGURE 7.9 Word rarity plotted against texts at top Memory level (participants 2 and 7)

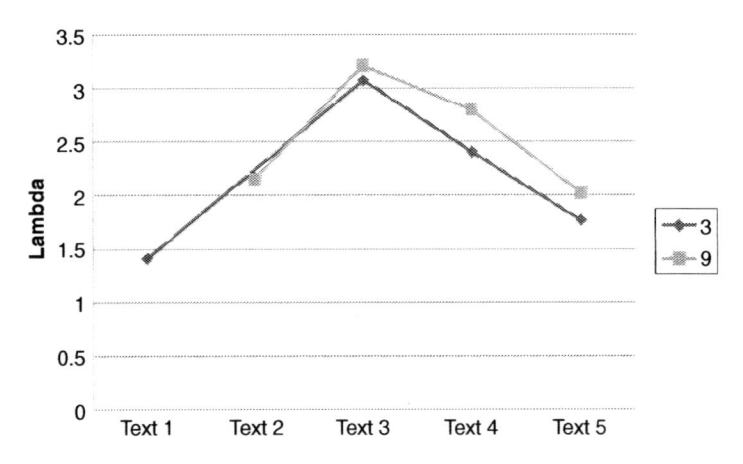

FIGURE 7.10 Word rarity plotted against texts at top Analysis level (participants 3 and 9)

rarity rose and then fell. Interestingly, a similar pattern emerged from the learners both high in Analysis. The high Memory learners did not show much relationship between their trajectories. Although they both started off from similar points, they tended to diverge over the period of the course.

In answer to the third question which asked whether productive lexical development is linear or not, we can firmly say that lexical development is not linear. Both diversity and rarity tend to rise and fall as learners produce texts over a period of 12 weeks. The diversity trajectories have shown that, in this study, over 12 weeks, learners' texts do not necessarily become more diverse in terms of vocabulary; in fact, the trajectory of the mean parameter D scores rose and then fell. So rather than a steady increase in diversity, there was instead a slight increase followed by a steady decline. The word rarity trajectories have shown that learners can increase their production of rare words but that the increase can just as easily fall with the next piece of writing. This, to some extent, can be expected given all the factors involved in lexical production.

Discussion

This work sought to find whether any patterns in lexical trajectories are related to strengths and weaknesses in memory- or analysis-orientated learning. Although there were exceptions, individuals with low Memory and Analysis scores tended not to gain in lexical diversity over the 12 weeks. Learners with high Analysis scores, however, tended to show relatively smooth, less fluctuation in their diversity trajectories than learners with only high Memory scores.

The two learners with high Analysis scores also had very similar lexical rarity profiles, while high Memory learners' trajectories did not show a coherent relationship. Regularity rather than irregularity in lexical knowledge may be associated with learners who are orientated towards or who have an aptitude for grammatical sensitivity. In a study of receptive vocabulary knowledge, Milton (2007) found that learners with normal lexical profiles (i.e. greater knowledge of each succeeding band of greater frequency) score higher on the LAT C (Analysis) than learners with a level two deficit (i.e. a dip in the knowledge of the second thousand frequency band). So while individual learners fluctuate in terms of lexical diversity and rarity over five pieces of writing, regularity and stability tend to go hand in hand with high Analysis scores but not high Memory scores.

In this study, when the trajectories of learners low on the Memory and Analysis dimensions were compared, we see that overall they declined in diversity but gained in rarity. It appears that in terms of lexical production, development in lexical diversity is more static than word rarity. Why this is so is not clear. The relationship between word diversity and rarity seems to be a complex one. Skehan's theory that analysis-orientated learners engage in regular restructuring and complexification (Skehan, 1998, p. 250) is borne out to some extent by some of my data in this study which suggest they are the ones whose diversity or rarity trajectories are likely to be more regular and less likely to fluctuate. However, memory-orientated learners are difficult to pin down in that data from their lexical trajectories in terms of rarity and diversity do not show much consistency with each other. They are the learners most likely to display fluctuations in their lexical trajectories. One possibility is that memory-orientated learners may be more likely to use vocabulary recently encountered but that new lexis is less likely to be used consistently in the long term.

It is possible that the use or non-use of rare words will cause the lambda statistic to fluctuate while the complexity of the language will remain relatively unchanged. Jarvis (2002) notes that excessively high levels of lexical diversity preclude the amount of repetition which is necessary to maintain text coherence. If the learner complexifies sentence structure, then a certain amount of repetition (e.g. function words) may be necessary which will depress the *D* statistic. A very high *D* score may mean that a text lacks coherence because a certain amount of repetition is necessary for text unity. In order to distinguish the quality of the learners' texts, they were also rated by native speakers (see below) to give a more holistic interpretation. The evidence from my study suggests that lexical development is certainly not a linear process either in diversity or rarity. Learners' scores rose and fell over the different points in time.

At the beginning of the course the learners' production of tokens was quite low, reflecting perhaps a lack of sub-topics in each text. A reduced word count means that the *D-Tools* software has less lexical information to base its *D* statistic on. Although the *D* parameter mitigates against type token ratio (TTR) being a function of text length by using a curve-fitting procedure, it does mean that texts with a low token count may give a less accurate idea of a learners lexical production than a larger text.

Subsequently, the word count rose, which might indicate more sub-topics within the text and so greater diversity. Then at the end of the course, although learners were more fluent, they perhaps were more focused on the task, thus causing the *D* statistic to fall. Looking again at the standard deviations for the group as a whole, we can see that the initial *D* scores are close together, and it is only after the first piece of writing that the trajectories become more diverse and then come closer together at the end of the language course.

Although the trajectories are not particularly smooth, intuitively one would expect more of an overall increase as the course progressed. At best, most learners seem to end up at a lexical diversity score roughly the same as where they started from; at worst, some learners' scores declined. The lexical rarity trajectories showed an increase then a fall. There may be many reasons for this. Learners may not progress for some very obvious reasons, for instance they may be tired or bored with the course; sometimes there is no obvious reason at all, for example development is not immediate but delayed.

One reason for the peak in lexical rarity could have been due to the task topic. Recall that these learners came from a banking background and that the subject of text 3 was an investment report. This task topic would call upon lexis connected with investment which these learners would have been exposed to in the course of their work or training. It is also possible that certain low frequency lexis of this topic is similar in both English and German. For example, participant 9 used the following cognates in the investment report: principal – *prinzipiell*, modern – *modern*, productivity – *Produktivität*, motivated – *motivieren*, information – *Information*, communicate – *kommunizieren*. However, the other learners did not use as many cognates for this task. The other topics the learners had to write about may not have been so familiar to the writers in terms of topic, for example a personal reference.

In fact, the teacher may have also had an indirect effect on the learners. An informal interview revealed that he did in fact encourage learners to focus on exactly what the task required them to do and not to include superfluous information. This might have had the effect of reducing the number of sub-topics within each text and also of increasing the amount of repetition of certain key words. However, a skilled writer would possibly use synonyms to reduce the monotonous effect of repeating the same words. Another teacher influence was the emphasis he gave to discourage the students from translating their thoughts from L1 into English. Instead, they were encouraged to think and work directly in English. As these learners were high proficiency, this was probably possible but lower level students may not have the lexical knowledge to work directly in English.

One learner (participant 12) was noted as being particularly uncomfortable with writing under exam conditions and usually became flustered when told she was coming to the end of the time allowed. Interestingly, this learner also scored the lowest on LAT B and C. This is unusual because this learner also reported that, apart from German, she has French and Czech as other languages. So although she scores very low on the LAT B and C, she is an experienced language learner who has reached a high level of proficiency in English. Meara et al. (2001) explain that when interpreting the LAT B scores, learners with high anxiety levels do not perform as well on this test. One reason could be that the pairs of words travel across the computer screen at a fixed speed over which the test taker has no control.

In order to determine qualitative differences between the texts, three native speaker raters who were qualified in teaching English as a second language were asked to give a single holistic quality rating (see appendix) to the texts from the participants of the various sub-groups. The quality rating was based upon the Cambridge CAE general impression mark scheme. This mark scheme was chosen because it includes the criteria for this exam class and the criteria have been fully piloted. The score ranges from 0 to 5 which is a general impression of the text. The criteria include: accuracy of language, range of vocabulary, structure of text, cohesion and register. Mean scores from the raters are given for the sake of conciseness.

We can see in Table 7.11 that participant 4 tends to score well compared to the other two. Participant 12 consistently scores less than the other two in the group. This is not surprising considering that this student scored the lowest on the LAT B and C and also claimed that the time limit was not sufficient. Overall though, participant 4 is judged the best out of this particular sub-group. This student also has the highest LAT C Analysis score in this group (45 per cent).

Table 7.11 Mean rater scores: bottom Memory and Analysis

Participant	Text 1	Text 2	Text 3	Text 4	Text 5
4	4	4.0	4.0	3.0	4.3
10	3	3.3	3.3	3.7	
12	2.7	2.7	2.7	3.7	3.3

Table 7.12 Mean rater scores: top Memory

Participant	Text 1	Text 2	Text 3	Text 4	Text 5
2	1	2.3	3.3	2.7	
7	3.7	4	4.3	3.7	3

Table 7.13 Mean rater scores: top Analysis

Participant	Text 1	Text 2	Text 3	Text 4	Text 5
3	4.3		4.3	4.3	4.3
9		4	4	3.7	4

Table 7.14 The reliability of the raters

Text type	Cronbach's alpha
1. Character reference	.926
2. Report (fund raising for a charity)	.785
3. Report (profit investment)	.719
4. Letter recommending changes for a club	.573
5. Complaint letter	.727

In Table 7.12, participant 2 tends to be erratic regarding the quality of the work. This is also reflected in the lexical diversity and to a lesser extent in the word rarity trajectory. The reason why the first text was judged so low is because this student misread the task question and produced a text which was not relevant. Interestingly, this sub-group does not tend to be judged any higher than participants 4 and 10 from the low Memory and Analysis group.

In Table 7.13, the participants were all rated 3 or above for the texts they wrote. Participant 3, who is high in Analysis but not Memory, also often hit the top score. Although these ratings are for a very small number of learners, the raters tended to evaluate the texts from the two analysis-orientated learners' texts higher than the other two sub-groups.

If we are to draw any conclusions about the holistic ratings of the texts, it is vital to know how reliable the raters are. I have used Cronbach's alpha as a measure of rater reliability. Table 7.14 shows that the Cronbach's alpha is generally acceptable for the texts except text 4.

Conclusions

This study examined learners' lexical development over time in relation to a memory-analysis learning style framework. Lexical development was measured in terms of diversity and rarity so as to capture both aspects of lexical richness. While the trajectories show fluctuations in terms of diversity and rarity, the memory-analysis framework can help us to understand which learners are likely to display trajectories which are relatively more regular, that is less likely to fluctuate than others. Analysis-orientated learners are more likely to show similar patterns of trajectories than memory-orientated learners. Learners who are memory-orientated tended to show greater variation in their trajectory pattern. However, the trajectories were not linear. Learners do not display profiles that progressively gain in diversity or rarity. The trajectories tended to rise and fall, which suggests that learners' output is relatively unstable and that a single sample of their productive vocabulary is likely to be misleading. Although the parameter D and lambda statistic from the software is sensitive to variations in learner output, impressionistic, holistic ratings of the writing quality tended to score analysis-orientated learners higher than those at the bottom on the memory-analysis dimensions.

The implication from this research study is that learners orientated towards grammatical sensitivity are more likely to be predictable in their lexical output. This type of learner is more likely to produce a stable profile over different times. This is not to say that this type of learner will always develop in terms of lexical diversity or rarity, but sensitivity to language patterns may be related to a more systematic use of vocabulary, that is one that does not show dramatic fluctuations in diversity or rarity. On the other hand, memory-orientated learners tend to fluctuate more in terms of lexical diversity and rarity which may indicate that these learners are more likely to use words recently encountered but that usage will be temporary. So when we consider L2 learner proficiency, a single measurement of lexical richness, whether it is diversity or rarity, will be sensitive to the task to elicit that lexis. Moreover, learners who are less strong in analysing language may show wider swings in their lexical diversity and rarity.

Notes

[1] The following sentence: 'The heat of the night' contains 5 running words or tokens even though one of them is repeated (the). Words which are different from each other are counted as types. So the type-token ratio of the example sentence is 4 types/5 tokens = 0.8.

[2] Parameter D (diversity) calculates a mean segmental TTR for a random selection of words from the text. The program (*vocd*) can read a transcript of the language sample and then plots the TTR verses tokens curve between N = 35 and N = 50 and

derives each point from an average of 100 trials on the randomized sub-samples of words of the token size for that point (Malvern et al. 2004, p. 55).
[3] The 'difficult' words are those which are not found in the list of high frequency words which are listed in the *P-Lex* Manual. The statistic which *P-Lex* uses is the Poisson distribution which describes the likelihood of rare events occurring.

References

Bell, H. (2002). Using frequency lists to assess L2 text. Unpublished PhD thesis, Swansea: University of Wales.

Cambridge Advanced Exam Teaching Resource (2008). *General impression mark scheme.* Retrieved March 10, 2008 from http://www.cambridgeesol.org/teach/cae/writing/aboutthepaper/assessment/general_imp_mark_scheme.htm

Harley, B., & Hart, D. (1997). Language aptitude and second language proficiency in classroom learners of different starting ages. *Studies in Second Language Acquisition* 19, 370–400.

Jarvis, S. (2002). Short texts, best-fitting curves and new measures of lexical diversity. *Language Testing,* 19, 57–84.

Larsen-Freeman, D. (2006). The emergence of complexity, fluency, and accuracy in the oral and written production of five Chinese learners of English. *Applied Linguistics,* 27, 590–619.

Malvern, D., Richards, B., Chipere, N., & Durán, P. (2004). *Lexical diversity and language development.* Basingstoke: Palgrave Macmillan.

Meara, P. (2007). *P-Lex* (Version 2.0) (Computer software). Swansea: Lognostics.

Meara, P., & Miralpeix, I. (2007). *D-Tools* (Version 2.0) (Computer software). Swansea: Lognostics.

Meara, P., Milton, J., & Lorenzo-Duz, N. (2001). *Language aptitude tests.* Newbury: Express.

Milton, J. (2007). Lexical profiles, learning styles and the construct validity of lexical size tests. In H. Daller, J. Milton, & J. Treffers-Daller (Eds). *Modelling and assessing vocabulary knowledge* (pp. 47–58). Cambridge: Cambridge University Press.

Skehan, P. (1986). Cluster analysis and the identification of learner types. In V. Cook, (Ed.). *Experimental approaches to second language acquisition* (pp. 81–94). Oxford: Pergamon.

Skehan, P. (1998). *A cognitive approach to language learning.* Oxford: Oxford University Press.

Wesche, M. B. (1981). Language aptitude measures in streaming, matching students with methods, and diagnosis of learning problems. In K. C. Diller (Ed.). *Individual differences and universals in foreign language aptitude* (pp. 119–54). Rowley, MA: Newbury House.

Appendix 1

D and lambda scores

	D scores					Lambda scores				
	Texts					Texts				
Participants	1	2	3	4	5	1	2	3	4	5
1	71.29	72.26	68.17	74.52	62.09	2.02	1.65	3.36	2.58	1.84
2	71.88	64.33	101.42	76.62		1.48	1.52	1.98	2.46	
3	83.89		90.00	76.91	75.29	1.41		3.08	2.34	1.84
4	93.39	99.92	69.86	113.13	79.32	1.64	1.77	3.11	2.52	1.99
5	66.21	73.18	67.42	75.31	64.52	1.31	1.73	3.38	2.29	1.81
6	88.69	100.60		61.47	84.51	1.67	1.61		2.95	2.35
7	65.21	76.95	79.33	57.06	64.13	1.5	1.59	3.27	2.21	1.77
8	70.75	66.40	60.68	79.93	79.29	1.92	2.15	2.81	2.22	2.36
9		66.48	81.98	83.60	59.63		2.09	3.16	2.8	2.07
10	84.61	71.42	72.37	56.74		1.35	2.1	3.97	2.61	
11	72.99	89.90		71.20	72.70	1.44	2.29		2.56	2.61
12	84.56	82.93	98.60	86.47	68.21	1.33	2.22	2.96	2.18	2.1

Holistic quality rating

Band 5   Minimal errors: resourceful, controlled and natural use of language, showing good range of vocabulary and structure. Task fully completed, with good use of cohesive devices, consistently appropriate register. No relevant omissions.
N. B. Not necessarily a flawless performance.
Very positive effect on target reader.

Band 4   Sufficiently natural, errors only when more complex language attempted. Some evidence of range of vocabulary and structure. Good realisation of task, only minor omissions. Attention paid to organisation and cohesion; register usually appropriate.
Positive effect on target reader achieved.

Band 3   Either (a) task reasonably achieved, accuracy of language satisfactory and adequate range of vocabulary and range of structures or (b) an ambitious attempt at the task, causing a number of non-impeding errors, but a good range of vocabulary and structure demonstrated. There may be minor omissions, but content clearly organised.
Would achieve the required effect on target reader.

Band 2	Some attempt at task but lack of expansion and/or notable omissions/irrelevancies. Noticeable lifting of language from the input, often inappropriately. Errors sometimes obscure communication and/or language is too elementary for this level. Content not clearly organised. Would have a negative effect on target reader.
Band 1	Serious lack of control and/or frequent basic errors. Narrow range of language. Inadequate attempt at task. Very negative effect on target reader.
Band 0	(a) Fewer than 50 words per question or (b) totally illegible work or (c) total irrelevance (often previously prepared answer to a different question).

Source: Cambridge Advanced Exam Teaching Resource (2008).

Chapter 8

Second Language Reading Proficiency and Word Recognition: The Concept of Saliency and Its Application Across Different Scripts

Mick Randall
British University in Dubai, Dubai

Abstract

This chapter examines the case for a greater emphasis on bottom-up processes in reading, especially with learners using a radically different script such as Arabic. It argues that word recognition is the major factor involved in SL reading and becomes the essential site where bottom-up and top-down processes unite. It examines word recognition processes in English and examines different 'saliency' factors and the way these may vary between Arabic and English.

Introduction

This chapter examines the cognitive aspects of reading in a second or foreign language especially in a second or foreign language situation where the scriptal system is very different. It discusses the dichotomy between top-down and bottom-up methods of processing print and argues that an essential skill involved in any reading process is that of word recognition and that recognizing words in any language rests on the rapid and automatic cognitive processing of salient orthographic features in the target language. There has long been an implicit assumption in pedagogic approaches to TESOL and TEFL that word recognition processes are part of initial literacy and that these processes are universal. However, there is increasing evidence that automatic perceptual and cognitive processes may not be universal, but at least influenced, if not determined, by the structure of the linguistic or orthographic system of the L1. It is the intention of this chapter to examine such a hypothesis through the examination of the differences between English and Arabic, two languages which use highly different linguistic and orthographic systems and the likely effect these systems may have on the cognitive processing of words. The chapter argues that pedagogic procedures should be based upon a 'contrastive cognitive analysis' between the target language and the first language of the speakers and it will offer some suggestions as to how more attention can be drawn to the problems of word recognition within ELT teacher training programmes, syllabi and materials.

Top Down and Bottom Up Processes in Reading

The tension between the different models of language processing (bottom-up vs. top-down) can be seen as one of the most important distinctions underlying the last 60 or so years of language processing debates. It is the difference between those which emphasise decoding processes of linguistic symbols (the bottom-up) and the approaches which emphasise the use of wider context and meaning (the top-down). The debate draws on the changing paradigms of applied linguistic theories from structural linguistics, through symbolic linguistics and cognitive linguistics to connectionism. Communicative Language Teaching (CLT) has largely favoured the top-down approach to language processing, emphasizing the central role of meaning in language processing (see Randall, 2007 for a discussion).

Nowhere is this more true than in approaches to reading and literacy. In first language literacy development, the debate is exemplified by the often 'Lilliputian' arguments between the Phonics vs. Look and Say and Real Books methods of teaching reading. Stemming from the work of Goodman (1976) and the idea of 'reading as a psycholinguistic guessing game', L1 reading pedagogies placed a great deal of emphasis on meaning (as outlined in Smith's seminal work on reading, Smith, 1978). Following from these approaches there has been an increasing emphasis on the social aspects of literacy rather than on the formal processes of decoding print (functional vs. autonomous literacy, Street, 1984). However, later writers, starting with Adam (1990) and, more importantly for second language readers, Goswami and Bryant (1990) have begun to reassert the importance of decoding processes in initial reading.

Within ELT methodologies, processes of decoding print in English by speakers of other languages received little attention. TEFL/TESOL has historically been largely dominated by young adult learners, often at the tertiary or at least post-compulsory education level. As the majority of these learners already have literacy skills in their L1 and often in a related language using the Roman alphabet, it has been tacitly assumed that they already possess basic literacy skills in English as a Second or Foreign Language. However, as Koda (2005) and others (Randall 2007) have pointed out, there are considerable differences between learning literacy skills in a first as against a second language:

- Initial L1 readers have established oral competence in the L1 on which to build their reading skills in the language.

- L2 readers have established L1 graphic-phonemic routines by which they approach the decoding of text.
- And L2 readers will have L1 cognitive processes for decoding texts which derive from the experience of reading the L1 and which may be dependent on the approaches used to teach initial literacy in the L1.

All of these factors will have an influence on word recognition processes adopted by second language readers of English.

Word Recognition Procedures and Salience

The major argument against concentration on decoding procedures in L1 literacy pedagogies is that concentration on such factors alone detracts attention from the main purposes of reading which is communication. Thus, reading for meaning, pragmatics and critical reading are three of the important skills in reading, which, added to decoding, leads to the Four Resources for Reading (Freebody and Luke, 1990). Such emphases, especially the importance of critical reading, have been echoed in ELT in the work of Wallace (2006). Such a tradition sees literacy as a social phenomenon, not an individual linguistic skill. However, as pertinent as such observations are, there needs to be a bridge between the contextual reality and the linguistic signs and symbols. Such a mediation is performed by meaning. Words, both spoken and written, have meanings and it is through them that the pragmatic message is conveyed. For example, a large red signboard warning of danger contains a lot of information about the pragmatic force of the message through its context, but it is through recognition of the words on the sign that this semiotic is refined and the specific message is transmitted (deep water, do not swim, beware of falling rocks, live ammunition, do not enter, etc.). This message can then be critically examined and challenged (on whose authority should people be excluded from certain areas etc.), but the essential mediation is through the recognition of the words contained in the sign.

In this sense, then, word recognition is the site at which language and meaning meet, where top-down and bottom-up processes converge. In that words carry the principle semantic load of the message they are the critical mechanism by which linguistic symbols are converted into meaningful messages. The access of meaning from print through recognizing words (the essential prerequisite for successful reading) is thus a core skill in the reading process. Such processing involves rapid and automatic word recognition procedures.

This centrality can be demonstrated by eye movement research. It has long been noted that readers do not pay equal attention to every feature of a text. Readers do not attend to every word in a text, but move their eyes across texts, pausing on certain aspects (fixations) and skipping over others (saccades).

Attention is not always unidirectional (10–15 per cent of saccades are regressive), indicating that readers do sometimes need to check previous linguistic context to disambiguate/confirm the meaning which they have constructed from the content words, but the important point is that most fixations are on content words. Even more important is the fact that all content words receive attention from fluent readers reading normally (Bernhardt, 1991). Content words are thus the most salient parts of any written message.

Bernhardt (1991) demonstrated differences between native and SL readers' eye movements when reading texts in English. The SL readers fixated more on function words than the L1 readers and they were longer in their fixations on the content words than the L1 readers. The time spent fixating function words can be explained on one level by the lack of language proficiency of the SL readers (lower syntactic knowledge leads to lower ability to infer the function words from grammatical context), but it also indicates a lack of ability to automatically access such words as whole units and concentrate on the more salient units – the content words. Furthermore, the longer fixation time on the content words indicates the greater problem SL readers have with word recognition procedures, that is the failure to rapidly and automatically cognitively process words at the micro-level. A cognitive approach would argue that such a failure is due to the inability to notice salient features in words in English.

The Cognitive Architecture of Information Processing and Noticing

The most enduring cognitive framework for understanding language processing is the Information Processing Model, with its three memory stores – the Sensory Register, the Working Memory and the Long-Term Memory, coupled with the concept of limited capacity. This framework, first proposed by Atkinson and Shiffron in 1968 has stood the test of time and, with minor modifications, still forms the basis of cognitive psychological thinking about information processing within the brain. The model is also supported by a considerable amount of neurological evidence (see Byrnes, 2001 and Randall, 2007). Information coming in to the brain is progressively paired down by extracting the salient information from the total data received. Within this framework, much attention has been paid within cognitive psychology to the role of Working Memory and language processing. The basic model envisages the Working Memory as a short-term 'notebook' or RAM (to use a computer analogy) in which incoming language data can be stored and compared to long-term information from the LTM as well as being integrated with further incoming data. The process is supervised by a control mechanism (the Supervisor Attention System, SAS) which can control where the language user directs their attention. Put simply, the process is shown in Figure 8.1.

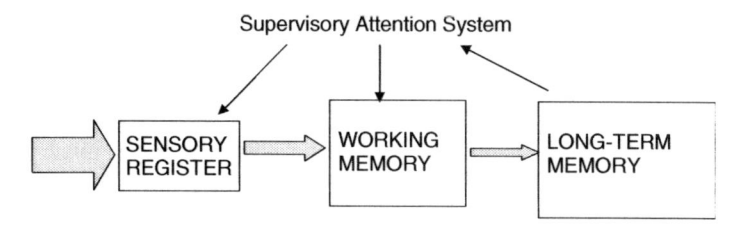

FIGURE 8.1 A simplified view of working memory with the SAS

We have suggested that words recognition is linked to recognizing salient features. In that situation, the role of the SAS is to direct attention of the Sensory Register and the WM to salient features of the visual information, paying no attention to visual patterns which are not relevant (i.e. background, visual 'noise'), and highlighting the most important patterns in the remaining information (i.e. the printed letters/words). Furthermore, if we accept that basic decoding features are not universal, but vary from language to language the SAS is 'tuned' by experience and training to notice salient features of the L1. Thus, the role of the SL language class will be to train the SAS to 'notice' the salient features in the L2 written text in as far as they are different from the L1 text.

Such a process is highly congruent with current applied linguistic thinking and SLL methodology in which 'noticing' (Schmidt, 1990) is a major mechanism by which the learner's interlanguage knowledge develops (for a description of noticing, see Skehan, 1998).

Lexical Access Procedures in English and Cross-Linguistic Research

One of the most established and well-researched phenomenon concerning lexical processing in English is the dual-route theory (Coltheart, Rastle, Perry, Langdon & Ziegler, 2001, and see Harley, 2001, for a discussion). Probably due to the orthographical complexity of English, it would seem that fluent readers in English need to use two routes to access words. One, the Direct Route, relies on recognizing words as wholes and the other, the graphic-phonemic conversion (GPC) route relies on the ability to sound out the word from the individual letters. It would seem from neurological evidence with acquired dyslexics that both routes are necessary for fluent word recognition in English and obviously form the basis of the differing approaches to initial reading in English (Phonics vs. Look and Say) discussed earlier. To this basic model, recent research has added a refinement to the Direct Route, suggesting that words are processed on a syllabic level as ONSET + RIME (Goswami and Bryant, 1990; Harley, 2001).

The other well-documented aspect of letter saliency in English is the Initial-Final-Medial saliency effect. Letters within words do not have equal importance in terms of their salience for accessing the word. Rather than a left-to-right serial processing effect in which the first letters are the most important followed by the medial letters and then the final letters (which would make sense in terms of reading direction), the initial letters are the most salient, followed by the final letters and the middle letters are the least salient. This effect has long been recognized and was first investigated by Bruner and O'Dowd (1958). They investigated the disruption to word recognition caused by inverting letters in different parts of the word and the manifestation of this salience order can be verified by the difficulty that we have spotting spelling mistakes in the middles of words rather than at the beginnings or ends.

The salience features noted above are those which have been developed by first language readers of English and are thus related to the particular scriptal and orthographic patterns of English. Arguably the most important of these is the lack of transparency in the orthography. There is emerging evidence that this feature may affect cognitive processing of print. Even in alphabetic languages there would appear to be differences in cognitive processing between languages with 'deep' orthographies (such as English) and those with more 'shallow' orthographies (such as German and Greek) and this appears at a very early age. Goswami, Ziegler, Dalton & Schneider (2003) demonstrated that children learning to read in English were more sensitive to 'chunks' of letters than were children learning to read in languages with greater transparency in their orthographies. Goswami et al. term this 'psychological grain size' and suggest that this reflects the use of a letter-by-letter strategy in languages with greater orthographic transparency than in English. Following from this, Wydell and Kondo (2003) suggest languages can be classified according to two dimensions, Granular size, ranging from fine (phoneme) to coarse (word) and Degree of Transparency, ranging from transparent to opaque.

In addition, differences in perceptual processing of arrays between Arabic L1 users and English L1 users responding to arrays of English letters and digits have been noted by Randall and Meara (1988) and these perceptual patterns are highly stable. It was also clearly established that processing strategies are transferred by Arabic L1 readers into their scanning of arrays in English. In array scanning experiments, subjects are presented with a single letter on a screen (e.g. 'S') and then asked to identify this target letter in a five-letter array (e.g. 'PSDAV'). The target letter can be moved to different positions in the array and the time taken to identify the target in the different positions is recorded. This procedure can also be used with digits and shapes as the targets. Typically, L1 English users produce radically different search patterns for linguistic stimuli (letters and digits) than they do for shapes. In the latter case, subjects produce U-shaped search strategies with the centre noted most quickly and the ends more slowly (see Figure 8.2a), but upward-sloping M-shaped

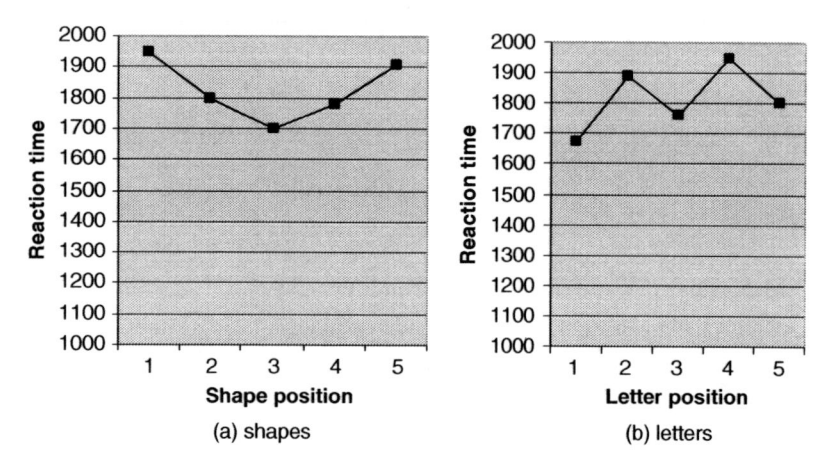

FIGURE 8.2 Typical array scanning reaction times for English L1 users

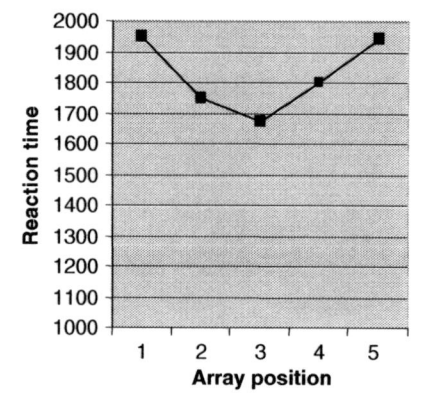

FIGURE 8.3 Typical array scanning reaction times for Arabic L1 users for English, Arabic and digits

patterns with linguistic data (Figure 8.2b). Differences in search patterns emerge at a very early age (Green, Hammond & Supramanian, 1983).

L1 Arabic users scanning arrays of both English stimuli and Arabic stimuli universally produce U-shaped patterns and this does not change with exposure to English (Randall and Meara, 1988) (see Figure 8.3.).

It would thus seem that basic perceptual processes are different across different language groups and one explanation is that these could be due to differences in the orthographic or linguistic structures of these languages. We shall next examine the orthographic and linguistic properties of Arabic to identify the way that these properties may affect basic word recognition strategies when Arabic L1 users read English.

Orthographic and Linguistic Differences between English and Arabic and Their Possible Effects on Word Recognition Strategies

Visual Properties of the Script

On the macro level of reading a text, the first task for the reader is to extract orthographic words. This is quite straightforward in languages using the Roman alphabet as orthographic words are separated by spaces (although languages will differ in the number of separate morphemes within the orthographic word). Such a process may well account for the initial and final letter saliency effect and the extra attention paid to the beginnings and ends of arrays of letters. Spaces between words and, by extension, initial and final letters are thus highly salient features of the text. Arabic also uses spaces between words, but not as categorically as in the Roman alphabet. As Arabic letters vary in their ability to link with the following letter, Arabic 'words' also have spaces within them, albeit smaller than between the words. Visually, the differences between Arabic and Roman calligraphy are quite striking as can be seen in the two sentences in Figure 8.4. The highlighted portions of the texts contain four words in each language which are quite clearly indicated in the English by three spaces, yet the similar Arabic text contains five 'large' and 3 'small' spaces, making it much more difficult to rapidly identify the word boundaries for the reader trained on the Roman alphabet script (see Figure 8.4).

This is not to say that spaces aren't salient in Arabic. Both languages (as do all alphabetic languages) use spaces as significant signs, but that the degree of salience of the space is different between the two languages. In Arabic the judgement is on the size of the space, not solely the presence of the space. Other features (such as the presence of a definite article, or a specific symbol

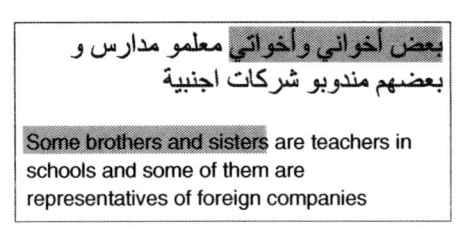

بعض أخواني وأخواتي معلمو مدارس و
بعضهم مندوبو شركات اجنبية

Some brothers and sisters are teachers in schools and some of them are representatives of foreign companies

FIGURE 8.4 A comparison of Arabic and English script

(ة), which in a particular format (ية) can only appear word finally) may be more salient for identifying words at the macro level. Another macro feature which differs between Arabic and English is the use of capital letters to identify the beginnings of sentences and proper nouns. Search strategies (e.g. the well-used pedagogic technique of asking students to scan for specific information – often proper nouns – within a text) will involve a completely different search strategy in a language which does not signal proper nouns with capital letters. In fact, the problem of programming computers to identify names in Arabic text is one that is on the forefront of text processing in Arabic (Shaalan & Raza, 2007).

Syllabic Structure

Classical Arabic has a predominantly CVCV, VC or CVC syllable structure. Initial consonant clusters do not exist although certain two consonant clusters may appear syllable finally. Consonants are therefore highly salient and, coupled with the fact that in normal script, unstressed vowels are not marked (see below), Arabic L1 readers will not be attuned to syllable structures such as CCCVC (as in [SCREAM]). Indeed, there will be a tendency to try to cognitively process the initial cluster as three separate syllables by inserting a neutral vowel between each consonant. In speech this leads to epenthesis, /s@k@ri:m/, and such a method of phonological processing will also have a profound effect of the way that Arabic L1 readers approach word recognition in English. Thus, these readers will have difficulties in accurately parsing orthographic words into syllables and in 'seeing' whole words and syllables.

Orthographic Transparency

Arabic has highly regular grapheme to phoneme correspondences; it is has a highly transparent orthography. This, combined with the CVCV structure of spoken classical Arabic, tends to lead to a heavily phonic L1 literacy training:

$$سكن = ن + ك + س = /sa/ + /ka/ + /na/$$

Given such an approach, the expectation will be that each letter will have the same phonetic value. Words will be processed using a serial GPC route and the modification of the vowel sound between [MAT] and [MATE] (i.e. the salience of the final [E]) will not be an aspect which Arabic L1 users will notice. Serial processing does not encourage the recognition of the ONSET + RIME structure of a syllable (see below), where the [ATE] versus the [AT] rime patterns[1] are highly salient in English.

The 'Consonantal' Nature of Written Arabic

Arabic is characterized as a 'consonantal' language (Cook & Bassetti, 2005; Sampson, 1985). In normal written Arabic, unstressed vowels are not marked. Therefore the Arabic reader needs to supply the correct vowelling, depending on the context. The word سكن, which is composed of three consonants, has three different phonetic realizations – /sakana/, /sakan/, and /sukina/ – which have three different meanings – 'he lived', 'hostel/house' and 'was lived' (a passive form of the verb). These realizations will vary according to the linguistic context. This consonantal feature of the written language will have an important affect on the way that Arabic L1 readers extract significant features from the words. One of the most important is the lack of attention to vowels in words written in the Roman alphabet (sometime referred to as 'vowel blindness', Ryan & Meara, 1991). Another important aspect which derives from the lack of vowel marking is that phonological mediation may be much a more important process in Arabic than it is in English (or it may even be mandatory). Again, the necessity of using a cognitive strategy which uses the GPC route to access words in Arabic will lead to a lessening of the ability to use the direct route to word recognition which, as we have seen, is considered to be an essential component of effective reading by L1 readers of English. Thus, individual letters rather than chunks of letters and words are much more salient in Arabic.

Morphological Structure

Arabic has an extremely regular morphological structure. The mathematical regularity of the grammar has led some scholars to accuse medieval Arab grammarians of contriving some artificiality about its classical form (Kaye, 1987). The lexical structure of the language consists of a relatively small set of three consonant verbal roots (and a smaller set of four consonant roots) from which a large number of words are generated by the use of regular morphological transformations. For example, the trilateral root, سكن, which we examined above will generate about 20 related head words by changing the vowelling (as we discussed above), by doubling consonants (doubled consonants are phonemic in Arabic) and by adding prefixes, infixes and suffixes. Such a system makes the triliteral and quadriliteral consonant roots highly salient for recognizing words. This provides a possible explanation for the array scanning search patterns which pay attention to the centre of arrays as such roots will generally appear in the centre of orthographic words. This heightened salience of root letters and reduced salience of written vowels in Arabic may lead to difficulties in processing words such as [SACKING] and [SICKEN] where the repetition of the consonants S, K and N letters may suggest that the words are morphologically related to the Arabic L1 reader. In addition to this morphological structure,

Arabic is an inflected language and adds other morphemes such as articles, direct and indirect object pronouns, and possessive markers to base words, making the orthographic word much more morphologically complicated than in English. The process of extracting the base form from an orthographic unit containing so much morphological information is likely to result in a very different search strategy involving different salient features from English.

Salience, and Cognitive Contrastive Analysis

The above contrastive analysis of Arabic and English suggests differences in the way that word meanings are accessed from printed texts in the two languages. The discussion rests on the examination of linguistic elements which differ between the two languages. In that sense it can be argued it is little different from the discredited Contrastive Analysis (CA) of structuralist linguistics and audio-lingualism which sought to derive syllabus items from linguistic description. However, the CA carried out in the 1950s and 1960s was aimed to predict surface features which needed intensive practice to 'perfect' performance in the SL. This analysis extends the concept of CA to examine the cognitive processing implications of the differences between the first and second languages. It is thus a 'Cognitive Contrastive Analysis' and is aimed at directing attention to significant features of the different systems in order to suggest how these may illuminate the basic psycholinguistic processes involved.

It is important to understand exactly what is meant by 'salience'. As we discussed when we examined the scripts of the Roman alphabet, all alphabetic languages make use of spaces to separate symbols (be they letters or words) but they are used to different extents by different languages and thus have different levels of salience to users of the different languages. On the oral level, both languages use consonant and vowel phonemes, yet there is a large difference in the salience of consonants and vowels across the two languages. English has a large number of vowel phonemes compared to Arabic (something like 22 to 7, but these vary according to dialects). Arabic, on the other hand, has most of the consonant distinctions found in English, but has certain consonant distinctions (the emphatic and non-emphatic consonants and the single versus doubled consonants) which do not exist in English. English L1 learners of Arabic often report that they differentiate between the emphatic and non-emphatic consonants by attending to changes in the vowels which follow them. L1 English speakers are highly sensitive to vowel differences and, to English speakers, vowels are much more salient than consonants.

In terms of reading and word recognition, all languages make use of some form of phonological processing (even readers of logographic languages have been shown to be sensitive to phonological features). All will use whole word recognition procedures, and all will use context to aid comprehension to some extent. It is just that the nature of the writing systems lead to the processes

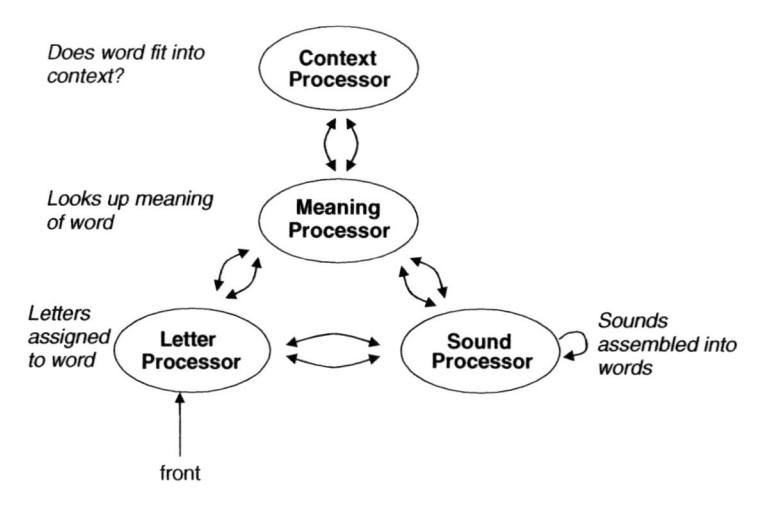

FIGURE 8.5 Cognitive processes involved in word recognition (after Adams, 1990)

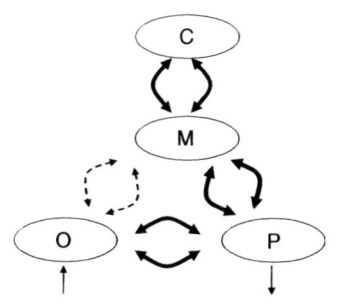

FIGURE 8.6 Cognitive processes involved in reading Arabic

being differentially employed. For example, if we take Adams' 'triangle model' (Adams, 1990) of word recognition and reading as applied to English, the Direct and GPC roots are represented as having an equal loading (see Figure 8.5).

With Arabic word recognition, as we have discussed, the GPC root may be more salient, given the relative transparency of the orthography, and the use of context may be more important, given the lack of vowel marking in normal reading. The triangle may then look more like the one in Figure 8.6.

It is important to note that the above analysis is one which is at present based on theoretical modelling. It is important that the predictions provided by these models are tested out in research. One of the reasons for the rejections of the strong version of traditional CA was its inability to account for many of the errors predicted, or, alternatively, for the lack of evidence for errors predicted by the analyses. However, it should also be pointed out that much of this criticism came from grammatical errors. Within the area of phonology, CA is still the best predictor of speech variations. As phonology plays a large part in word recognition and phonological awareness has been shown to be an essential prerequisite for reading, it would seem to be reasonable to expect that a cognitive contrastive analysis will provide useful predictions about cognitive processes involved in reading.

As discussed above, there is evidence that linguistic factors seem to have an influence on perceptual processes, and there is evidence from spelling errors that supports the predictions derived from linguistic analysis. In as much that spelling can reveal underlying orthographical knowledge, the investigation of spelling errors can shed light on cognitive processing of print. Randall (2005) has shown the influence that the syllable structure of Bahasa Malaysia has on Malaysian student spelling mistakes in English. Work has also been carried out on Chinese student errors, and again, there are suggestions of a strong influence of L1 processing strategies effecting the processing of English words. As regards Arabic, evidence is emerging that many of the predictions of this cognitive model are borne out in practice (Sadhwani, 2005). Arabic L1 users have great difficulty with selecting or recognizing vowels in writing or reading printed material. There is also a lot of evidence of inability to process clusters and spelling errors especially in initial consonant clusters. However, evidence on aspects such as syllabification, morphology or the use of context is yet to be established.

Implications for Pedagogic Practice

The first implication relates to macro system-wide changes in syllabus goals and teacher training. At present syllabi and training programmes pay scant attention to the particular problems of word recognition. Reading proficiency is assessed holistically according to the ability to perform tasks such as extracting information from a text. This is based on pragmatics and meaning and little attention is paid to sub-skills such as orthographical knowledge and pattern recognition which are essential for accomplishing the higher order tasks. In addition, the generally accepted pedagogy of reading in SL deals with a common core of pragmatic skills such as prediction, reading for gist, skimming, scanning, and the use of context to aid comprehension. These skills are not language specific and arguably are generic skills common to literacy in general. They do not pay attention to the specific difficulties faced by users of different L1s, except in the area of different cultural schema. A similar 'one size fits all' approach can be seen in the approaches to academic subject knowledge, such as phonology, commonly taught on initial training courses. Rather than deliver a general description of phonology, often narrowly linked to pronunciation skills, initial training programmes should pay greater attention to the specific aspects of phonology as it affects literacy and orthographic knowledge (i.e. the phonology/orthography interface). The areas studied should be related to the specific difficulties faced by the L1 users.

In terms of materials design and lesson delivery, current ELT practice is moving towards a more eclectic, modified task-based approach to teaching. The successful accomplishment of meaningful and communicative tasks in the SL classroom still forms the backbone of most SL/FL teaching approaches and materials, but the belief that the performance of tasks *per se* will be sufficient to lead to proficiency has been replaced by evidence that there needs to be some focus on formal elements (the Focus on Form(S) debate). Within this renewed interest in teaching of formal features there is much debate about what should be taught, the timing and placement of formally taught elements and how they should be taught (Doughty & Williams, 1998). Vocabulary, for example, is one such formal area on which to focus. At present vocabulary study is motivated by an emphasis on meaning and semantics; words are usually grouped around semantic or contextual domains with little attention paid to the formal word recognition properties. International textbooks select pertinent areas to present to the students based on areas such as estimates of frequency or utility. The implication of the approach suggested here is that some attention should be paid to the formal characteristics of orthography in English to enable students to build up cognitive strategies for recognizing words through their salient features. It is also suggested that the training in the use of cognitive strategies needs to be related to the differences in processing strategies between the first and second languages. The greater the distance between the linguistic, orthographic and scriptal systems, the greater will be the need for such training.

Notes

[1] While this pattern is often taught as the 'magic e' rule in initial literacy programmes, it can be seen as an example of a more general VCV rime pattern on stressed syllables in which certain vowels following a single consonant change the vowel quality preceding the consonant.

References

Adams, M. (1990). *Beginning to read: Thinking and learning about print*. Cambridge MA: The MIT Press.
Atkinson, R. C., & Shiffrin, R. M. (1968). Human memory: A proposed system and its control processes. In K. W. Spence, & J. T. Spence (Eds.). *The psychology of learning and motivation* (pp. 89–195). London: Academic Press.

Bernhardt, E. B. (1991). *Reading development in a second language: Theoretical, empirical & classroom perspectives.* Norwood, NJ: Ablex.

Bruner, J. S., & O'Dowd, D. (1958). A note on the informativeness of parts of words. *Language and Speech,* 1, 98–101.

Byrnes, J. P. (2001). *Minds, brains and learning.* New York, NY: The Guilford Press.

Coltheart, M., Rastle, K., Perry, C., Langdon, R., & Ziegler, J. (2001). DRC. A computational model of visual word recognition and reading aloud. *Psychological Review,* 108, 204–56.

Doughty, C., & Williams, J. (Eds.). (1998). *Focus on form in classroom SLA.* Cambridge: Cambridge University Press.

Freebody, P., & Luke, A. (1990). Literacies programs: Debates and demands in cultural context. *Prospect: Australian Journal of TESOL,* 5, 7–16.

Goodman, K. S. (1976). Reading as a psycholinguistic guessing game. In H. Selinger and R. B. Ruddell (Eds.). *Theoretical models and processes of reading* (487–508). Newark, DE: International Reading Association.

Goswami, U., & Bryant, P. (1990). *Phonological skills and learning to read.* Hove, East Sussex: Lawrence Erlbaum Associates.

Goswami, U., Ziegler, J. C., Dalton, L., & Schneider, W. (2003). Nonword reading across orthographies: How flexible is the choice of reading units? *Applied Psycholinguistics,* 24 (2), 235–47.

Green, D. W., Hammond, E. J., & Supramanian, S. (1983). Letters and shapes: Developmental changes in search strategies. *British Journal of Psychology,* 3, 101–17.

Harley, T. A. (2001). *The psychology of language: From data to theory.* Hove: Psychology Press.

Kaye, A. S. (1987). Arabic. In B. Comrie (Ed.). *The world's major languages* (pp. 664–85). London: Routledge.

Koda, K. (2005). *Insights into second language reading: A cross-linguistic account.* Cambridge: Cambridge University Press.

Randall, M. (2005). Orthographic knowledge and first language reading: Evidence from single word dictation from Chinese and Malaysian users of English as a foreign language. In V. Cook., & B. Bassetti. (Eds.). *Second language writing systems* (122–46). Clevedon: Multilingual Matters.

Randall, M. (2007). *Memory, psychology and second language learning.* Amsterdam: John Benjamins.

Randall, M., & Meara, P. (1988). How Arabs read Roma letters. *Reading in a Foreign Language,* 4 (2) 133–45.

Ryan, A., & Meara, P. (1991). The case of the invisible vowels: Arabic speakers reading English words. *Reading in a Foreign Language,* 7, 531–40.

Sadhwani, P. (2005). Phonological and orthographical knowledge: An Arab-Emirati perspective. MEd Dissertation, British University in Dubai. Retrieved Accessed January 1, 2009 from (http://www.buid.ac.ae/buid/html/article.asp?cid=610)

Sampson, G. (1985). *Writing Systems.* London; Hutchinson.

Schmidt, R. (1990). The role of consciousness in second language learning. *Applied Linguistics,* 11, 129–58.

Shaalan, K., & Raza, H. (2007). Person name entity recognition for Arabic. In *Proceedings of the ACL Workshop on Computational Approaches to Semitic Languages*, Prague, Czech Republic.

Skehan, P. (1998). *A cognitive approach to language learning*. Oxford: Oxford University Press.

Smith, F. (1978). *Reading*. Cambridge: Cambridge University Press.

Street, B. (1984). *Literacy in theory and practice*. Cambridge: Cambridge University Press.

Wallace, C. (2006). *Critical reading in langugage education*. London: Palgrave Macmillan.

Wydell T. N., & Kondo T. (2003). Phonological deficit and the reliance on orthographic approximation for reading: A follow–up study on an English–Japanese bilingual with monolingual dyslexia. *Journal of Research in Reading*, 26, 33–48.

Chapter 9

L2 Proficiency: Measuring the Intelligibility of Words and Extended Speech

Sara Kennedy
McGill University, Montréal, Canada

Abstract

Intelligibility (the extent to which a speaker's message is understood) is a central element in assessing second language (L2) learners' proficiency. To date, intelligibility has mostly been measured through the recognition of isolated words or sentences. However, it is unclear whether the intelligibility of words reflects the intelligibility of extended speech in context. In this study, 30 personal stories from 4 native English speakers and 6 L2 learners were presented to 76 listeners whose reactions yielded intelligibility measures of words and of extended speech. Results showed that word-level intelligibility measures might not reflect the intelligibility of extended speech in context.

Introduction

When evaluating a second language (L2) learner's oral proficiency, there are many aspects of L2 speech which can be measured. Consider, for example, this excerpt of a story told by an L2 learner.

> Uh, I think the person will face so many kind of, uh, problems and decision he should, he choose or make, uh, during the whole life. Uh, in my life, uh, until now I think the very good decision I made is, uh, go to Canada. Why I say so? Because, uh, I, I have some, some stray no, strong reason, for support my decision. Uh, even, uh, very hard two years in Canada life, uh, but I think it's worth.

To assess this learner's oral proficiency, researchers could examine, for instance, the type and frequency of errors produced by the learner, the complexity of her morphosyntax, the range and richness of her lexicon, or the fluency (speed, smoothness) with which she speaks (e.g. Daller, Van Hout & Treffers-Daller, 2003; DeKeyser, 2005; Towell, Hawkins & Bazergui, 1996).

All of these measures of oral proficiency target the accuracy, complexity and fluency of learners' language, but these measures often give little information about the effectiveness of learners' communication with interlocutors. For example, researchers who use these measures usually do not consider whether interlocutors more easily understand learners' utterances which are syntactically complex or those which are simple, or whether learners with a limited productive lexicon are less able to accomplish their communicative goals than are learners with a larger lexicon. Therefore, by using these measures, researchers may overlook important elements of learners' communicative ability, and thus of their proficiency (Kramsch, 1986). One important element of communicative ability is the extent to which learners' production is understood by a listener: what is referred to as *intelligibility* (Nelson, 1982; for review, see Isaacs, 2008). It is the measurement of intelligibility, a component of learners' oral proficiency, that is the focus of this chapter.

It seems uncontroversial that an L2 learner who is frequently unintelligible to most listeners cannot be considered functionally proficient in the L2. Therefore, intelligibility can be seen as a fundamental element of L2 proficiency, and teachers who aim to help learners increase their L2 proficiency may also need to focus on improving learners' intelligibility (Hoekje, 2007). Because there are many reasons why learners might be unintelligible to listeners, teachers could address different aspects of their learners' production. For example, teachers could focus on learners' grammatical accuracy, their lexical range, fluency, pronunciation, or pragmatic appropriateness.

It is currently unclear which aspects of learners' production are most essential to intelligibility. This is simply because to date most intelligibility researchers have focused on only one aspect – improving intelligibility through an instructional focus on pronunciation. Several instructional approaches have been investigated. These include training learners in articulation of individual sounds (Kerr, 2003), exposing them to pronunciation models with no feedback (Macdonald, Yule & Powers, 1994) and teaching them about suprasegmental aspects of pronunciation, such as sentence stress, rhythm and intonation, and general speech characteristics, such as volume and energy (Derwing, Munro & Wiebe, 1997; Stevens, 1989). In fact, it is this third approach (a combined, intensive focus on suprasegmental aspects of pronunciation and on general speech characteristics) that appears to be most effective in improving learners' intelligibility over time. This research finding aligns well with a principle evident in many pronunciation textbooks, especially those for the teaching of English as a second language (ESL), namely, that an instructional focus on suprasegmental aspects of pronunciation is an effective way of improving L2 learners' intelligibility (Avery & Ehrlich, 1992; Celce-Murcia, Brinton & Goodwin, 1996).

This apparent connection between the findings from intelligibility research and the focus of many pronunciation textbooks is misleading, however. The ultimate aim of pronunciation instruction is to prepare learners for interactive, spontaneous and extended L2 communication in a given context (Celce-Murcia et al., 1996). In contrast, in intelligibility research, intelligibility has almost always been measured using listeners' recognition of isolated words or sentences (e.g. Derwing et al., 1997; Rogers, Dalby & Nishi, 2004), and not listeners' understanding of L2 learners in contextualized, extended speech. This raises an important question: does listeners' understanding of L2 learners' isolated words or sentences accurately reflect their understanding of L2 learners in contextualized, extended speech? In other words, what is the link between the measured intelligibility of L2 learners' words and the measured intelligibility of their extended speech? This question is the focus of the study reported here.

Method

Participants

The participants included 10 speakers who recorded personal stories in English. Six were L2 speakers of English who were graduate students at an English-medium university in Canada, and four were native speakers of English with a completed undergraduate degree (mean age = 33). Of the six L2 graduate students, three speakers (henceforth, the treatment group) were taking an ESL oral communication course. The course was a one-semester course for L2 graduate students; its goal was to develop students' pronunciation and communication skills, with a particular focus on intelligibility. Three speakers were only following their graduate program (henceforth, the control group). The L2 speakers in both groups were matched to each other for their first languages (L1s) and length of residence in the English-speaking environment. The background characteristics of the L2 speakers appear in Table 9.1.

Table 9.1 L2 Speaker background characteristics

	Treatment group			Control group			
Participant	L1	Age[a]	Length of residence[a]	Participant	L1	Age[a]	Length of residence[a]
Javier (M)	Spanish	26	0.4	Lupe (M)	Spanish	30	0.4
Hui (M)	Mandarin	22	1.3	Ping (F)	Mandarin	29	1.5
Xiao (F)	Mandarin	29	2.0	Feng (M)	Mandarin	30	3.5

Note: [a]In years.

The participants also included 76 listeners (17 males, 59 females) who were native speakers of North American English. The listeners were divided into two groups, with 46 listeners in one group (mean age = 21) and 30 listeners in the other (mean age = 22). The two listener groups were composed according to listeners' self-reported frequency of exposure to non-native, accented English. That is, each group comprised equal numbers of participants with frequent and infrequent exposure to non-native, accented English. Each of the two groups performed one of two listening tasks (described below).

Materials

Three personal stories were elicited from each speaker using short written prompts focusing on concrete life experiences familiar to any speaker or listener (see Appendix A). The personal stories were recorded three times: near the beginning and end of the four-month oral communication course (Times 1 and 2), and one month after the end of the course (Time 3). The recording took place with individual speakers in a quiet room. Before recording the personal stories, each speaker did a warm-up task to familiarize them with the form and requirements of the story-telling task. For both the warm-up task and the main task, speakers received a different written prompt. They were allowed to think and to make notes (1 min for the warm-up task, 5 min for the main task) but were not permitted to look at their notes while speaking. The researcher, who was listening to each story, did not make audible comments during the recording. Each story was recorded directly onto a computer using a Plantronics (DSP-300) head-mounted microphone. The mean durations of the personal stories were 2.0, 3.6, and 2.3 minutes for the treatment, control and native speaker groups, respectively.

The researcher, a native speaker of English, first transcribed all recorded personal stories (excluding the warm-up stories). Then, another native speaker of English with five years of ESL teaching experience checked 65 per cent of the transcripts against the recordings. The percentage agreement for the transcripts was 96–100 per cent, with most differences centring on function words which had been repeated (*and, and* . . .). Those speakers whose stories contained some unclear words took part in verification sessions. These speakers were shown transcripts of their stories with the unclear words highlighted and were played those sections; they were asked to determine what they had said. The transcript was changed when the speakers proposed a different word than the one in the original transcript. For all samples verified, out of the 18 unclear words (0.3 per cent of the total number of words in all stories), 8 were confirmed and 10 were changed.

Listening Tasks

Listeners did one of two listening tasks, with the same speech samples used for each task. The first listening task, the pause task, targeted the intelligibility of speakers' words. The listeners ($n = 30$) were instructed that they would hear ten stories. They were asked to pause the recording when they did not understand or were not sure of a word, to talk about what the word might be, then to unpause the recording to continue listening. They were also instructed that if they later identified a word that they had not understood before, they should again pause the recording, name the word and talk about how they had come to understand it. To familiarize listeners with the task, all listeners practised the task using one sample story before listening to the ten target stories. All stories for the pause task were played on a laptop computer using *SoundScriber* audio transcription software (Breck, 1998). The audio files were automatically rewound two seconds after unpausing, which ensured that listeners who were slow to pause a recording after an unclear word would be able to resume listening at or immediately before the unclear word. The pause task lasted between 20 and 45 minutes, depending on the number of words which were unclear for each listener.

The second listening task, the retell task, targeted the intelligibility of extended speech. The listeners ($n = 46$) were also instructed that they would hear ten stories. They were asked to take detailed notes while listening to each story, to pause the recording (played on a JVC stereo CD player) only when the story was finished, and then to look over their notes and record the story retell using their notes. They were also asked to indicate if they did not understand something in the story. Listeners were given unlimited time to complete each retell. Before listening to the ten target stories, listeners practised this task using one sample story. The retell task lasted between 40 and 75 minutes, depending on the set of stories heard and the speed of the listener in retelling.

For both tasks, the listening sessions were held individually in a quiet room, with the order of stories individually randomized for each listener and presented through stereo headphones. Within each task, equal numbers of listeners heard the ten speakers' stories from either Time 1, 2 or 3, such that no single listener heard the same speaker more than once. For both tasks, the entire listening session was recorded for later analysis using an Olympus DS-2 digital voice recorder and a Sony ECM-T2 lapel microphone.

Data Analysis

Analyses were based on written transcripts of the speakers' original stories and of listeners' retells and comments. For both tasks, speakers' level of intelligibility was defined as the extent to which listeners were inaccurate in their understanding of words (in the pause task) or story elements (in the retell task). Henceforth, speakers' intelligibility is characterized here as the degree of inaccurate content in listeners' understanding of words or story elements (defined below).

For the pause task, inaccurate content was measured by the number of times listeners signalled uncertainty about words and were also inaccurate in their guesses of the words. For example, one listener paused a story and said, 'My wife, something... accentuate?' The original word was *concentrate*, so this comment was coded as one instance of inaccurate content. This intelligibility measure had to be normalized for story length because the original stories told by the speakers varied in length (the more words in a story, the more possibilities for a listener not to understand a word). Therefore, the number of instances of inaccurate content for each listener for a given story was divided by the number of total words in that story. This yielded intelligibility ratios of inaccurately guessed words to the total number of original words. The final intelligibility ratios for this task were derived for each listener separately, as an average of the ratios for all speakers in a given speaker group. That is, the final intelligibility ratios for each listener included three values: one each for the treatment, control and native speaker groups.

For the retell task, inaccurate content was measured by the number of times a listener inaccurately retold a story element. In order to divide a story into story elements, each original story and its retells were first separated syntactically into clauses, using Berman and Slobin's protocol for clausal analysis (1994, p. 660). Then, each story was categorized semantically, using a narrative analysis scheme of story elements (shown in Appendix B) modified from three different versions of story grammars (Labov, 1972; Trabasso, van den Broek & Suh, 1989; van Dijk, 1976). This scheme was used only to divide the stories and retells into countable semantic story elements. The actual types of elements told or retold (e.g. setting, initial event) were not further considered in the calculation of the intelligibility scores.

In order to calculate the intelligibility scores for the retell task, each retell was compared to its original story. This analysis focused on the original story elements that were retold inaccurately (in terms of semantic, not lexical, accuracy). Not considered in this analysis were those retell elements that listeners added to their retell (i.e. listeners' comments or additional details) and those original elements that listeners did not include in their retell (i.e. missing elements). A second trained coder re-analyzed the accuracy of 10 per cent of the retells. The percentage agreement for the accuracy coding for the retells was 99–100 per cent. Table 9.2 shows an excerpt of an original story and retell where the third original element is retold inaccurately. This retell element (that research is better at foreign universities) was coded as an instance of inaccurate content.

Table 9.2 An illustration of an original story and retell

	Original story		Retell	
Id	**Clause**	**Id**	**Clause**	**Category**
14	I, I think the Chinese education system is totally different, with Canadian education.	14	She says that Chinese education, like the schooling in China, I guess, is very different from Canada.	accurate
15	And I get the university degree, bachelor degree and master degree in China,			
16	but I, I knew about the research, the foreigner university is much better.	16	And she said some reasons why a university degree in Canada could be better, considered better than the one in China.	inaccurate
17	They have the better conditions, such as equipments and informations resource.	17	She says there's better equipment, resources, information.	accurate

As with the pause task, the original stories varied in length from speaker to speaker. The intelligibility scores were therefore normalized for story length by dividing the number of instances of inaccurately retold elements of a story by the number of original elements in the story. This yielded intelligibility ratios of inaccurately retold elements to total original elements. As with the pause task, the final intelligibility ratios for this task were derived for each listener separately, as an average of the ratios for all speakers in a given speaker group. Again, these final intelligibility ratios for each listener included three values: one each for the treatment, control and native speaker groups.

Results

For all statistical tests reported below, the alpha level for significance was set at .05. The effect sizes reported below are partial eta squared (η_p^2), calculated by dividing the effect sum of squares by the effect sum of squares plus the error sum of squares.

Pause Task

The intelligibility ratios from the pause task were submitted to a two-way analysis of variance (ANOVA). In this analysis, time (Time 1, Time 2, Time 3) served as a between-subjects factor and speaker group (native, treatment, control)

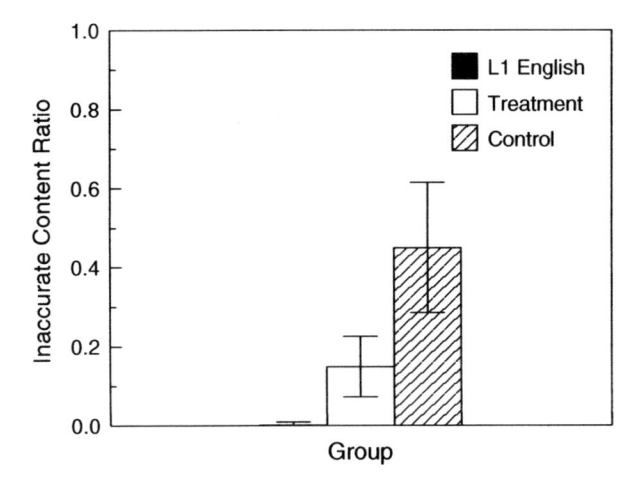

FIGURE 9.1 Mean inaccurate content (intelligibility) ratios for the three participant groups in the pause task. Brackets enclose ± 2 SEs. The invisible bar for the L1 English group represents very low inaccurate content for this group

served as a within-subjects factor. The ANOVA yielded only a significant main effect for speaker group, $F(2, 54) = 47.33$, $p < .0001$, $\eta_p^2 = .64$, with no significant main effect for time or significant two-way interaction ($p > .05$). Bonferroni tests, which were used to explore the significant main effect for speaker group, showed that all speaker groups were significantly different from one another. When listeners heard stories from each group, they made the largest number of inaccurate guesses for the control group stories, fewer inaccurate guesses for the treatment group stories, and the fewest inaccurate guesses for the native speaker group stories ($p < .0001$). The mean inaccurate content (intelligibility) ratios from the pause task for each group are shown in Figure 9.1 (higher bars represent more inaccurate guesses). Because there were no significant differences for any group over time, this graph shows intelligibility ratios that were averaged for each group across the three times.

Retell Task

The intelligibility ratios from the retell task were submitted to a similar two-way ANOVA, in which time (Time 1, Time 2, Time 3) served as a between-subjects factor and speaker group (native, treatment, control) as a within-subjects factor. This analysis yielded a significant main effect for speaker group, $F(2, 86) = 6.35$, $p = .003$, $\eta_p^2 = .13$, and a significant two-way interaction, $F(4, 86) = 2.89$,

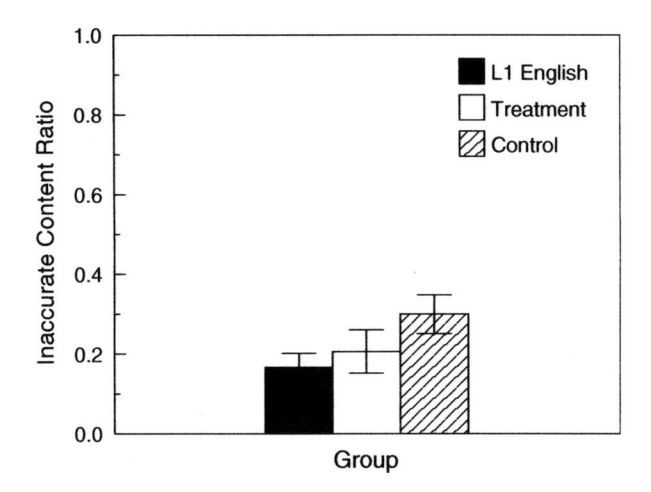

[FIGURE 9.2: Bar chart showing Inaccurate Content Ratio by Group — L1 English ≈ 0.17, Treatment ≈ 0.21, Control ≈ 0.30]

FIGURE 9.2 Mean inaccurate content (intelligibility) ratios for the three participant groups in the retell task. Brackets enclose ± 2 SEs

$p = .027$, $\eta_p^2 = .12$, with no significant main effect for time ($p > .05$). Bonferroni tests, which were used to explore the significant interaction, revealed that the native speaker and the treatment group retells did not differ in inaccurate content at any testing time ($p > .05$). These tests also showed, however, that the control group retells had more inaccurate content than the treatment group retells only at Time 2 ($p = .02$) and that the control group retells had more inaccurate content than the native speaker group retells, again only at Time 3 ($p = .001$). The mean inaccurate content (intelligibility) ratios from the retell task for each group are shown in Figure 9.2 (higher bars represent more inaccurate retell content). Again, because there were no stable significant differences for any group over time, this graph shows intelligibility ratios that were averaged for each group across the three times.

Discussion

The analyses reported here revealed two main findings. The first finding is that for both tasks there were no differences in intelligibility over time which were both significant and stable. It may be that improvement in intelligibility with or without instruction requires far more time and practice than was available over the four months of the study. While interesting, this finding is outside the scope of this chapter (see Kennedy, 2008, for further discussion). The second finding is more pertinent to the aims of the study reported here. Namely, there were significant differences in intelligibility between groups. These differences depended on the task that was used. For the pause task, all speaker groups were different from one another in their inaccurate word guesses. For the retell task, however, there were no differences in inaccurate retell content between the native speaker and the treatment group stories, but retells for both these groups had significantly less inaccurate content than retells for the control group.

The aim of this study was to investigate this question: what is the link between the measured intelligibility of L2 learners' words and the measured intelligibility of their extended speech? The results suggest that there is no one-to-one correspondence between the intelligibility of words and of extended speech in an L2. More specifically, for units of intelligibility measurement which are above word level, which are focused on accurate understanding of semantic elements (rather than accuracy of word recognition) and which are heard in context, some L2 learners can be as intelligible as native speakers (as were the treatment group speakers for the retell task). However, when the unit of intelligibility measurement is at the level of words, there are clear differences in intelligibility between native speakers and L2 learners. Therefore, intelligibility measures based on isolated words or sentences may not reveal some L2 learners' *potential* for intelligibility in authentic discourse.

This suggests that when teachers and researchers aim to assess how intelligible L2 learners might be in authentic discourse and then address these learners' intelligibility problems, they would do well to include tasks and measures which are based on extended speech samples and which measure listeners' accurate understanding of semantic elements (rather than solely accurate word recognition). This focus on the intelligibility of extended speech would then correspond more closely to the ultimate aim of pronunciation instruction, and indeed general L2 instruction, namely, to prepare learners to succeed in interactive, spontaneous and extended L2 communication in a given context.

However, intelligibility measures at the level of words or sentences are also important to training and assessment in L2 speech. As the results showed, these measures clearly differentiated native speakers from L2 learners, but also differentiated different groups of L2 learners (e.g. treatment and control groups). These measures may help teachers and researchers to prepare and assess learners, not for their overall intelligibility in discourse, but for their pronunciation at the level of words or sentences. Elements of pronunciation which need attention can be more easily identified and isolated using these measures, in contrast to intelligibility measures based on extended, spontaneous speech. These latter measures reflect not only learners' pronunciation, but also their lexical and morphosyntactic choices and communication strategies, as well as situational factors such as conversational topics.

It is worth noting that while phrases like 'intelligibility measures' may sound overly technical and therefore not practical in the classroom, teachers already use numerous tasks, many of them interactive, to work on and assess learners' intelligibility. For example, 'Running Dictation' is a common activity which can be used as a sentence-level intelligibility measure. In this group activity, learners in each group take turns going to a written-out passage or set of sentences (located away from the group), with each learner memorizing one sentence, then going back to the group and reciting the sentence for the group to write down. The overall goal is for the group to write down the text as fast and as accurately as possible. Teachers can select or adapt passages or sets of sentences targeting particular features of pronunciation so that learners can practise or be assessed on those particular features.

When teachers wish to focus on learners' intelligibility in extended, contextualized discourse, they can use a number of existing communicative activities, adapting them for their own classroom context. One such activity is a modified retell task where learners must work together to retell and understand parts of a text in order to reconstruct the whole text. In pairs or small groups, each learner may read, listen to or watch one particular part of a story. The different parts can have few or no words (pictures/video) or can be long enough that the words in the text cannot be fully memorized. Learners must then work together to reconstruct the story by retelling their particular parts to other learners (listeners) and putting the parts in order. This task targets listeners' accurate understanding of the parts of the story, but does not specify one particular way for learners to retell their part. It thus allows learners to make their retells intelligible not only through the accuracy of their pronunciation, but also through their lexical and morphosyntactic choices and communication strategies.

The two activities described above involve non-native listeners (learners) and allow for two-way interaction, 'building' intelligibility between interlocutors, rather than requiring the listener to understand a fixed text without negotiating meaning. This type of two-way communication, especially involving L2 English listeners, is typical of oral communication among most users of L2 English, as noted by Jenkins (2000), and is likely common among users of many other second languages. The research design of most intelligibility studies has, by and large, not taken into account these two characteristics of L2 communication: interactive, not one-way, communication and L2 users as both speakers and listeners (see Jenkins, 2000, for a laudable exception). In the current study, the development of an intelligibility measure for extended naturalistic speech, using narrative speech samples, is a step towards the kind of intelligibility research which acknowledges and values features of authentic L2 communication. It is hoped that future intelligibility studies will include extended samples of naturalistic speech, non-native listeners and interactive tasks. Including these elements in the design of intelligibility studies can be challenging for researchers, but it is by no means impossible (e.g. see Major, Fitzmaurice, Bunta & Balasubramanian, 2002). Closer links in intelligibility research between actual L2 use on the one hand, and L2 instruction, assessment, and learning on the other, can only be beneficial for researchers, teachers and learners.

Acknowledgements

This research was supported by a *Fonds québécois de la recherche sur la société et la culture* (FQRSC) doctoral fellowship (no. 105039). Many thanks are extended to Randall Halter for his invaluable statistical advice, Lise Winer for her guidance throughout this project, and Tracey Derwing for her advice. The author gratefully acknowledges Pavel Trofimovich and Alessandro Benati for their suggestions on earlier drafts of this chapter.

References

Avery, P., & Ehrlich, S. (1992). *Teaching American English pronunciation.* Oxford: Oxford University Press.

Berman, R. A., & Slobin, D. A. (1994). *Relating events in narrative: A crosslinguistic developmental study.* Hillsdale, NJ: Erlbaum.

Breck, E. (1998). *SoundScriber.* English Language Institute, University of Michigan.

Celce-Murcia, M., Brinton, D. M., & Goodwin, J. M. (1996). *Teaching Pronunciation: A Reference for Teachers of English to Speakers of Other Languages.* Cambridge: Cambridge University Press.

Daller, H., Van Hout, R., & Treffers-Daller, J. (2003). Lexical richness in the spontaneous speech of bilinguals. *Applied Linguistics,* 24, 197–222.

DeKeyser, R. (2005). What makes learning second-language grammar difficult? A review of issues. *Language Learning,* 55, 1–25.

Derwing, T., Munro, M., & Wiebe, G. (1997). Pronunciation instruction for fossilized learners: Can it help? *Applied Language Learning,* 8, 217–35.

Hoekje, B. J. (2007). Medical discourse and ESP courses for international medical graduates (IMGs). *English for Specific Purposes,* 26, 327–43.

Isaacs, T. (2008). Towards defining a valid assessment criterion of pronunciation proficiency in non-native English-speaking graduate students. *Canadian Modern Language Review,* 64, 555–80.

Jenkins, J. (2000). *The phonology of english as an international language.* Oxford: Oxford University Press.

Kennedy, S. (2008). Second language learner speech and intelligibility: Instruction and environment in a university setting. Unpublished doctoral dissertation, McGill University, Montréal, Canada.

Kerr, J. (2003). The rest of the iceberg: Articulatory setting and intelligibility. In J. Burton. & C. Clennell (Eds.). *Interaction and Language Learning* (pp. 99–114). Alexandria, VA: TESOL.

Kramsch, C. (1986). From language proficiency for interactional competence. *Modern Language Journal,* 70, 366–72.

Labov, W. (1972). *Language in the inner city: Studies in the Black English vernacular.* Philadelphia: University of Pennsylvania.

Macdonald, D., Yule, G., & Powers, M. (1994). Attempts to improve English L2 pronunciation: The variable effects of different types of instruction. *Language Learning,* 44, 75–100.

Major, R. C., Fitzmaurice, S. F., Bunta, F., & Balasubramanian, C. (2002). The effects of non-native accents on listening comprehension. *TESOL Quarterly*, 36, 173–90.

Nelson, C. (1982). Intelligibility and non-native varieties of English. In B. Kachru (Ed.). *The other tongue: English across cultures* (pp. 58–73). Chicago: University of Illinois Press.

Rogers, C. L., Dalby, J., & Nishi, K. (2004). Effects of noise and proficiency on intelligibility of Chinese-accented English. *Language and Speech*, 47, 139–54.

Stevens, S. G. (1989). A dramatic approach to improving the intelligibility of ITAs. *English for Specific Purposes*, 8, 181–94.

Towell, R., Hawkins, R., & Bazergui, N. (1996). The development of fluency in advanced learners of French. *Applied Linguistics*, 17, 84–19.

Trabasso, T., Van den Broek, P., & Suh, S. Y. (1989). Logical necessity and transitivity of causal relations in stories. *Discourse Processes*, 12, 1–25.

van Dijk, T. A. (1976). Philosophy of action and theory of narrative. *Poetics*, 5, 287–338.

Appendices

Appendix A

Personal Story Prompts

Purchase

Think of a time when you made a very good purchase or a very bad purchase. Where were you? What did you buy? You will have five minutes to think of what you will say. You can write notes, but you will not be able to use them when you talk.

Job/Course

Think of a job you had or a course you took which was really bad or really good. What was the job/course about? What was the boss or instructor like? Why was it so good or so bad? What did you get out of the experience?

Decision

Think of a time you made a very good or very bad decision. What did you decide? What were your reasons for making the decision that you did? What was the result of your decision?

Appendix B

Narrative Analysis Scheme

Story element	Definition
Abstract	A short summary of the story.
Setting	Introduces characters, gives relevant characteristics of persons and circumstances.
Initiating event	Character undergoes change in state; this event determines the main causal chain of states and actions in a story.
Internal response	Character's feelings, cognitions, beliefs in response to initiating event, attempt, or outcome.
Goal	Character wants something that will resolve the problem; either state, activity, or object.
Attempt	Tries at attaining the goal.
Complicating event	Unexpected, abnormal event that leads to a state contradictory to the purposes of a main character.
Outcome	Result, positive or negative, in attaining goal.
Evaluation	Narrator's judgments, beliefs, emotions about events, characters, or circumstances in story.

Chapter 10

English with a Native-like Accent: An Empirical Study on Proficiency

Tanja Angelovska
Angela Hahn
University of Munich, Germany

Abstract

This study investigates native speakers' evaluations (judgements) of English accents by means of empirical-experimental methods. Four groups of speakers were evaluated: two groups with native English speakers and two groups with non-native speakers of English (highly proficient, adult foreign language learners). The primary goal of the current study is to investigate the relationship between native speakers' assumptions about their rating competence and their *de facto* assessments of native and non-native speech samples. The main objective is to compare the L2 spoken proficiency of native and non-native speakers and to verify whether or not linguistically aware native speaker judges can reliably rate samples of native and near-native English speech.

Introduction

Achieving the ultimate level of oral language proficiency is an issue widely applied in language teaching and highly debated among SLA researchers since Lenneberg's Critical Period Hypothesis (CPH) in 1967, which has been followed by many variations and refinements. All of those variations support the postulation that the ultimate level of competence which can be attained by late L2 learners is lower than that of native speakers (cf. Long, 1990). As a counter-argument, a number of studies included adult learners of an L2 who have achieved a near-native competence and concentrated on testing the CPH in their L2 (Birdsong, 1992; Bongaerts, 1999; Guion, Harada & Clark, 2004; Ioup, Boustagui, El Figi & Moselle M. 1994,).

Most of these CPH studies relied solely on native speakers' judgements. In a wider study we focus on testing the CPH with a specific group of learners whose proficiency is to such a degree native-like that many interlocutors simply do not notice any possible minor or occasional infelicities that may occur. Hence, the motivation of the present study is to question the reliability of native speaker judgements: we attempt to answer the question whether native speakers are always able to recognize near-native and native speech.

The Current Study

The present study is part of a larger Munich project on testing the CPH and investigates the notion of native and near-native accents.[1] More specifically, it investigates native speakers' (judges) evaluations of English accents by means of empirical-experimental methods. Four groups of speakers were evaluated: two groups with native English speakers and two groups with non-native speakers of English (highly proficient, adult foreign language learners).

As the evaluations were fully based on a quantitative rating procedure, we widened the present research study to additional qualitative elements in order to reveal the nature of the rating process. As a result, interviews with the judges were included to account for unexpected and spontaneous reactions of the judges while listening to each sample.

There have been numerous studies of native-speaker attitudes towards foreign accents as well as different varieties of English.[2] However, to our knowledge, no research has been carried out on the assumptions that native speakers have about their judging abilities of nativeness and very little research has questioned the native speakers' perceptions of near-native speech.

Theoretical Background

Rating Spoken Language Proficiency

In the 1980s much theoretical and empirical work focused on defining the nature of L2 language proficiency. However, the specific character of the components of L2 oral proficiency still remains debatable due to the varying features of the construct 'proficiency' (Hulstijn, 2008).

Although pronunciation is an important aspect of second language proficiency, there is still a lack of reliable measurements for oral proficiency.

Utterances can be evaluated along various dimensions. According to Munro and Derwing (1995), '. . . there are some inconsistencies in the ways in which such dimensions have been interpreted and in the methods used to rate L2 learners' speech' (p. 290). These inconsistencies may actually be even more severe concerning the ratings and measurements of near-native speech. In investigating the nature of the near-native speech, concepts used to describe the various degrees of accentedness, such as 'foreign accent', 'native speaker' (norm) and 'near-native' become fuzzy. The term 'accentedness' has been defined by Terry and Cooper (1971) as 'the degree to which the phonological and syntactic structures of one language appear to influence speech produced in the other.' For the purpose of this discussion, however, we will exclude the influences of the syntactic structures and we will operate with the term 'accentedness' in terms of the strength by which the degree of the speaker's foreign accent is perceived to be.

A deviant pronunciation of a language from the native 'norms' is usually referred to as 'foreign accent' (FA). Deviations may indeed occur at the phonetic and phonemic level, and at the segmental and prosodic levels, characterizing the user of a second or a foreign language (L2) as a non-native speaker. According to Munro and Derwing (1995), 'foreign accented speech may be defined as non-pathological speech that differs in some noticeable respects from native speaker pronunciation norms' (p. 289). However, questions such as: when and which aspect of the non-native speech is seen as noticeable, to what degree is it noticeable, is it noticeable for all native speakers or only for some, which native speaker 'norm' one rater bases their evaluation upon, and how exactly each native speaker sees the 'norm' from their perspective, have not been answered yet.

The Constructs: Native and Near-Native Speaker

The notion of the 'native speaker' (NS) occupies an important place in any theory of foreign or second language proficiency. In the traditional view of foreign language learning and teaching, the native speaker criterion is taken as a measure of success in learning, as well as a role model for language teaching and as a measuring stick in research. This notion is based on the Chomskyian idea that the native speaker is the ideal and ultimate authority on language competence and use. Various interpretations were created to supplement and clarify the construct 'native speaker' in SLA and language pedagogy, discussing relevant defining criteria such as 'the native language must be the *first language learned in childhood*' (cf. Davies, 1991) or it 'must be *continually used* in one's life' (cf. Tay, 1982 quoted in McKay, 2002). Others assume it is enough for one speaker to be called native only if the presupposition to possess a *high level of competence* in English is true. (For a more detailed discussion of the various notions of the native speaker model, see McKay, 2002, Chapter 2).

Many studies of ultimate attainment have demonstrated that an important number of L2 learners can acquire the same degree of proficiency as native speakers, even in phonology (cf. Bongaerts, 1999). Those successful L2 learners who can 'pass for natives' are usually being referred to as near-natives. However, 'passing for a native' is an issue that requires careful examination because there seem to be discrepancies between the various interpretations of the concept 'near-native speaker'. So far, there have been no answers to the questions: Is there a difference between the native and near-native speaker? If so, what constitutes this difference? It is indeed difficult to arrive at a clear definition of the concepts 'native' and 'near-native speaker' and to identify the differences between both terms, because a satisfactory characterization of the construct of L2 proficiency is still missing (Hulstijn, 2008). Another question is who is actually qualified to make accurate and objective judgements of near-native proficiency? The practice has not moved far away from the 1980s when Ludwig stated that 'the competence of the non native speaker is *sui generis* not that of a native . . .' (Ludwig, 1983, p. 103) Based on the performance, that is production of native speech, it is generally taken for granted that each native speaker is a competent judge for non-native speech. Consequently, in most studies on ultimate attainment in pronunciation, accentedness ratings are commonly obtained by asking native speakers to judge speech samples using a Likert scale with ends containing contrasting labels such as 'no foreign accent at all' and 'very heavy foreign accent'. The number of gradients on such scales has varied widely, ranging from three to ten.[3] The identification of the gradient reveals the degree of L2 spoken proficiency as assigned by native speaker judges.

Ludwig (1982) conducted a study in an academic setting where NSs teachers and non-teachers rated L2 oral proficiency. She stated that the NSs judges who were teachers attended more to form, due to their continuous exposure to interlanguage, whereas NSs non-teachers focused more on content. So studies have arrived at different results according to the experience of raters. The results of the MacKay, Flege & Imai's (2006) study indicated that non-native speaker (NNS) judges are as capable as native speaker judges in detecting accentedness.

So far, the tradition in SLA research has seen native speakers not only as the most competent and reliable judges but as the only judges who have the qualifications for measuring the language proficiency of foreign language speakers reliably (Davies, 2003, 89–90).

Research Questions

The current study was motivated by a lack of research work on the rating of foreign language spoken proficiency. Its primary goal is to investigate the relationship between native speakers' assumptions about their rating competence and their *de facto* assessments of native and non-native speech samples. The main objective is to verify if linguistically aware native speaker judges can reliably rate samples of native and near-native English speech. Our research questions are as follows:

1. From a quantitative perspective:
   - How do NSs assess non-native speech?
   - How do NSs assess native speech?
2. From a qualitative perspective:
   - Why do native speakers rate the way they do?

Method

For this study[4] quantitative and qualitative data are generated from four sources: (1) *stimuli set* compiled of *read aloud* speech samples by two groups of advanced foreign language learners of English and one group of English native speakers, (2) *stimuli set* compiled of *spontaneously narrated* speech samples by two groups of advanced foreign language learners of English and one group of English native speakers, (3) *measurements* derived from statistical data containing the *native speakers' ratings* assigned to each speech sample of the stimuli sets and (4) individual *interview sessions* with each of the NS judges.

Participants

The present study included two types of participants: 'near-native' (type 1) and native speakers (type 2) of English.

The first type consisted of 24 very advanced successful foreign language learners of English who provided the audio samples for the stimuli set. The participants of this type belonged to two groups: group 1 compiled of native speakers of German ($n = 16$) and group 2 of native speakers of Macedonian ($n = 8$). We applied the following procedure to select potential near-native speakers: First, participants were recruited from advanced undergraduate classes in English Phonetics and Phonology at two major universities in Germany and in Macedonia. All of them were designated by their professors as highly successful learners with a near-native command of English. Second, the researchers used the network of the scholarship holders of the Friedrich Ebert Foundation in Germany where potential candidates were recruited after having positively answered the question whether they have ever been mistaken for a native speaker of English and after a telephone conversation in English with the researchers. Third, the researchers used a network of friends in search of very advanced learners of English. The candidates were selected on the basis of the quality of their pronunciation in English. Anyone with a fairly obvious foreign accented speech was disqualified as a potential participant. Our NNSs were not living in an English speaking environment, but had daily contact with the English language mainly through their studies or work. The age of these participants at the time of testing ranged from 20 to 36. All non-native subjects in our study started learning English on entering secondary education in a foreign language environment, at or around age 11.

The second type of participants comprises the native speakers of English of whom some provided samples for the stimuli set (the 'NS pronunciation group' or group 3, $n = 8$) and others served as judges (group 4, $n = 8$). Group 3 was included in the stimuli set as a control group and it consisted of three speakers of General American English, two speakers of Standard British English and one speaker of Canadian English. The second group of native speakers acted as judges and it comprised eight subjects, six of whom were speakers of American English and two of British English.[5] The reason for including heterogeneous subjects in groups 3 and 4 was the desire to have speech samples which coincide with the varieties of English that the near-natives were exposed to through their education (teachers who spoke British English or American English).

As the assessment of how foreign an accent is also depends on the raters' own linguistic background,[6] we decided to recruit native-speaker judges with a professional linguistic background and an appropriate teacher training[7]. All of our judges have completed undergraduate studies and were either ESL lecturers at the language centre of the University of Munich or at other institutions. Their teaching experience at the language centre provided them with familiarity of various foreign accents and meta-linguistic awareness and thus can be qualified as experienced judges.

Materials and Procedures

Tasks

We included two types of tasks: task 1 – reading aloud a text paragraph (adapted from the book 'Mrs. Bixby and the Colonel's Coat' by *Roald Dahl*, see appendix) and task 2 – spontaneous speech – personal narration where students were given the chance to choose between five topics (funny story, influential person, favourite place for living, next summer destination or a topic of their own choice). Their task was to think about one of the topics and talk spontaneously for two minutes.

Recording Procedure

We conducted two group recording sessions with the undergraduates at both universities: Ludwig Maximilian University of Munich and St. Cyril and Methodius University of Skopje.

Shortly before the recording participants were given the paragraph that they were asked to read. Afterwards, they were supposed to record themselves while narrating for two minutes. No preparation was allowed. There were no verbal exchanges between the experimenter and the speaker during the narration. The entire recording session (2 tasks) took five minutes for each participant. To simplify the stimulus preparation procedure we used the waveform editing feature of the audio software Audacity (on a Toshiba laptop, Genuine Intel(R) CPU T 2050, 1.60 GHz) to divide the speech samples into shorter excerpts that were of sufficiently short duration to be evaluated by the judges.

Stimuli Length

Previous studies included various types of stimuli: beginning from a sound, word, sentence, many sentences, and paragraph to clips of various durations (ten seconds to two minutes). In spite of the fact that studies with sentence-length stimuli prevail, Flege (1984) found out that even 30 milliseconds of speech can be sufficient for raters to decide whether a token was produced by a native speaker or a non-native speaker. However, in the same study he also found that the accuracy of judges increased when they were presented with longer tokens. Though longer speech samples could be more informative for the raters, they would then increase the difficulty to determine whether phonological features or other lexical/grammatical etc. features intrude the stimuli and so determine the overall ratings. Thus, we decided to cut the reading samples to a short paragraph.

The final stimulus set of the reading samples varied somewhat in length due to the varying speed at reading of each speaker. We edited 9 to 13 second-excerpts from each of the original two-minute samples of spontaneous speech. We decided not to break the original narration recordings from task 2 down into samples of exactly identical durations, because as a result of such cutting the utterances would not begin or end at clausal boundaries. Instead, we identified endings of the excerpts at locations of natural pauses in the utterances or where a meaningful unit was finished. The final stimuli set contained 64 audio speech samples, evenly distributed between reading and speaking samples.

Stimuli Set Compilation

We opted for a randomized order of both audio samples and speakers in each part of the listening procedure: first, the raters listened to all speakers of task 1 in a randomized order, then to all speakers of task 2 in a different randomized order: Thus, we tried to minimize the chance that the raters would recognize individual speakers and assign ratings based on previous task performance. In contrast to other studies which included fully randomized order of speakers and tasks (cf. Moyer, 2007), we opted for not mixing the two tasks (reading aloud and speaking) to avoid distraction by a constant change of tasks[8] and to enable raters to concentrate more on the form than on the content of the samples.

Rating Procedure

So far the stimuli have been played to eight judges individually before each extensive interview session. Our judges did not receive any training before (in contrast to other previous studies such as Suter, 1976). They were presented with the stimuli data for the first time. As there has only been very little research on the effects of task-specific training of the raters, we opted for a pragmatic solution: we included neither extensive training for the raters nor allowed rating upon second listening.

Before the listening started, judges received a short explanation of their task and an evaluation sheet where the samples were numbered with an empty space for the mark to be given. Above the table with numbers and spaces for marks, we also included a five-point gradient Likert scale, ranging from 'very strong foreign accent: definitely non-native' to 'no foreign accent at all: definitely native', numbered from one to five (see also Bongaerts, Planken & Schils, 1995; Bongaerts, van Summeren, Planken & Schils, 1997). Descriptors were also included for the midpoints.

We explained the five-point rating scale to each judge and informed them that the samples came from non-native and native subjects (no further information on language background or proportion of native and non-native samples was given). We allowed them to (a) say anything they wanted in-between listening to the samples and (b) interrupt the playing of the samples by giving us a sign. This proved very productive, because we obtained valuable spontaneous reactions from the judges in the middle of the listening procedure. There was a short break between task 1 and task 2.

Interview Sessions

The following quotation perfectly justifies the need for further research on native speakers' perceptions of various speeches:

> Further investigation of how native and nonnative listeners perceive speech is important because it is increasingly common for different groups of ESL speakers to use English when they interact, and, undoubtedly their perceptions of native and nonnative speech affect their interactions. (Roy C. Major, 2007, p. 541)

To our knowledge all previous studies which tested L2 spoken proficiency included NSs as judges and relied only on the quantitative assessments of the various speeches by the natives. We assume that the quantitative assessments partly depend on the attitudes of the judges. In our opinion neither a single mark assigned to a speech sample nor a word describing an accent's feature can tell us enough about what stands behind it and why that exact gradient of a scale was assigned to the relating sample. Hence, we included qualitative interview sessions to find out more about the rating processes and the native speakers' assumptions about their rating competence. So far, we have conducted eight interview sessions (ranging from 20 to 60 minutes) with each native speaker judge.

Results

Ratings[9] From the Quantitative Data Analysis

The ratings result from the quantitative data gathered from the judges' assessments of the speech performance of group 1 (near-native speakers of English with L1 German), group 2 (near-native speakers of English with L1 Macedonian) and of the control group 3 (native speakers of English) at the two tasks, task 1 (reading) and task 2 (spontaneous speech). Their group performance (means) together with the obtained marks have been fully incorporated into Table 10.1.

A look at Table 10.1 shows that there are some cases in group 1 and 2 that show similar or better results than subjects in group 3. For example, subjects with numbers 3, 24, 4, 10 and 22 received the highest scores ('no foreign accent at all: definitely native') on the two tasks, thus outperforming all seven native speakers except one native speaker (number 1, overall mean: 4.94) who differed from the first best non-native speaker (overall mean: 4.75) slightly. This is a clear contradiction to the claim that the natives' spoken performance is in any case superior to that of the non-natives. The results in Table 10.1 show that native speakers were rated as non-natives 52 times in both tasks. The number of times each native speaker subject was correctly assigned a truth value is 76. These two ranges in percentage reveal the following ratios: the percentage of the times all NSs were rated as NNSs is 41 per cent and the percentage NNSs were assigned truth values is 59 per cent.

If we compare the three groups, we can conclude that there are no extreme differences between the NSs group 3 (mean: 4.38) and group 1 (mean: 4.1); group 2 (NNS with L1 Macedonian) has the lowest overall group mean (3.93).[10] The scores from Table 10.1 reveal also unexpected results in terms of the group differences in task performance. Namely, group 1 and 2 showed better results at the speaking task than at the reading one. The NS group 3 on the contrary was rated better at the reading task. These results confirm the previous findings

Table 10.1 Raw data and mean scores for groups, tasks and cells (= group-task combinations)

Tasks (1-r, 2-s)		1								2								Group means:
Judges / Nr		1	2	3	4	5	6	7	8	1	2	3	4	5	6	7	8	
Group 1 - L1 G	1	3	5	3	5	5	5	5	5	2	4	4	4	3	4	5	3	
	2	3	4	3	5	5	5	4	5	1	5	5	5	4	2	5	3	
	3	4	5	4	5	5	3	5	5	5	3	4	5	4	5	5	5	
	4	5	4	5	5	4	4	5	5	5	4	5	4	5	4	5	4	
	5	3	4	3	4	4	4	4	4	2	3	4	3	3	5	5	3	
	6	3	5	4	4	3	4	5	5	3	4	5	5	3	4	5	4	
	7	4	4	4	4	3	4	4	3	4	3	5	5	3	5	5	3	
	8	3	4	3	4	3	4	5	4	5	4	5	5	3	5	5	4	4,101563
	9	2	4	4	5	3	3	4	3	5	3	5	5	4	5	5	3	
	10	2	5	4	5	5	4	5	4	5	5	5	5	5	5	5	5	
	11	5	4	4	5	3	3	5	3	2	5	4	5	4	4	4	4	
	12	2	5	4	5	4	4	5	4	4	4	4	4	4	5	4	4	
	13	1	3	3	5	3	3	4	4	1	3	4	5	5	3	5	4	
	14	4	4	4	5	4	4	5	5	2	4	3	4	5	5	5	5	
	15	2	4	5	3	3	3	5	4	1	3	5	5	5	5	5	4	
	16	1	5	5	4	5	4	5	4	2	4	4	5	5	5	5	5	
Cell means:					4,078125								4,125					
Group 2 - L1 M	17	3	3	3	4	4	5	5	3	2	4	3	4	5	5	5	3	
	18	4	4	5	4	4	5	5	3	3	4	5	4	5	5	5	4	
	19	4	4	4	3	1	4	3	2	4	3	4	4	1	4	4	3	
	20	1	3	4	3	1	2	3	2	1	3	4	5	5	4	3	3	3,929688
	21	5	5	5	5	5	3	5	4	1	5	5	4	5	5	5	5	
	22	5	5	5	5	4	4	5	4	4	3	4	5	5	4	4	4	
	23	2	3	5	4	4	5	5	3	1	3	4	4	4	5	5	4	
	24	5	5	5	4	3	5	5	5	5	3	5	5	5	5	5	5	
Cell means:					3,796875								4,0625					
Group 3 - L1 E	25	3	4	5	5	3	4	5	5	4	2	4	4	3	4	5	5	
	26	2	5	4	5	4	5	5	5	3	4	4	5	4	5	5	4	
	27	4	5	4	5	3	3	5	5	4	4	4	4	4	5	4	5	
	28	5	5	4	5	4	5	5	5	2	4	5	3	3	4	5	5	4,375
	29	2	5	4	4	4	5	5	5	3	4	5	5	5	5	5	5	
	30	5	5	5	5	3	5	5	5	5	4	5	5	4	5	5	5	
	31	3	3	3	4	3	4	4	4	2	2	3	4	3	4	5	4	
	32	5	5	5	5	3	4	5	5	3	3	4	3	3	4	5	4	
Cell means:					4,484375								4,265625					
Task means:					4,109375								4,14453125					4,126953

by Oyama, 1976 and Thompson, 1991 who have found that read speech is judged as more accented than spontaneous speech. However, this claim cannot be applied to the group of native speakers of English where the opposite was shown.

In the following Figures 10.1, 10.2 and 10.3 the overall success of each speaker on task 1, 2 and overall performance is presented visually. The data points of each speaker are expressed in means. The scale gradients are presented vertically on the left side and the gradients where no scores were given are excluded. With respect to the spoken proficiency of all three groups at both tasks, reading and speaking, it can be concluded from Figures 10.1, 10.2 and 10.3 that non-native speakers from both groups (German and Macedonian) were not

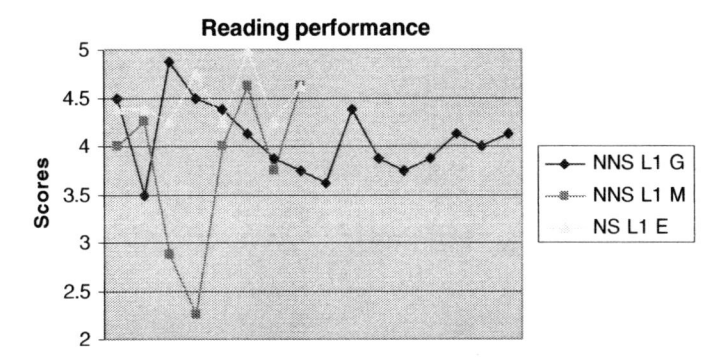

FIGURE 10.1 Distribution of overall success in reading (expressed in means) on the rating 5-point scale

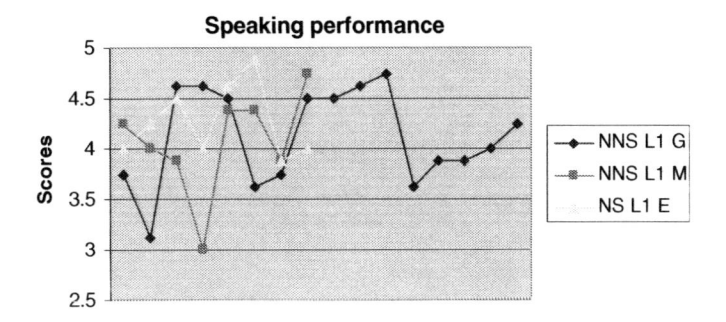

FIGURE 10.2 Distribution of overall success in speaking (expressed in means) on the rating 5-point scale

Overall performance

[Line chart showing Scores (2.5 to 5) for NNS L1 G, NNS L1 M, NS L1 E]

FIGURE 10.3 Distribution of overall performance (expressed in means) on the rating 5-point scale

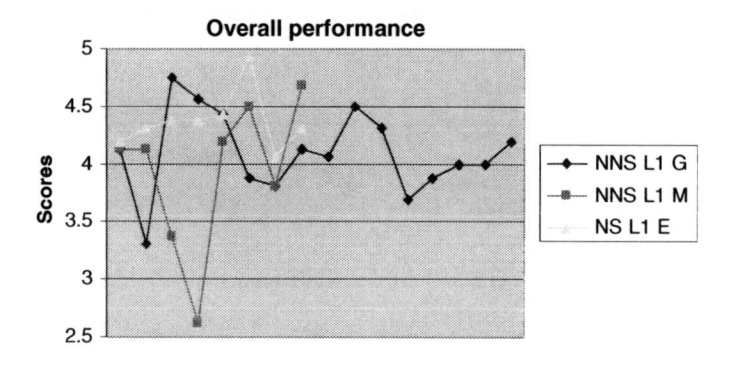

Table 10.2 Regrouping of the subjects into three additional categories: highest (4.5 to 4.9), average (4.06 to 4.4) and lowest (2.6 to 4.00).

Nr	S mean-r	S mean-s	S mean overall	Nr	S mean-r	S mean-s	S mean overall	Nr	S mean-r	S mean-s	S mean overall
30	5	4.875	4.9375	5	4.375	4.5	4.4375	14	4.125	3.875	4
3	4.875	4.625	4.75	29	4.25	4.625	4.4375	15	4	4	4
24	4.625	4.75	4.6875	27	4.25	4.5	4.375	6	4.125	3.625	3.875
4	4.5	4.625	4.5625	28	4.75	4	4.375	13	3.875	3.875	3.875
10	4.375	4.625	4.5	11	3.875	4.75	4.3125	7	3.875	3.75	3.8125
22	4.625	4.375	4.5	26	4.375	4.25	4.3125	23	3.75	3.875	3.8125
				32	4.625	4	4.3125	12	3.75	3.625	3.6875
				16	4.125	4.25	4.1875				
				21	4	4.375	4.1875	19	2.875	3.875	3.375
				25	4.375	4	4.1875	2	3.5	3.125	3.3125
				1	4.5	3.75	4.125	20	2.25	3	2.625
				8	3.75	4.5	4.125				
				17	4	4.25	4.125				
				18	4.25	4	4.125				
				9	3.625	4.5	4.0625				
				31	4.25	3.875	4.0625				

Note: L1 German ■ L1 Macedonian ■ L1 English ■

outperformed by the NS group. On the contrary, only one of the 8 NSs proved to occupy the highest place in the charts, followed immediately by the most successful non-natives.

In order to obtain a global picture of the highest, average and lowest rated subjects, we re-grouped our subjects from group 1 (in Table 10.2 with blue colour), 2 (with yellow colour) and 3 (with grey colour) into three additional categories according to the range to which their overall score belonged. As Table 10.2 shows the order of the scores showing overall performance of all three groups seems to deviate somewhat from the expected pattern. Thus, we categorized our subjects into three ranges according to their overall means: highest (those whose means scored from 4.5 to 4.9), average (4.06 to 4.4) and lowest (2.6 to 4.00). The regrouped three new categories reveal that there is neither homogenous distribution of the subjects' performance according to their L1 background, nor was the expectation met that the native speakers' means would all belong in the category 'highest=best'. We were rather surprised to see that in the category 'best' only one native speaker occupied the highest position (4.9) and was followed by five non-native speakers, three of whom with German as L1 and two with L1 Macedonian. Their scores did not differ significantly at all. The difference between the best NS (4.9) and the next German NNS (4.8) was only one tenth. The second group with the 'average' scores proved to be interesting likewise, because it shows very clearly that the overall means of the NSs and those of the NNSs were equal, that is where one non-native scored 4.4, three other NSs received the same score, then one NNS and two NSs scored 4.3 and so on. (For a more detailed distribution of scores see Table 10.2.)[11]

These results show that there is only one native speaker who was rated to be in the 'best' group and five NNSs. The main conclusion that can be drawn from this small-scale rating study is that there are cases of proficient adult foreign language learners[12] who – according to our judges – can pass for native speakers on the phonological level and whose pronunciation in English is indistinguishable from that of a native speaker.

Analysis of the Transcribed Interview Sessions

In this section we introduce results of native speakers' assumptions about their rating competence when accessing various accents. One of the questions to the interviewees was: Do you think that you are always capable of judging if a particular accent is a native or a non-native one? We deliberately set this question twice: at the beginning and in the end of the interview in order to see if some changes occurred.

In Table 10.3 B1 was the first interviewee, B2 the second and so on. The method we employed for our analysis is the constant comparison method (i.e. grounded theory approach) by Glaser and Strauss (1967) in order to group answers to common questions and analyse different perspectives on central issues. Table 10.3 shows the comparison between each native speaker's answer given to the same question at the beginning and in the end of the interview. The sub-analysis and sub-categorization of the answers to the question

Table 10.3 Outline of NS answers given at the beginning and in the end of the interview

Answer given at the beginning of the interview	Answer given in the end of the interview
B1: hm..huh.. I would say yes. (1)	B1: no (4) Int: no? why? B1: hm well just thinking back to those that I heard and again I think it is just so much easier in person . . .
B2: usually yes (2)	B2: if you saw them face-to-face, you'd be able, you'd note their body language and you would take that into consideration with how they are sounding and how their accent was. (3)
B3: If they speak very well, I may think they are native (3)	B3: generally.(1) Not always.(3)
B4: yeah I like to think so, I mean there are a few extremely good,(3) but I can usually notice it. (2)	B4: yeah obviously not, not any more.(4)
B5: hm usually(2)	B5: erm no (laughs) Int: okay B5: but it just depends on how (pause) I don't know, I thought I was (laughs). (4)
B6: I would say with about 95 to 90 per cent accuracy yes (1)	B6: I say most of the time yes(2)
B7: generally (1)	B7: (pause) I don't think always. (3)
B8: I think a lot of people who are non-native speakers often sound native like ... I know lot of people who would pass as natives in their daily life. (4)	B8: no certainly not, not at all. (4)

under analysis revealed the following four categories derived from our 'code book': (1) 'full confidence about judging ability', (2) 'occasional confidence', (3) 'occasional confidence with awareness about unexpected cases' and (4) 'full awareness about non-natives sounding like natives'. The numbers next to each statement reveal the numbers of the respective category scheme. Answers in the left and right column of the same row – given by the same speaker – belong to different category schemes, except the last interviewee.[13] A gradient from moderate to radical progression in their answers can be observed. Thus, speaker B1 'jumps' from category 1 to category 4, speaker B5 from category 2 to category 4, B7 from 1 to 3 and so on. The changes between their initial and final answers during the interview reflect the effects of the interview session on their self-reflections and on their self-concept.

Another important aspect is the native speakers' 'justification' for their failure to accurately judge the various accents. Many interviewees pointed out that face-to-face interaction would have provided a more precise judgement of the particular speech. Thus the NS-judges unconsciously admitted that such features as body language, gestures, race and appearance are important determiners for them when judging accents.

Many interviewees realized that they failed to recognize all samples accurately and talked about personal experiences when they mistook non-natives for native speakers. They admitted limits of their judging competence and a lack of a model of spoken language proficiency to base their judgements on.

Discussion and Conclusion

Our study is different in three aspects from previous studies which questioned L2 spoken proficiency of near-native subjects:

1. It analysed L1-L2 language combinations which have been unexplored, so far. It included a group comparison between L1 German which is typologically close to L2 English and an L1 Macedonian typologically more distant to English. The results proved that there are subjects from both NNS groups (German and Macedonian) who proved to have better scores in L2 spoken performance than some native speakers.
2. The current study is the first one to question the reliability of NS judges.
3. The design of the study differs from the previous ultimate attainment studies in the inclusion of interview sessions. The interviews enabled us to indicate the native speakers' assumptions on their ratings compared to their actual ratings.

The present study contributes to the theory of research on ultimate attainment in L2, particularly for older learners. It contributes empirically by comparing adult L2 spoken performance to L1 performance of English.

One main conclusion is that no significant differences between native and non-native performances in a number of individual near-natives were indicated, although such differences do occur when natives and near-natives are compared as groups. These results support Birdsong's (1999) conclusion: no differences were found between the performance of natives and that of near-natives. Thus, concepts like 'profound differences' that are used to contrast natives and near-natives can be misleading. Therefore, a sound theory of L2 spoken proficiency and reliable measurement instruments for L2 spoken proficiency have to be incorporated.

In contrast to Davies (1991) who contended that 'native speakers normally recognize one another' (p. 165), the result of our study suggests a different conclusion. In our small-scale study native-speaker judgements were shown to be unreliable when accessing native and near-native speech. It was demonstrated that being a native speaker of English does not automatically qualify for the one and only reliable judge of accentedness. Consequently, the construct of nativeness is neither monolithic nor immutable.

Limitations and Future Directions

In every research design some limitations are involved inherently. Our study focuses on phonological attainment and does not attempt to separate suprasegmentals from segmentals. The raters' judgements were possibly not only influenced by phonological features, but also by morphological, lexical and syntactical features. A 'pure' measure of phonological data, thus, seems to be impossible.

Another rating-problem occurred: One of the L1 German speakers of English was recognized by three of the judges as a member of the students' staff employed in the language centre at the LMU. The judges reported that if they had not known that this person was German, they would definitely have rated him as a native speaker of British English.

The study does not compare students at various levels of attainment, because this is not a study of developmental order, rate or achievement.

Necessarily the outcome has been affected by the implementation of the data collection. The data were recorded under artificial conditions. Hence, unnatural production may well have resulted from the instrument itself, due to sharpened attention to tasks and increased self-consciousness.

Lydia White and Fred Genesee (1996) have suggested that the discrepancies among various critical period studies may be a direct result of the failure of researchers to acknowledge the distinction between competence and proficiency. In recognition of this claim, we conclude nothing about the competence of our subjects as we only evaluated their performance. However, in future research the competence of native-like 'performers' has to be investigated for native-likeness additionally.

Further employment of unexplored L1-L2 combinations is needed as much as L2 learners with various L1 backgrounds not typologically close to English.

We recognize the complexity of assessing oral language proficiency and most importantly the difficulty in interpreting potential interactions of scale components, task type and group composition of raters. Clearly, further empirical research into the judgements and criteria of native versus non-native judges, and of teachers versus non-teachers is needed.

Finally, a characterization of *the native speaker proficiency level* and an examination of the actual linguistic performance of the native speaker are needed, rather than a comparison of a foreign language learner to an 'ideal' native speaker. This would provide for more realistic accounts of ultimate attainment in the target language.

Acknowledgements

The authors are highly grateful to all participants in this study. We thank the team of the Language Centre (FFP) at the LMU for their assistance with technical equipment.

Notes

1. Here, the term 'accent' is used in the sense of '[a] particular way of pronouncing a language, seen as typical of an individual, a geographical region, or a social group' (Trask, 1996, p. 4).
2. For a comprehensive overview of studies on language attitudes, see Bradac (1990).
3. Though Likert scales dominate in such studies, other techniques have also been adopted, such as sliding scale (Flege & Fletcher, 1992) or direct magnitude estimation (Brennan & Brennan, 1981).
4. In a wider study where we attempted to test the CPH we included a quantitative data collection stage as an initial step. Our aim was to gather answers from our subjects (the very advanced foreign language learners) based on a given questionnaire containing data on their language and school experience, teachers' profiles, learning background etc.
5. Currently only data from eight judges are presented. However, we are in the process of recruiting more native speakers who will serve as judges.
6. Flege (1984); Thompson (1991): Linguistically experienced listeners are more reliable than inexperienced judges in estimating L2 learners' speech intelligibility, irritation and/or accentedness.
7. Studies such as that of Munro and Derwing (1994) and Flege and Fletcher (1992) reported that foreign accents tended to be evaluated as stronger by judges with increased experience.
8. Processing L2 speech by natives indeed takes more effort as shown by Munro and Derwing (1995).
9. We decided not to include such dimensions as intelligibility, irritation or comprehensibility in our measurements, because, in the present study, we are only interested in the ratings on the accentedness.
10. We did not undertake a statistical correlation analysis, because it does not demonstrate a cause-effect relationship. Thus the predictive power of any of the variables cannot be proven.
11. The third category of the 'lowest=worst' scores is not interesting for the current analysis, because none of the native speakers belonged to it.
12. The explanations for the various proficiency outcomes among the non-natives will not be elaborated in this chapter, because this question is going to be answered in the wider project undertaken at the LMU, Germany.
13. This interviewee showed enormous knowledge and personal interest for the topic. Even during the interview she admitted having read much about the question of 'nativeness'. Thus her theoretical linguistic knowledge equipped her with an open-minded approach to this question.
14. This is the part of the text which has been selected for the ratings.

References

Birdsong, D. (1992). Ultimate attainment in second language acquisition. *Language*, 68, 706–55.

Birdsong, D. (1999). (Ed.). *Second language acquisition and the critical period hypothesis.* Mahwah, NJ: Lawrence Erlbaum Associates.

Bongaerts, T. (1999). Ultimate attainment in L2 pronunciation: The case of very advanced late L2 learners. In D. Birdsong (Ed.). *Second language acquisition and the critical period hypothesis* (pp. 133–59). Mahwah, NJ: Lawrence Erlbaum Associates.

Bongaerts, T., Planken, B., & Schils, E. (1995). Can late learners attain a native accent in a foreign language? A test of the critical period hypothesis. In D. Singleton., & Z., Lengyel (Ed.). *The age factor in second language acquisition* (pp. 30–50). Clevedon: Multilingual Matters.

Bongaerts, T., van Summeren, C., Planken, B., & Schils, E. (1997). Age and ultimate attainment in the pronunciation of a foreign language. *Studies in Second Language Acquisition*, 19, 447–65.

Bradac, J. J. (1990). Language attitudes and impression formation. In Giles, H., & Robinson, W. P. (Ed.). *Handbook of language and social psychology* (pp. 387–412). Chichester, u.a: John Wiley.

Bradac, J. J. (1990). Language Attitudes and Impression Formation. In Giles H. Robinson W. P. (Ed.). *Handbook of language and social psychology.* (pp. 387–412). Chichester u.a.: John Wiley.

Brennan, E. M., & Brennan, J. S. (1981). Accent scaling and language attitudes: Reactions to Mexican American English Speech. *Language and Speech*, 24, 207–21.

Davies, A. (1991). *The native speaker in applied linguistics.* Edinburgh: Edinburgh University Press.

Davies, A. (2003). *The native speaker: Myth and reality.* Clevedon: Multilingual Matters.

Flege, J. (1984). The detection of French accent by American listeners. *Journal of Acoustical Society of America*, 76, 692–707.

Flege, J., & Fletcher, K. (1992). Talker and listener effects on the perception of degree of foreign accent. *Journal of the Acoustical Society of America*, 91, 370–89.

Glaser, B. G., & Strauss, A. (1967). *The discovery of grounded theory: Strategies for qualitative research.* Chicago: Aldine.

Guion, S., Harada, T., & Clark, J. (2004). Early and late Spanish-English bilinguals' acquisition of English word stress patterns. *Bilingualism in Language and Cognition*, 7, 207–26.

Hulstijn, J. (2008). *What is language proficiency?.* Plenary talk at BAAL Language Learning and Teaching SIG Conference, 1–2 July 2008.

Ioup, G., Boustagui, E., El Figi, M., & Moselle, M. (1994). Reexamining the critical period hypothesis. A case study of successful adult SLA in a naturalistic environment. *Studies in Second Language Acquisition*, 16, 73–98.

Lenneberg, E. (1967). *Biological foundations of language.* New York: John Wiley.

Long, M. (1990). Maturational constraints on language development. *Studies in Second Language Acquisition*, 12, 251–85.

Ludwig, J. (1982). Native-speaker Judgments of Second Language Learners' Efforts at Communication: A Review. *Modern Language Journal*, 66, 274–83.

Ludwig, J. (1983). Linguistic criteria which affect native-speaker judgments of language use. In Dudley E., & Haller P. (Ed.). *American attitudes toward foreign languages and foreign cultures.* Bonn: Bouvier.

MacKay, I. R. A., Flege, J. E., & Imai, S. (2006). Evaluating the effects of chronological age and sentence duration on degree of perceived foreign accent. *Applied Psycholinguistics*, 27, 157–83.

Major, R. C. (2007). Identifying a foreign accent in an unfamiliar language. *Studies in Second Language Acquisition*, 29, 539–56.

McKay, S. L. (2002). *Teaching English as an International Language*. Oxford: OUP.

Moyer, A. (2007). Do language attitudes determine accent? A study of bilinguals in the USA. *Journal of Multilingual and Multicultural Development*, 28 (6) 502–18.

Munro, M., & Derwing, T. (1994). Evaluations of foreign accent in extemporaneous and read material. *Language Testing*, 11, 253–66.

Munro, M., & Derwing, T. (1995). Processing time, accent and comprehensibility in the perception of native and foreign-accented speech. *Language and Speech*, 38, 289–306.

Oyama, S. (1976). A sensitive period for the acquisition of a non-native phonological system. *Journal of Psycholinguistic Research*, 5, 261–83.

Suter, R. W. (1976). Predictors of pronunciation accuracy in second language learning. *Language Learning*, 26, 233–53.

Terry, C., & Cooper, R. L. (1971). The perception of phonological variation. In Fishman J. A., Cooper R. L., & Ma R. (Ed.). *Bilingualism in the barrio*. (pp. 333–36). Bloomington, IN: Research Centre in Anthropology, Folklore, and Linguistics.

Thompson, I. (1991). Foreign accents revisited: The English pronunciation of Russian immigrants. *Language Learning*, 41, 177–204.

Trask, R. (1996). *A Dictionary of Phonetics and Phonology*. London: Routledge.

White, L., & Genesee, F. (1996). How native is near-native? The issue of ultimate attainment in adult second language acquisition. *Second Language Research*, 12, 233–65.

Appendix

Task 1: Please read the following text paragraph at a pace that is natural for you. You are not allowed to record yourself twice, or improve your first recording. Exercising the sentences or individual words is also not acceptable. Please adhere to this instruction because it is the only way reliable data for the study can be gathered.

> There had been no message, and as soon as she was on the train, Mrs. Bixby found a place where she could open the box in private. Mrs. Bixby: 'How exciting! A Christmas present from the Colonel . . . What is it?'[14] Source: *Mrs. Bixby & the Colonel's Coat* by Roald Dahl (adapted)

Part Three

Attaining L2 Proficiency in the Classroom

Chapter 11

Formal Intervention and the Development of Proficiency: The Role of Explicit Formation

Bill VanPatten
Texas Tech University, United States of America
(with Daniela Inclezan, Hilda Salazar, Jeffrey L. Farmer, Caleb L. Clardy, &
Andrew P. Farley, Texas Tech University)

Abstract

This chapter presents the findings of research in which the role of explicit information (EI) in three interventions for focus on form were compared: processing instruction (PI), meaning-based output instruction (MOI), and dictogloss (DG). The questions we address are these: (1) Is EI a significant variable in the outcomes of the three treatments? (2) Does the role of EI as a variable change depending on the treatment type? Our findings suggest that the treatments themselves are variable in terms of outcome and that the role of EI is also variable.

Introduction

The development of proficiency in instructed SLA is dependent on a number of factors, one of which is the role that a focus on formal properties of language plays. Does such a focus aid acquisition and thus aid the development of proficiency? Lurking behind that question is another related to the components of any kind of formal intervention. Very often, a focus on formal properties involves rule presentation and some kind of practice. It is reasonable to question the relative contributions of rule presentation and practice (e.g., VanPatten, 2007a). Does each play a significant role in acquisition?

This chapter presents the findings of research in which the role of explicit information in three interventions for focus on form were compared: processing instruction (PI), meaning-based output instruction (MOI), and dictogloss (DG). The comparative basis for the present study is motivated by previous research in which PI has been compared to MOI (e.g., Benati, 2005; Farley, 2004b; Keating & Farley, 2008; Morgan-Short & Wood Bowden, 2006) as well as

DG (Qin, 2008). In those studies, MOI and DG were seen to be as good as PI in terms of improved performance. This is a significant finding in that the foundational study on which these other studies were built found PI to be superior overall to what was called "traditional instruction" (VanPatten & Cadierno, 1993). Although the results of the VanPatten and Cadierno study were replicated in a number of studies (e.g., Benati, 2001, 2005; Cadierno, 1995; VanPatten & Wong, 2004, among others), the results of Farley's, Keating and Farley's, and Qin's studies were not replicated in recent research. In VanPatten, Inclezan, Salazar, and Farley (forthcoming), and VanPatten, Farmer and Clardy (2009), PI was found to be superior to DG and MOI, respectively. In short, the results of these recent comparative studies resemble those of the original VanPatten and Cadierno study.

Motivation for examining the role of explicit information (EI) comes from the research by VanPatten and Oikkenon (1996), which was replicated in various other studies (e.g., Benati, 2004; Farley, 2004a; Fernandez, 2008; Sanz & Morgan-Short, 2004; Wong, 2004a). In that research, EI was found not to be necessary; that is, groups that received the structured input activities only without EI fared as well as those in the full PI groups that received both EI and the structured input activities. The notable exception is the research by Farley, in which it appears that EI is not necessary as the structured input only group improved significantly, but the full PI group improved even more. Thus, it could be that EI is not necessary but maybe beneficial. Research on the role of EI in other interventions (in particular MOI and DG) is scant, at best. Therefore, the present study sought to initiate a research agenda in which the role of EI is systematically compared across different interventions.

Research on Explicit Information

Explicit information refers to any overt explanation about how language works. This explanation may come from an instructor, a textbook, a Web site, or from some other source. In terms of formal properties of language, it generally takes the shape of description of the formal property and any rules that govern its use. For example, a learner might get EI on the *passé composé* in French in which the learner is made to understand that it is a compound tense consisting of auxiliary plus a main verb (past participle). The learner would further learn that there are two auxiliaries, *avoir* and *être*, that have different distributions depending on the main verb. The learner might also learn that with *être*, the past particple is inflected for gender and number, and so on. EI is seen by most instructors as a necessary part of any grammar lesson and precedes any kind of practice.

Interestingly, EI has not received a good deal of attention in the literature on instructed SLA and has sometimes been conflated with the issues of explicit/

implicit learning (see, for example, DeKeyser, 2003, and Hulstijn, 2005). For example, in Scott (1989), learners of French L2 were taught relative pronouns and the subjunctive under one of two conditions: (1) explicit rules plus form focused practice; (2) input passages (short stories) read by the instructor with no rules provided. In this design, the effects of EI cannot be teased out because the variable is conflated with a particular activity type: that is, the two treatments themselves are different. To better understand the effects of EI (and, to be fair, this was not Scott's purpose), "practice" should be held constant across treatments while EI is either present or absent.

Alenan (1995) and Robinson (1995) come close to such a design. Alenan, for example, compared four L2 groups on the acquisition of locative suffixes in Finnish using text enhancement: (1) passages with the locative highlighted and EI provided prior to reading, (2) same as (1) but no EI provided, (3) passages with no highlighting but EI prior to reading; and (4) same as (3) but no EI. Robinson's design included exposure to sentences on a computer screen with (1) EI prior to exposure; (2) no EI but instructions to search for a rule; (3) no EI with follow-up questions that directed learners to location of particular words; and (4) no EI with follow-up content questions about each sentence. In both studies, some benefit was observed for the groups that received EI.

VanPatten and Oikennon (1996) was the first published study to attempt to isolate EI as a variable. Responding to criticisms that in the earlier research on processing instruction (PI) that claimed explanation provided prior to treatment was a confounding variable (VanPatten & Cadierno, 1993), VanPatten and Oikkenon compared three groups: (1) regular PI (explanation plus structured input activities), (2) structured input activities (SI) only with no EI, and (3) EI alone with no activities. They found that EI played no role in PI. The SI group evidenced equivalent gains as the PI group after treatment while the EI only group showed no gains at all (which tested whether learners could rely on conscious knowledge to take the two tests they used).

VanPatten and Oikkenon's research spawned a number of replications and related studies: Benati (2004), Farley (2004a), Sanz & Morgan-Short (2004), Wong (2004a), Fernandez (2008). The pattern has been clear: EI is not a necessary component of PI and SI alone appears to be sufficient to induce change as part of the treatment. However, Farley's and Fernandez's studies suggest that EI, although not necessary, may speed up processing for some structures.

Motivation for the Present Study

As stated above, VanPatten and Oikkenon's research was predicated on one particular criticism of the original study on PI: VanPatten and Cadierno (1993). In that study, the researchers sought to compare two distinct ways of conceptualizing a focus on grammar instruction. One, they called traditional instruction

(TI), involved explanation plus a particular kind of output practice that was widespread at the time in foreign language circles in the United States: the move from mechanical to meaningful to communicative drills/exercises. The other, now called processing instruction (PI), involved explanation plus a particular kind of input-oriented treatment designed to push learners away from less than optimal input processing strategies. The idea behind PI was that if we could identify incorrect or less than optimal processing strategies, we could teach learners to process input better. In VanPatten's model of input processing (e.g., VanPatten, 1996, 2004, 2007b), a series of principles are claimed to guide or constrain how learners get data from the input they are exposed to. Of relevance here is the First Noun Principle (FNP). The FNP states that learners tend to process the first noun or pronoun they encounter in a sentence as the subject/agent of the sentence.[1] For SVO sentences, this is not a problem. However, because Spanish (the focus of VanPatten & Cadierno's work) is not strictly SVO, with OV and OVS being frequent word orders, the FNP can cause a problem. For example, *gustar*-like structures are misinterpreted as are any object pronoun-first constructions. Thus, learners misinterpret *Lo ve María* as "He sees Mary" rather than the correct "Mary sees him." The result is problems in the acquisition of the Spanish pronoun system and a processing system with a rather strict reliance on word order as the principal means to comprehend sentences.

Within PI, the problem is tackled by providing activities that manipulate input such that learners are literally forced to abandon a reliance on the FNP (e.g., Farley, 2005; Lee & VanPatten, 1995, 2003; VanPatten & Cadierno, 1993; Wong, 2004b, 2005). *Referential activities* within PI usually begin a string of activities and are structured so as to have right or wrong answers. For example, learners hear a mixture of SVO, OVS, OV sentences in which both the subject and object are capable of performing the action (e.g., boy looking for a girl or a girl looking for a boy). They are asked to select between two pictures in order to indicate they have correctly processed and comprehended the sentence. Such activities are designed to force the learners' internal processors to abandon a strict reliance on the FNP. *Affective activities* follow referential activities and are those that do not have right or wrong answers, but instead allow learners to offer opinions, indicate something about themselves, and so on. For example, students might see a list of OV sentences that may or may not indicate how they feel about a female relative (e.g., *la respeto, la admiro, la detesto, la adoro, la comprendo bien*) and are [2]asked to indicate which ones apply to them. The purpose, again, of PI activities is to push learners away from the FNP (in this case) and to rely on more appropriate cues to determine meaning. In this way, better intake is created for the developing linguistic system. At no point during PI activities do learners produce the target structure, though they may produce isolated words or short phrases that do not contain the structure (unless they are confirming something). In short, students *do not create new meaning and new utterances* with the target structure. (For detailed information on PI and structured input activities, see Lee & VanPatten, 1995, 2003 as well as Farley, 2005 and Wong, 2004b.)

VanPatten and Cadierno used a standard pretest/posttest design, with several delayed posttests. The tests consisted of a sentence interpretation task designed to bias for the PI group and a sentence production task designed to bias for the TI group. What they found, however, was a clear advantage for the PI group. The PI group made significant gains on both interpretation and production tasks, whereas the TI group made gains only in production. The PI and TI groups' production gains were similar with no significant differences. All results were maintained across the delayed posttests. VanPatten and Cadierno concluded that PI was superior to TI because of the "two for one" gains made by PI and argued that PI's intervention at the level of correcting an incorrect processing strategy (the FNP) caused changes in the underlying grammar of learners that could then be accessed for production, albeit under the limited measures used in their study.

The purpose of the present study is to bring EI into the realm of this comparative research. Although there seems to be substantial research that suggests that EI is not necessary for PI, we do not know what the role of EI is for MOI and DG, for example. In the present study, we explore that role.

Method and Procedure

Participants

Participants were recruited from eight second-year, second semester university-level Spanish classes from Texas Tech University. The classes were randomly divided into the following groups: (1) PI + EI; (2) PI − EI; (3) MOI + EI; (4) MOI − EI; (5) DG + EI; (6) DG − EI; (7) Control (no instructional treatment at all).

Learners showing knowledge of or ability with the targeted grammatical item by scoring 60 percent or above on any section of the pretest were excluded from the data analysis. On the basis of a background questionnaire, we also excluded participants who reported hearing or reading difficulties, those who declared Spanish as a heritage language, those who claimed to have substantial contact with Spanish outside the classroom, and those who had substantial study (two years or more) of another language. Finally, we excluded from final analysis any participant who had been absent during any part of the experiment (pretest, treatment, posttests). The final N was 272.

The Spanish curriculum consisted of four formal hours of instruction per week, two of which were classroom-based and two of which were online. Explicit grammar instruction did not form part of the in-class activities, as students had to work on the grammar component individually online outside of the classroom.

Classroom time, then, was focused on meaning-based and communicative activities. None of the three treatments (PI, MOI, or DG) was used as part of regular class activities; thus, there was no instructional bias toward one or the other of the treatments due to typically used classroom activities.

Materials

The target structure was direct object pronouns in Spanish and flexible word order, as described previously. Treatment materials for the PI group were borrowed from VanPatten and Cadierno (1993). They consisted of an instructional packet containing explicit information in English on Spanish direct object pronouns, including information and examples on the flexible Spanish word order, and information on the first-noun strategy and to watch out for it. Following VanPatten (1993) and Lee and VanPatten (1995, 2003), activities consisted of structured input activities that moved from referential (right-wrong answers designed to push learners away from the first-noun strategy) to affective activities (focus on students and their beliefs, opinions, knowledge, and so on). A total of seven activities formed the instructional treatment for PI with a total of 28 tokens. Because of the way in which the activities are conducted in class, learners tend to interact with each token twice, so in the end there were 56 possible tokens. This number is much reduced compared to that used in the original VanPatten and Cadierno study (just over 100 tokens). The reason for this is that the present study is part of a study in which we attempted to replicate the findings of Keating and Farley (2008), who borrowed the VP & C materials but limited their study to third-person object pronouns.

As per standard PI, learners did not produce the target structure as part of the instructional treatment. Instead, participants listened to and/or read stimulus sentences and indicated comprehension and reactions that did not involve producing the target structure. Target items in the PI materials included SOV, OV, and OVS word orders. If, in the referential activities, learners made mistakes and selected the wrong picture, instructors simply said "No. La respuesta es 'b'" (if the answer was actually "a"). During the affective activities, instructors would read aloud all items, before participants were asked to make indications of agreement, "true for me," or some other response. Instructors would subsequently read aloud each item one at a time as participants offered their reactions. Sample activities are provided in the appendix.

In contrast to the PI materials, the MOI materials consisted of activities in which the participants had to produce sentences using object pronouns to convey meaning. For example, participants might see a picture and then be asked to describe who was doing what to whom using the following words correctly to form a sentence: *besar/lo/la niña*, with the word order varying in each item (e.g., *la/mirar/el perro, el chico/la/llamar*, and so on). Other activities involved sentence completion based on pictures, as in the following: *Paco piensa en Juan* y _____. This was accompanied by a drawing in which Paco had picked up the phone and was calling Juan. The expected response would have been *y lo llama* or some variation. Still, other activities had participants single out someone (a male or a female relative) and write sentences using particular verbs to express their feelings toward that person (e.g., *admirar, respetar, detestar*).

During the MOI treatment, if participant responses were correct, the instructor would say something like "Bien. Sí, aha" without supplying extra input or reinforcement. However, if the sentence was wrong (e.g., *El niño busca la*), the instructor would say "No. ¿Alguien más sabe?" If the correct response was not hit upon by a fellow participant, the instructor would then finally say something like "OK. La respuesta es 'el niño la busca'." The idea here was to keep incidental input on the part of the instructor to a minimum.

Because of the nature of dictogloss activities, the DG group did not receive an instructional packet and instead received a handout containing explicit information in English on object pronouns and word order in if they were in the DG + EI group.

The dictogloss passages used during the experiment consisted of 6 short texts, 5 to 7 sentences long, with 30 to 36 words in each. Each passage contained four tokens of the target structure for a total of 24 tokens. Because of the nature of dictogloss activities, during the experimentation learners would hear the passages once, hear them again, then work to reconstruct the passages, and then compare their reconstructions to the original version that was projected on a screen. Thus, participants in the DG group minimally received 72 tokens during the treatment period (excluding the time on reconstruction). These tokens included the following word orders: SVO, SOV, OVS and OV distributed evenly across the passages. As in the case of the PI materials, both masculine and feminine genders were used.

Because dictoglosses are aurally presented in class, we prerecorded the dictoglosses using a Mexican male who was not part of the present study. During the recording, he read each dictogloss at slightly less than normal speed with no special emphasis on the target grammatical structure.

We departed from typical use of dictoglosses in one way. In Wajnryb's (1990) description of dictoglosses, learners are allowed to jot down words during the second reading of the text. But in a test practice with dictogloss we noticed that some learners were able to write down the whole dictogloss while listening to it, thus undermining the reconstruction phase of the task. We thus decided to remove this option.

Assessment Tasks

Assessment consisted of three different tasks: an interpretation task, a sentence level production task, and a paragraph-level reconstruction task, given as pretest, first posttest, and a delayed second posttest. The first two tasks were borrowed from VanPatten and Cadierno while the third was constructed for the present study. The rationale for these tasks was the following. First, the interpretation task and sentence-level production task would allow direct comparison to the results of VanPatten and Cadierno, as well as Keating and Farley (2008) and Qin (2008), thus exploring assessment task as an intervening variable. If each group was only learning to perform a particular kind of task related to its treatment, this ought to show up in the results.

The interpretation task consisted of 15 oral sentences: 10 target sentences and 5 distractors. All target sentences were in OVS word order. Five of them were of the following types (translations provided here for reader):

Al hijo   lo   calma   la madre.
The son-case marker OBJnoun   him-OBJpro   calms   the mother-SUBJ.
"The mother calms the son".

The remaining five target sentences were of the type:

Lo   ve   el perro.
Him-OBJ   sees   the dog-SUBJ.
"The dog sees him."

The five distractor sentences contained no DO pronouns, had SVO word order, and were of the type:

La abuela   escucha   al muchacho.
The grandmother-SUBJ   listens to   the boy-OBJ.
"The grandmother listens to the boy."

The participants' task was to listen to each sentence and then select from one of two pictures to indicate who did what to whom. For example, participants heard *lo ve el perro* and would simultaneously see a picture representing a dog seeing a man and a man seeing a dog. Sentences were prerecorded using the voice of a Mexican female who was not part of the present study. No emphasis was placed on the target feature and the recorder read the sentences at normal speed. The recording was timed so that only eight seconds were provided for both listening to a sentence and selecting a correct picture. The instructions asked participants to listen to each sentence and to select the picture that best represented what they heard. No mention was made of object pronouns or word order. The interpretation task was loaded into a PowerPoint slide show so that both the audio and visual elements of the task were linked. Participants indicated answers on a prepared sheet by circling A or B, the letters corresponding to the two images projected via PowerPoint for each sentence.

The sentence-level production task was a paper-and-pencil test consisting of ten incomplete sentences, five of which were targets such as the following (translation provided here for reader):

La niña saluda al niño y entonces _____.
　　　　　　　　　　　　　　　　　(besar)
"The girl greets the boy and then _____."
　　　　　　　　　　　　　　　　　(to kiss)

Each sentence was accompanied by a pair of images. The first image illustrated the first part of the sentence and the second illustrated the second part of the sentence. In the above, for example, the first image was one of a girl greeting a boy and the second image was one of the same girl kissing the boy. In these targets, the sentences were constructed so that an object pronoun and OV word order would be the natural response (e.g., *La niña saluda al niño y entonces lo besa.*).

The remaining five sentences were distractors that did not create occasions to use object pronouns. Unlike the targets, the two images did not form a narrative and thus neither did the sentence completion. An example of a distractor item is the following (translation provided here for the reader):

La mujer piensa en el hombre y el gato _____.
　　　　　　　　　　　　　　　　　　(seguir)
"The woman thinks about the man and the cat _____."
　　　　　　　　　　　　　　　　　　　(to follow)

Here, the first image was one of a woman seated at a desk thinking about a man while the second image was one of a cat following a dog. The expected response was *La mujer piensa en el hombre y el gato sigue al perro.* Instructions to the participants indicated that they should examine the two pictures and complete the sentence based on what was occurring in the second picture. There was no time limit although participants were told to work as quickly as possible.

The reconstruction task consisted of listening to and reconstructing a short paragraph length text. The participants were instructed to listen to a prerecorded text in Spanish as it was read twice at normal speed. They were not allowed to take notes while listening. At the end they had to reconstruct the passage in Spanish as close as possible to the original, working individually. The passage contained five instances of object pronouns in the following configurations: OV, OVS, SOV (two tokens), SVO. Again, no time limit was imposed but participants were told to work as quickly as possible.

Each section of the assessment task (interpretation, production, and reconstruction) had two versions: A and B. A modified split-bock design was used so that the A and B versions were used as the pre- and first posttest. Of the participants 50 percent received the A version as the pretest and 50 percent received the B version. For the posttest, those who had received A as the pretest received B as the posttest and vice versa. The versions of the interpretation and sentence-level production tasks had been validated and used previously in several studies. The passages for reconstruction were new to the present study. To ensure equal difficulty across the passages, a template was constructed. All versions were then based on this template keeping sentence length relatively equal, tokens of object pronouns the same, placement of target structure within the passage in the same locations, and so on. Common everyday vocabulary familiar to participants was selected. After the passages were constructed, five instructors not participating in the present study were asked to evaluate the passages and determine whether they were of equal difficulty, and to indicate any vocabulary that could potentially be problematic. These instructors agreed that the passages were of equal difficulty and did not make any suggestions for vocabulary changes.

Procedure

A week prior to treatment, participants took the pretest and completed the brief background questionnaire. Treatment for all experimental groups took place over two class periods during the following week, with the posttest given immediately upon completion of treatment at the end of the second hour.

A team of four instructors was used for the present study. These were not the regular instructors for the sections of Spanish involved in the study. To control for bias and instructor effects, assignment of groups was randomized. In addition, each instructor worked with more than one treatment. Because none of the instructors had training in either PI, MOI, or DG materials, a two-hour training session was conducted the week prior to treatment.

During the experimental treatments, the Control group was engaged in material and activities unrelated to the target structure. The regular instructors of all sections of Spanish involved in the study were told not to discuss the nature of the experiment with their students and not to answer questions about the target structure during all phases of the study.

Scoring

For each participant separate scores were calculated for the interpretation, the production, and the reconstruction tasks. On the interpretation task, which contained 10 target sentences, each correct response received one point. Therefore the range of possible scores was 0–10.

On the sentence-level production task, each item had a maximum value of 2 points. The learners received 2 points if they used the correct object pronoun in the correct position, 0 points if no pronouns were produced or if it was clear that object pronouns were being used as subject pronouns, and 1 point for in-between cases. For example, a sentence containing the correct pronoun, but with the pronoun situated in a wrong position (after the verb, instead of preceding the verb) received 1 point:

La niña saluda al niño y entonces   besa lo.
"The girl greets the boy and then [she] kisses him-OBJpro."

Sentences containing *le* instead of *la* or *lo* in pre- or postverbal position also received a score of 1:

La niña saluda al niño y entonces   le besa.
"The girl greets the boy and then [she] kisses him-OBJpro."

In the end, the number of in-between scores was minimal, less than 10 percent of the scores assigned on the sentence-level production task. Because there were five target items on the sentence-level production task, each with a value of 0-2, the possible range of scores on this task was 0–10.

Each passage used in the reconstruction task contained five instances of the target items. We used the same scoring procedure as for the sentence-level production task: 2, 1, 0. As in the case of the sentence-level production task, the vast majority of scores were either 0 or 2, with less than 5 percent of the scores being 1. The range of scores for reconstruction task was the same as the other two tasks: 0–10.

For purposes of analysis, all scores were converted to percentages.

Results

PI

Descriptive statistics for all PI data appear in Table 11.1. A one-way ANOVA conducted on each set of interpretation pretest scores did not reveal any main effect for presence or absence of EI: Interpretation, $F(2, 103) = .41$, $p = .66$; Production, $F(2, 103) = 1.14$, $p = .32$; Reconstruction, $F(2, 103) = .55$, $p = .58$. Thus, any differences found for groups after treatment are due to the effects of the main variable, +/- EI. We will begin with the interpretation data.

A repeated measures ANOVA for the interpretation tests reveal the following:

- effect for EI: $F(2, 103) = 67.34$, $p < .01$
- effect for Time: $F(1, 103) = 223.187$, $p < .01$
- interaction EI × Time: $F(2, 103) = 73.507$, $p < .01$

Table 11.1 Descriptive statistics for PI

	Pretest		Posttest	
	Mean	*SD*	*Mean*	*SD*
Interpretation				
PI + EI	10.00	15.25	75.00	21.66
PI – EI	12.00	13.54	48.80	25.55
Control	8.84	12.76	11.16	14.18
Production				
PI + EI	2.11	5.77	36.05	38.73
PI – EI	3.60	9.52	22.80	37.36
Control	6.05	16.20	14.19	29.62
Reconstruction				
PI + EI	7.90	14.73	11.84	15.57
PI – EI	4.40	12.94	10.00	21.41
Control	5.81	12.20	3.02	8.32

Note: PI + EI = 38; PI–EI = 25; Control = 43

Because of the interaction, additional analyses were conducted. An ANOVA on the posttest scores yielded an effect for EI: $F(2, 103) = 103.53$, $p < .01$. Fishers PLSD revealed that the effect was due to the following contrasts: PI + EI better than PI – EI ($p < .01$); PI + EI better than Control ($p < .01$); PI – EI better than Control ($p < .01$). Thus, while both treatment groups improved and were better than Control, the group that got EI performed better than the group that did not receive EI.

A repeated measures ANOVA for the production data yielded the following:

- no effect for EI: $F(2, 103) = 1.96$, $p = .15$
- an effect for Time: $F(2, 103) = 39.94$, $p < .01$
- an interaction EI × Time: $F(2, 103) = 6.41$, $p < .01$

Because of the interaction, a one-way ANOVA was conducted on the posttest scores. The analysis yielded an effect for EI: $F(2, 103) = 3.97$, $p = .02$. Fishers PLSD revealed only one contrast: PI + EI better than Control ($p < .01$). Thus, there were no differences between PI + EI and PI – EI but only PI + EI was better than Control.

A repeated measures ANOVA for the reconstruction data yielded the following:

- no effect for EI: $F(2, 103) = 2.21$, $p = .12$
- no effect for Time: $F(2, 103) = 1.99$, $p = .16$
- a trend for an interaction EI × Time: $F(2, 103) = 2.81$, $p = .07$

Because of the trend for an interaction a one-way ANOVA was conducted on the posttest scores with the following results: an effect for EI: $F(2, 103) = 3.88$, $p = .02$. Fishers PLSD revealed that the effect was due to one contrast: PI + EI better than Control ($p = .01$). Thus, there were no differences between PI + EI and PI − EI but only PI + EI was better than Control.

For the PI data, then, we see an effect for EI across the board when we examine interactions and look at posttest scores. However, the effect is not the same: for the interpretation scores, EI had an effect but −EI was still better than Control. This finding did not show up on the other two measures. It is worth noting here that the reconstruction task yielded disappointingly low scores, suggesting the task was difficult. We will see this with each treatment.

MOI

Descriptive statistics for the MOI data appear in Table 11.2. A one-way ANOVA conducted on each set of interpretation pretest scores did not reveal any main effect for presence or absence of EI: Interpretation, $F(2, 121) = 1.23$, $p = .30$; Production, $F(2, 121) = .77$, $p = .46$; Reconstruction, $F(2, 121) = .05$, $p = .95$. Thus, any differences found for groups after treatment are due to the effects of the main variable, +/− EI. Once again we will begin with the interpretation data.

A repeated measures ANOVA for the interpretation data yielded the following:

- an effect for Treatment: $F(2, 121) = 6.65$, $p < .01$
- an effect for Time: $F(1, 121) = 20.73$, $p < .01$
- an interaction Treatment × Time: $F(2, 121) = 3.20$, $p = .04$

Table 11.2 Descriptive statistics for MOI

	Pretest		Posttest	
	Mean	*SD*	*Mean*	*SD*
Interpretation				
MOI + EI	10.83	11.56	26.11	22.96
MOI − EI	13.11	13.79	26.44	28.30
Control	8.84	12.76	11.16	14.18
Production				
MOI + EI	6.39	14.76	47.50	39.96
MOI − EI	3.11	8.21	54.89	45.11
Control	6.05	16.20	14.19	29.62
Reconstruction				
MOI + EI	5.00	11.83	7.50	12.04
MOI − EI	5.33	10.79	14.89	19.26
Control	5.81	12.20	3.02	8.32

Note: MOI + EI = 36; MOI − EI = 45; Control = 43

Because of the interaction, a one-way ANOVA on the posttest scores was conducted, which yielded the following: $F(2, 121) = 6.27$, $p < .01$. Fishers PLSD revealed the following contrasts: MOI + EI better than Control ($p < .01$); MOI – EI better than Control ($p < .01$); but no difference between the +/–EI conditions. Thus, for the interpretation data, the presence or absence of EI did not make a difference; both MOI +EI and MOI–EI made equal gains.

A repeated measures ANOVA for the production test yielded the following:

- an effect for Treatment: $F(2, 121) = 8.98$, $p < .01$
- an effect for Time: $F(1, 121) = 104.67$, $p < .01$
- an interaction Treatment × Time: $F(2, 121) = 16.82$, $p < .01$

Because of the interaction, a one-way ANOVA was conducted on the posttest scores, which yielded the following: $F(2, 121) = 13.42$, $p < .01$. Fishers PLSD revealed the following contrasts: MOI +EI better than Control ($p < .01$); MOI–EI better than Control ($p < .01$); but no difference between the +/–EI conditions. Thus, for the production data, the presence or absence of EI did not make a difference; both MOI + EI and MOI – EI made equal gains.

A repeated measures ANOVA on the reconstruction data yielded the following:

- an effect for Treatment: $F(2, 121) = 3.41$, $p = .04$
- an effect for Time: $F(1, 121) = 4.97$, $p = .03$
- an interaction Treatment × Time: $F(2, 121) = 7.16$, $p < .01$

Because of the interaction, a one-way ANOVA was conducted on the posttest scores with the following results: $F(2, 121) = 7.87$, $p < .01$. Fishers PLSD revealed the following contrasts: MOI – EI better than MOI + EI ($p = .02$); MOI – EI better than Control ($p < .01$). There was no difference, however, between MOI + EI and Control. Thus, for the reconstruction data, the absence of EI proved to be superior overall to the presence of EI.

The results for the MOI are not as clear as for PI. On the one hand, the presence/absence of EI does not seem to make a difference when it comes to interpretation or production, but it does when it comes to reconstruction. However, the difference is not what is expected: –EI was better than +EI in this domain. As in the case of the PI groups, the reconstruction scores were quite low.

DG

Descriptive statistics for the DG data appear in Table 11.3. A one-way ANOVA conducted on each set of pretest scores did not reveal any main effect for presence or absence of EI: Interpretation, $F(2, 96) = .04$, $p = .96$; Production,

Table 11.3 Descriptive statistics for DG

	Pretest		Posttest	
	Mean	*SD*	*Mean*	*SD*
Interpretation				
DG + EI	9.63	14.00	17.78	26.36
DG – EI	9.66	14.01	4.14	6.82
Control	8.84	12.76	11.16	14.18
Production				
DG + EI	5.19	11.56	22.59	31.82
DG – EI	4.83	11.84	6.55	17.58
Control	6.05	16.20	14.19	29.62
Reconstruction				
DG + EI	5.93	13.38	13.70	21.87
DG – EI	4.14	11.19	10.00	17.11
Control	5.81	12.20	3.02	8.32

Note. DG +EI = 27; DG – EI = 29; Control = 43

$F(2, 96) = .07$, $p = .93$; Reconstruction, $F(2, 96) = .20$, $p = .82$. Thus, any differences found for groups after treatment are due to the effects of the main variable, +/– EI. As with the other two treatments, we will begin with the interpretation data.

A repeated measures ANOVA on the interpretation data yielded the following:

- no effect for Treatment: $F(2, 96) = 2.31$, $p = .11$
- no effect for Time: $F(2, 96) = .68$, $p = .41$
- an interaction Treatment × Time: $F(2, 96) = 3.49$, $p = .03$

To examine the interaction, a one-way ANOVA was conducted on the posttest scores with the following results: $F(2, 96) = 4.50$, $p = .01$. Fishers PLSD revealed only one contrast: DG + EI better than DG – EI ($p < .01$). Neither treatment was better than Control, however, which suggests why an effect for Treatment was not obtained on the repeated measures.

A repeated measures ANOVA on the production data yielded the following:

- no effect for Treatment: $F(2, 96) = 1.45$, $p = .24$
- an effect for Time: $F(2, 96) = 13.60$, $p < .01$
- an interaction Treatment × Time: $F(2, 96) = 3.01$, $p = .05$

Because of the interaction a one-way ANOVA was conducted on the posttest scores. The analysis suggested a trend for Treatment: $F(2, 96) = 2.41$, $p = .09$.

Fishers PLSD revealed one contrast leading toward that trend: DG + EI better than DG − EI ($p = .03$); again with neither treatment better than Control.

A repeated measures ANOVA on the reconstruction data yielded the following:

- no effect for Treatment: $F(2, 96) = 1.81$, $p = .17$
- an effect for Time: $F(2, 96) = 4.96$, $p = .03$
- an interaction Treatment × Time: $F(2, 96) = 4.56$, $p = .01$

Even though there was no effect for Treatment, the interaction was explored by examining the posttest scores with a one-way ANOVA. The analysis yielded an effect for Treatment: $F(2, 96) = 4.20$, $p = .02$. Fishers PLSD revealed one and only one contrast: DG +EI better than Control ($p < .01$).

For DG, it seems, EI has little effect. The effects of EI never show up as a main variable but they do show up in interactions. However, this is usually due to DG +EI better than Control and not to any differences between +/−EI within DG itself. Interestingly, the DG scores on the reconstruction task were not much different from those of the PI and MOI groups, and were low compared to those of the other assessment tasks.

Discussion and Conclusion

From the results presented earlier, it seems that EI is playing differential roles for each treatment. For PI, it seems to be beneficial. For MOI, it seems to make no difference, and for DG we might even conclude that EI is necessary (i.e., only DG + EI is consistently better than Control). However, such conclusions would need to be considered through the lens of what each treatment itself does. This is because the impact of the treatments seems to differ from task to task. For example, on the interpretation task PI–EI consistently outperforms all non-PI groups, even MOI+EI and DG+EI. The PI–EI posttest mean on interpretation was 48.80, but the MOI+EI mean was only 26.11. So, although EI made a difference for PI on this measure, overall PI (regardless of +/−EI) is still a superior intervention when it comes to processing problems. On the other hand, for the production task, MOI–EI proved to be better than all othernon-MOI groups, even PI+EI (a unique finding to this study and not present in previous PI/MOI contrasts). Thus, MOI seems to be a superior intervention when it comes to sentence level production. However, we should note that the posttest scores for the MOI groups on production (a task biased for this particular group) are between 47 percent and 55 percent, whereas the PI scores for interpretation (which biased for those groups) was between 48 percent and 75 percent. DG, regardless of +/−EI, seemed to be the least effective treatment on any measure as its scores were never better than and were often consistently lower than any of the non-DG groups. On the task that biased for DG (reconstruction), the two DG treatment groups' scores did not climb over 13 percent on the posttest. (Note that both PI and MOI groups scored between 10 percent and 14 percent on the reconstruction task.) In short, the three treatments themselves have variable outcomes in terms of effects and thus the presence/absence of EI is seen to have variable effects.

Because we have no prior research on either MOI or DG with +/–EI as a variable, we cannot couch this research within a larger context. We can, however, contextualize the PI section of this study within prior research. We note here that there are some differences and similarities to previous research. First, the results do not support that EI is necessary for PI. This finding is well supported by previous research. However, in contradistinction to the findings of VanPatten and Oikkenon (1996), Benati (2004), and Wong (2004), for example, the presence of EI within PI seems to be beneficial (i.e., results in higher gain scores than when EI is absent). The results thus resemble those of Farley (2004a) and to a certain extent Fernandez (2008). I attribute this finding to the limited tokens used in the present study. Although we based our materials on the original VanPatten and Cadierno materials, which were subsequently used in toto by VanPatten and Oikkenon, we halved the materials when we focused on third-person only. What this means is that learners in the present study received about 50 percent of the exposure/practice compared with previous research. This may have contributed to the fact that the PI–EI group did not perform like its cohort in VanPatten and Oikkenon. In other words, by reducing the number of tokens, we made the intervention less robust, making comparison with previous research tenuous. Unfortunately, we were forced into this methodological decision because we wanted direct comparison with Keating and Farley (2008) who focused on third-person only (see VanPatten, Farmer et al., 2009). Future research would need to address this particular issue.

I conclude by saying that the present study is the tip of the iceberg in comparative research on the effects of EI. We are currently analyzing data from a delayed posttest and I will report on that in future research. For now, it is enough to state the following: not all treatments are made equal, and thus EI will most likely play a differential role in the effectiveness of those treatments. If borne out, scholars in instructed SLA will have to come to grips with what the treatments themselves are actually doing vis à vis pushing along the development of an underlying linguistic system in the learner. If, for example, we continue to see EI not necessary for PI but necessary for DG, what does this say about what structured input is doing for learners within PI and what the passages and the interaction are doing for learners in DG? This is an important question.

Notes

[1] There is some disagreement as to whether learners are guided by the FNP or the word order of their first language (e.g., Carroll, 2001). However, for the purposes of the present study, either position would result in misinterpretation of an OVS sentence (e.g., VanPatten, 2008).

[2] In contradistinction to claims made by others, VanPatten and Cadierno's study was not focused on comprehension vs. production.

References

Alenan, R. (1995). Input enhancement and rule presentation in second language acquisition. In R. Schmidt (Ed.). *Attention and awareness in foreign language learning* (pp. 259–302). Honolulu: University of Hawai'i at Manoa.

Benati, A. (2001). A comparative study of the effects of processing instruction and output-based instruction on the acquisition of the Italian future tense. *Language Teaching Research*, 5, 95–127.

Benati, A. (2004). The effects of structured input activities and explicit information on the acquisition of the Italian future tense. In B. VanPatten (Ed.). *Processing instruction:Theory, research, and commentary* (pp. 207–25). Mahwah, NJ: Lawrence Erlbaum Associates.

Benati, A. (2005). The effects of processing instruction, traditional instruction, and meaning-output instruction on the acquisition of the English past simple tense. *Language Teaching Research*, 9, 67–93.

Cadierno, T. (1995). Formal instruction from a processing perspective: An investigation into the Spanish past tense. *The Modern Language Journal*, 79, 179–93.

Carroll, S. (2001). *Input and evidence: The raw material of second language acquisition.* Amsterdam: John Benjamins.

DeKeyser, R. (2003). Implicit and explicit learning. In C. J. Doughty & M. H. Long (Eds.), *The handbook of second language acquisition* (pp. 313–48). Oxford: Blackwell.

Farley, A. P. (2004a). Processing instruction and the Spanish subjunctive: Is explicit information needed? In B. VanPatten (Ed.). *Processing instruction: Theory, research, and commentary* (pp. 227–39). Mahwah, NJ: Lawrence Erlbaum & Associates.

Farley, A. P. (2004b) The relative effects of processing instruction and meaning-based output instruction. In B. VanPatten (Ed.), *Processing instruction: Theory, research, and commentary* (pp. 143–68). Mahwah, NJ: Lawrence Erlbaum & Associates.

Farley, A. P. (2005). *Structured input.* New York: McGraw-Hill.

Fernandez, C. (2008). Re-examining the role of explicit information in processing instruction. *Studies in Second Language Acquisition*, 30, 277–305.

Keating, G. D., & Farley, A. P. (2008). Processing instruction, meaning-based output instruction, and meaning-based drills: Impacts on classroom L2 acquisition of Spanish object pronouns. *Hispania*, 91, 639–50.

Hulstijn, J. (2005). Theoretical and empirical issues in the study of implicit and explicit second-language learning. *Studies in Second Language Acquisition*, 27, 129–40)

Lee, J. F., & VanPatten, B. (1995). *Making communicative language teaching happen* (1st ed.). New York: McGraw-Hill.

Lee, J. F., & VanPatten, B. (2003). *Making communicative language teaching happen* (2nd ed.). New York: McGraw-Hill.

Morgan-Short, K., & Wood Bowden, H. (2006). Processing instruction and meaningful output-based instruction: Effects on second language development. *Studies in Second Language Acquisition*, 28, 31–65.

Qin, J. (2008). The effect of processing instruction and dictogloss tasks on acquisition of the English passive voice. *Language Teaching Research*, 12, 61–82.

Robinson, R. (1995). Aptitude, awareness and the fundamental similarity of implicit and explicit second language learning. In R. Schmidt (Ed.). *Attention and awareness in foreign language learning* (pp. 303–58). Honolulu: University of Hawai'i at Manoa.

Sanz, C., & Morgan-Short, K. (2004). Positive evidence vs. explicit rule presentation and explicit negative feedback: A computer assisted study. *Language Learning*, 54, 35–78.

Scott, V. (1989). An empirical study of explicit and implicit teaching strategies in French. *The Modern Language Journal*, 73, 14–22.

VanPatten, B. (1993). Grammar instruction for the acquisition-rich classroom. Foreign Language Annals, 26, 433–50.

VanPatten, B. (1996). Input processing and grammar instruction. Norwood, NJ: Ablex.

VanPatten, B. (2004). Input processing in second language acquisition. In B. VanPatten (Ed.). *Processing instruction: Theory, research, and commentary* (pp. 5–31). Mahwah, NJ: Lawrence Erlbaum & Associates.

VanPatten, B. (2007a). Some thoughts on the future of research on input enhancement. In C. Gascoigne (Ed.). *Assessing the impact of input enhancement in second language education: Evolution in theory, research and practice* (pp. 169–89).

VanPatten, B. (2007b). Input processing in adult second language acquisition. In B. VanPatten & J. Williams (Eds.). *Theories in second language acquisition* (pp. 115–35). Mahwah, NJ: Lawrence Erlbaum Associates.

VanPatten, B. (2008). Processing matters. In T. Piske & M. Young-Scholten (Eds.) *Input Matters* (pp. 47–61). Clevedon, UK: Multilingual Matters.

VanPatten, B., & Cadierno, T. (1993). Explicit instruction and input processing. *Studies in Second Language Acquisition*, 15, 225–43.

VanPatten, B., Farmer, J. L., & Clardy, C. L. (2009). Processing Instruction and Meaning-based Output Instruction: A Response to Keating and Farley (2008). *Hispania*, 92, 124–135.

VanPatten, B., Inclezan, D., Salazar, H., & Farley, A. P. (forthcoming). Processing Instruction and Dictogloss: A Response to Qin (2008). *Language Teaching Research*.

VanPatten, B., & Oikkenon, S. (1996). Explanation versus structured input in processing instruction. *Studies in Second Language Acquisition*, 18, 495–510.

VanPatten, B., & Wong, W. (2004). Processing instruction and the French causative: another replication. In B. VanPatten (Ed.). *Processing instruction: Theory, research, and commentary* (pp. 97–118). Mahwah, NJ: Lawrence Erlbaum & Associates.

Wajnryb, R. (1990). *Grammar dictation.* Oxford: Oxford University Press.

Wong, W. (2004a). Processing instruction in French: the roles of explicit information and structured input. In B. VanPatten (Ed.), *Processing instruction: Theory, research, and commentary* (pp. 187–205). Mahwah, NJ: Lawrence Erlbaum Associates.

Wong, W. (2004b). The nature of processing instruction. In B. VanPatten (Ed.). *Processing instruction: Theory, research, and commentary* (pp. 33–63). Mahwah, NJ: Lawrence Erlbaum Associates.

Wong, W. (2005). *Input enhancement: From theory and research to classroom practice.* New York: McGraw-Hill.

Chapter 12

Secondary and Cumulative Effects in Attaining L2 Proficiency in the Classroom: The Acquisition of French[1]

Alessandro Benati
University of Greenwich, United Kingdom,

James Lee
University of New South Wales, Australia,

Cécile Laval
University of Greenwich, United Kingdom

Abstract

This chapter presents the results of an unique line of research within the processing instruction model which has assessed secondary and cumulative effects of this approach on grammar instruction. Research on processing instruction has so far focused on measuring its direct and primary effects by comparing this type of instruction with traditional and meaning-output based instruction. The results of the empirical research have shown that processing instruction is a better approach to output-based approaches to grammar instruction. Processing instruction is a very effective approach towards altering inappropriate processing strategies and instils appropriate ones in L2 learners. Despite the positive results obtained on measuring the primary effects of processing instruction, no research has yet been conducted to look into possible secondary and cumulative effects of this approach. The main aim of this chapter is to present results of a study investigating secondary and cumulative effects for processing instruction in the acquisition of French.

Introduction

Research on processing instruction (PI) has measured its primary effects focusing on the effect of this instructional treatment on the acquisition of a specific linguistic feature affected by one or a combination of processing principles (see review of these studies in Lee and Benati, 2007a, 2007b and 2009; VanPatten, 2002). The new line of research we present in this chapter has attempted to measure possible secondary and cumulative effects for PI (see a full review of these studies in Benati and Lee, 2008).

We refer to secondary effects when the processing principle is the same for two linguistic features investigated. For example, after being trained to circumvent the Lexical Preference Principle in the acquisition of present tense in French, can learners apply/transfer the same Principle to other forms in French affected by the same principle?

We refer to cumulative effects when learners who have been exposed/trained to a processing principle might pick up a second processing principle more quickly and efficiently than they pick up the first one.

Aims and Motivation of the Present Study

Research on the effects of PI has addressed a specific processing principle to date. It has been conducted in both syntactic and perceptual processing principles (Lee, 2004). PI research has taken the appropriately conservative approach of assessing the direct effects of instruction, that is, does PI alter inappropriate processing principles and/or instil inappropriate ones? (see Van Patten, 2004). Empirical evidence has shown that the answer to this question is positive. Therefore it might be relevant to move one step away from assessing direct/primary effects of PI and investigate secondary and cumulative effects of PI. In this chapter we present the results of a classroom study that has investigated whether English native speakers learning one specific grammatical feature in French affected by one processing principle can transfer the training received to another affected by the same principle without the need for any further intervention in PI. The question we are aiming to answer is: Would Training on one Principle (P1.b) for one specific form in French transfer/apply to another form affected by the same Principle without any further Training?

The findings will be considered in relation to Lexical Preference Principle (see Van Patten, 2004). The Lexical Preference Principle (P1.b) states that learners tend to process lexical items as opposed to grammatical form when both encode the same semantic information. We will show whether the use of one principle (P1.b) for one specific form (French *imparfait*) can be transferred by the learner to another form (subjunctive) without the need for additional PI.

We will also show whether the training of one processing principle (P1.b) for one specific form (French *imparfait*) can be transferred by the learner to another form (causative with *faire* in French) affected by a different processing principle (P2. First Noun Principle: Learners tend to process the first noun or pronoun they encounter in a sentence as the subject/agent, VanPatten, 2004) without the need for additional PI. This refers to cumulative effects of receiving PI on different types of forms/processing principles. The question we are aiming to answer is: Will learners pick up a second processing principle more quickly and efficiently than they pick up the first one?

Research Questions

The specific research questions formulated in this study are:

Q1: Are there any secondary effects of PI from receiving instruction on French past tense imperfective aspect to French subjunctive mood morphology as measured by an interpretation and production task?

Q2: Are there any cumulative effects of PI from receiving instruction on French past tense imperfective aspect to French causative constructions with *faire* as measured by an interpretation and production task?

Method and Procedure

Participants

We randomly assigned English native-speakers of French to three groups. The final pool (reduced from 55) consisted of 30 undergraduate students enrolled in intermediate-level French. Participants completed an informational/consent form as part of the selection criteria should not have been exposed in the classroom to any of the three targeted linguistic items before the treatment. Subjects who scored more than 50 per cent in the pre-tests (interpretation and production tests) were not included in the final pool. Only participants who had participated in each stage of the experiment (pre-tests, instructional treatment, and post-tests) were included in the final data collection. The final pool consisted of three groups: the PI group ($n = 13$); the Traditional group ($n = 10$); and the control group ($n = 7$).

Procedure

Participants were tested on their ability to interpret and to produce the three linguistics target features (imperfect, subjunctive of doubt, and causative construction with *faire*) at sentence level. The experiment took place during participant's regular class period. They were given the six pre-tests (two per target linguistic item) two weeks before the instructional treatments took place. The instructional treatments lasted for one class period of two hours and post-tests were administered immediately after the end of the instructional treatment. The three immediate post-tests on the three grammatical features were administered to the three groups after the end of instruction.

All three groups were taught by the same instructor (a researcher) instructional period. She was not, however, the participants regular classroom instructor. The instructional treatments contained identical subject matter, vocabulary and same number of tokens.

Materials

Two separate instructional packets were designed for this study, one for the group receiving PI instructional treatment and one for the group receiving Traditional instruction (TI) treatment. The instructional material was developed for the French *imparfait*.

PI

The material for the PI treatment reflects one approach to the teaching of grammar which encourages L2 learners to focus their attention on a targeted form in order to process that form for meaning. In the material pack for the PI group the activities comprised of structured input activities as described by Lee and VanPatten (1995, 2003) that consisted of both referential and affective activities. Structured input activities (both referential and affective) were structured so that learners were to rely on the form (French *imparfait*) in order to understand (interpret the sentence) the meaning and therefore complete the task. In these activities the relation between form and meaning was always in focus. In addition to the explicit information regarding forms and functions of the past imperfective tense, the PI group received information about the processing problems. Lexical items like *l'année dernière* (last year) which communicate past time frame encourage learners to leave past tense markers undetected in the input as learners tend to rely on lexical cues over grammatical forms to encode semantic information. In the PI materials all lexical cues to past time and imperfective aspect were removed. Never during instruction were students in the PI group asked to produce the correct verb inflection in the French imperfect. Rather they were engaged in processing input sentences so that they could make better form-meaning connections. Feedback during the instructional treatment was quite limited and restricted. On the referential activities, the instructor told the learners whether their interpretations were correct or not but did not offer any further information on the item nor offered further explanation.

TI

The instructional packet used for the TI treatment reflects a different approach to the teaching of grammar. In the case of this experimental study, TI consisted in the paradigmatic presentation of the French imperfect, all persons, all forms regular and irregular followed by traditional output practice. The TI group was not given any information about processing problems, the tendency to rely on lexical items or information about listening for the forms in the input because this information is not part of traditional approaches to grammar instruction. All practice which followed the explicit information provided to learners in this group was oriented to producing the correct verbal inflection. All the activities used for the implementation of this approach were constructed to make learners produce the target form in either oral or written mode. The activities included the following types of practice: fill-in-the- blank tasks, sentence completion tasks, traditional substitution drills and transformation tasks. As in VanPatten and Cadierno's original PI study (1993), activities in the traditional pack followed the pattern of moving from mechanical to meaningful and then to communicative practice.

Control Group

The control group took the pre-tests and post-tests on the same days as the treatments groups, but they received no instructional treatment for the target form. These participants continued their regularly scheduled class lesson during the instructional period.

Assessment Tasks and Scoring

Pre- and post-tests were developed for measuring the primary effects of instruction on the first feature (French past tense imperfective aspect), the secondary effects on the second feature (French subjunctive mood morphology), and the cumulative effects on the third feature (French causative constructions with *faire*). Pre-tests and post-tests for each of the three linguistics features consisted of a sentence level interpretation task and a sentence level production task.

The interpretation tasks for the primary and secondary linguistic targets consisted of 20 recorded sentences. Ten contained targets and the other ten served as distracters. For the interpretation tests all the items were recorded by a native speaker of French and presented to the subjects on a CD player. Participants listened to the sentences only once, no repetition was provided. The different versions of the interpretation tasks were balanced in terms of difficulty and vocabulary used with a tendency to favour the use of high frequency items.

Primary Linguistic Target

The interpretation task for the primary linguistic target (French *imparfait*) required participants to listen to a series of sentences about people doing various activities and to determine whether the action was in the present or in the past. For example, participants heard the sentence *Emma parlait au téléphone* (Emma was speaking on the phone) and then had to decide whether the sentence expressed 'present', 'past' or they were 'not sure'. Participants were given the option of indicating whether they were 'not sure' to discourage guessing. Subjects received 1 point if the target sentence was interpreted correctly and 0 points if they were wrong or they were not sure how to interpret the sentence correctly. The maximum score possible was 10 points with a minimum possible score of 0 points. Only target items were scored, not the distracters. Each item was read only once.

In the production task, learners had to fill the blanks in a short passage by producing the correct form of the verb. Scoring for the production task consists of a 2, 1, 0 point system for a possible maximum score of 20 points. A participant received 2 points if the sentence completion contained a verb in the correct past tense form. If the verb was in the past tense but was the wrong person or if the learner had switched verb category endings, a score of 1 point was allocated to the answer. Any other response received a score of 0 points.

Secondary and Cumulative Linguistic Targets

To assess the possible secondary effects of instruction on the second targeted linguistic item, the French subjunctive in nominal clauses after expressions of doubts, an interpretation task and a production task were developed and used as a pre-test-post-test measure of knowledge gained at interpreting the French subjunctive of doubt. The interpretation task required the learners to listen to the nominal dependent clause of each sentence and then to select the appropriate beginning for the sentence. In essence, we separated the lexical indicator of subjunctive mood '*Je doute que*' (*I doubt that*) from the subjunctive mood morphology. Learners could not rely on the lexical indicator but rather had to process the subjunctive form to link it to the lexical indicator. By dividing and restructuring the sentences in this way, we were able to move the target form into a more salient processing position. In that this is the secondary target item, these learners have never been exposed to it in an instructional setting. They listened to these sentences without knowing anything about subjunctive morphology.

They heard each clause once and then had only five seconds to decide which beginning was appropriate. Again, they were given the option to indicate if they were not sure. We wanted to discourage guessing.

Scoring of the ten target items on the interpretation task consisted of one versus zero point system per item for a possible maximum score of ten points.

A subject received one point if the target sentence was assigned its correct beginning and received zero points if the selection was incorrect.

The written production task consisted of ten sentences with blanks followed by the infinitive form of a verb. The participants were directed to complete the sentences with the correct form of the verb. Of these sentences five require the use of the indicative present tense (distracters) and five items require the use of the subjunctive. Five minutes were allocated to complete this task. Scoring for the production task consists of a two, one, zero point system for a possible maximum score of ten points. A participant received two points if the sentence completion contained a verb in the correct subjunctive form. If the verb was in the subjunctive but was the wrong person, a score of one point was allocated to the answer. Any other response received a score of zero points.

To assess the possible cumulative effects of instruction on the third linguistic item, the French causative with *faire*, an interpretation task and a production task were also developed. The interpretation task required participants to listen to the 20 sentences and then indicate who was performing the action by answering the questions or by ticking *Je ne suis pas sûr(e)* 'I am not sure' if they did not know. Participants had five seconds to answer the question and no repetition of the item was provided so that we could measure real-time comprehension. Scoring for the interpretation task consisted of a one versus zero point system per item for a possible maximum score of ten points. A participant received one point if the person performing the action was identified correctly and received zero points if the person performing the action was wrong or the participant indicated an inability to determine who performed the action.

The written production task consisted of ten written items with blanks in which participants have to complete the sentence to describe who was doing what on each of the ten pictures shown using an overhead projector. Each sentence was begun for the learners. These beginnings contained a grammatical subject and the verb form *fait*. Of the ten pictures/sentences five used the French causative and five did not. These latter items served as distracters and were not scored. Participants had ten seconds to complete each sentence. Scoring for the production task consisted of a two, one, zero point system for a possible maximum score of ten points. A participant received two points if the sentence completion contained a verb in the correct form using the causative. If the causative was used but the wrong person is indicated, a score of one point was allocated to the participant. Any other response received a score of zero points.

Results

Primary effects were measured on the acquisition of French Imparfait at the end of the instructional treatment period. The statistical results showed that the PI group performed better than the TI and the Control group on the interpretation task. Both the PI group and the TI group perform equally and better than the control group on the production task. The findings of this investigation (primary effects, see Benati, Lee and Laval, 2008) led to the following conclusions:

PI is a more effective instructional treatment than TI in helping L2 learners at interpreting sentences containing French imperfect form;

PI is equally successful as TI in helping learners at producing sentences containing French imperfect forms;

PI is successful at altering processing problems that affect the French imperfect forms (Lexical Preference Principle and Sentence Location principle).

To address the two main research questions that guided this study and in order to establish whether there were secondary and cumulative effects for the PI group we conducted a series of one-way ANOVAs on the pre-test scores for the interpretation and the production tasks (French subjunctive mood morphology and French causative construction with *faire*) in order to determine whether there were any statistically significant differences between the three groups before the beginning of the experimental period. The results did not yield any significant differences. We used a repeated measure ANOVA to assess whether there were any significant effects for Instruction and Time and whether there was a significant Interaction between Instruction and Time. Where effects were found, we then carried out a post-hoc test, Tukeys test, to establish where statistical differences were between the three groups.

Secondary Effects (French Subjunctive Mood Morphology)

We used a one-way ANOVA on the pre-test interpretation task scores of the three groups to insure that there were no pre-existing differences between the groups' knowledge of French subjunctive mood morphology. The results showed no significant differences among the instructional treatment groups' means before instruction ($F(2,28) = .277$, $p = .760$). Means and standard deviations for the interpretation tests are presented in Table 12.1. These means show a modest increase in score for the PI group but a decrease in scores for the TI and control groups. The repeated measure ANOVA with instruction as the between-subjects factor and Time as the within-subjects factor was conducted for the interpretation task. The analysis revealed a significant main effect for Instruction ($F(2,28) = 14.528$, $p = .000$) and Time ($F(2,28) = 2.559$, $p = .047$) as well as a statistically significant interaction between Instruction and Time ($F(4,28) = .582$, $p = .021$). The post-hoc analyses showed that the effect for

Table 12.1 Means and standard deviation (French subjunctive) for interpretation task pre-test and post-test

Variable	N	Pre-test Mean	Pre-test SD	Post-test 1 Mean	Post-test 1 SD
PI	13	1.76	1.09193	3.69	1.65250
TI	9	2.11	1.53659	1.77	1.39443
C	6	1.66	1.21106	1.16	0.98319

instruction was due to the scores of the processing group being significantly higher than those of the traditional group ($p = .016$) and the control group ($p = .022$). There was no difference in scores between the TI and control groups ($p = .727$).

As we can see from the means the processing group has slightly improved from pre- to post-test compared to the other two groups and in particular with the control group. Although the improvement of the PI group from the pre-test to the post-test is about 20 per cent, it is statistically significant. What these results demonstrate is that there are secondary effects in the interpretation test for the processing group. The PI treatment is more effective than the TI treatment and the control group in affecting learners' interpretation of subjunctive forms.

A second one-way ANOVA was used on the pre-test production scores of the three groups. Once again this analysis showed no significant differences between the three groups. We then conducted a repeated measures ANOVA on the raw scores for the production task (pre- and post-tests). Similar to the previous results on the interpretation task, the statistical analysis revealed significant main effects for Instruction ($F(2,28) = 12.170$, $p = .000$) and for Time ($F(2,25) = 11.912$, $p = 002$) as well as a significant interaction between Instruction and Time ($F(4,28) = 8.952$, $p = .000$). The post-hoc analysis showed the following contrasts. First, the PI group's scores were higher than those of the control group ($p = .000$). Second, the PI group's scores were also higher than the TI group's ($p = .037$). And, third, there was no significant difference in scores between the TI and control groups ($p = .437$).

As we can see in Table 12.2, the PI group made a modest but significant 10 per cent improvement from pre-testing to post-testing on producing the secondary linguistic target. The TI group improved only 2 per cent but this change in performance was not statistically significant. These findings are very consistent with the findings of the other two studies presented in this book. It is the third set of findings demonstrating secondary transfer-of-training effects for PI.

Table 12.2 Means and standard deviation (French subjunctive) for production task pre-test and post-test

		Pre-test		Post-test 1	
Variable	N	Mean	SD	Mean	SD
PI	13	.000	.00000	1.00	.57735
TI	9	.000	.00000	0.222	.44096
C	6	.000	.00000	0.000	.00000

Cumulative Effects (French Causative Construction with *Faire*)

The means for the interpretation pre-test and post-test results for the French causative construction with *faire* are given in Table 12.3. The means suggest that the PI group improved their interpretation whereas the other two groups means decreased from pre-test to post-test. We used again a one-way ANOVA on the pre-test interpretation task scores of the three groups to determine that there were no pre-existing differences between the groups. The result showed no significant differences among the instructional treatment groups' means before instruction ($F(2,28) = .337$, $p = .717$). We then conducted a repeated measures ANOVA to compare the effects of Instruction and Time. The statistical analysis revealed significant main effects for Instruction ($F(2,28) = 18.312$, $p = .000$); and for Time ($F(2,28) = 10.211$, $p = .001$) as well as a significant interaction between Instruction and Time ($F(4,28) = 6.215$, $p = .020$). The post hoc analysis showed the following contrasts. The PI group's scores are better than both the TI group's ($p = .001$) and the control group's ($p = .018$). There was no difference between the scores of TI and control groups ($p = .846$). As we can see from the means in Table 12.3, the PI group improved 34 per cent from pre- to post-test in interpreting correctly the underlying structure of French causative constructions.

We now present our final analysis. The means for the production tests on French causative constructions with *faire* are given in Table 12.4. The one-way ANOVA conducted on the pre-test production scores of the three groups showed no pre-existing differences between the groups. This finding was not surprising in that all learners scored a zero on the production pretest. We then carried out an ANOVA with repeated measures on the raw scores for the production task. The statistical analysis revealed significant main effects for Instruction ($F(2,28) = 17.803$, $p = 000$) and for Time ($F(2,28) = 26.561$, $p = 000$) as well as a significant interaction between Instruction and Time ($F(4,28) = 6.561$, $p = 000$). The post hoc analysis showed the following contrasts. The PI group's scores are better than both the TI group's ($p = .013$) and the control group's ($p = .038$). There was no difference between the scores of TI and control groups ($p = .673$). The PI groups 10 per cent improvement again proved significant whereas the TI group's 2.7 per cent improvement did not.

Table 12.3 Means and standard deviation (French causative) for interpretation task pre-test and post-test

		Pre-test		Post-test 1	
Variable	N	Mean	SD	Mean	SD
PI	13	1.23	1.30089	4.61	2.66266
TI	9	0.8889	0.60093	0.3333	0.500433
C	6	1.16	0.40825	0.8333	0.98379

Table 12.4 Means and standard deviation (French causative) for production task pre-test and post-test

		Pre-test		Post-test 1	
Variable	N	Mean	SD	Mean	SD
PI	13	.000	.00000	1.079	.49355
TI	9	.000	.00000	0.272	.35094
c	6	.000	.00000	0.000	.00000

The present study is the first to demonstrate that PI provides learners not only primary or direct effects of instruction on interpretation and production, but also secondary and cumulative transfer-of-training effects on both interpretation and production.

Discussion and Conclusion

The two main objectives of this study were to investigate the possible secondary and cumulative effects of PI. The forms under scrutiny here were the primary target of past tense imperfective aspect and the secondary transfer-of-training target of the subjunctive mood morphology. Both these verb final morphological marking are affected by the same processing problems. The cumulative transfer-of-training target was causative constructions whose underlying subject-verb relations are misinterpreted by learners. The target language was French as learned by classroom-based native speakers of English. The two main questions that guided our investigation are reiterated as follows:

Q1: Are there any secondary effects of PI from receiving instruction on French past tense imperfective aspect to French subjunctive mood morphology as measured by an interpretation and production task?

Q2: Are there any cumulative effects of PI from receiving instruction on French past tense imperfective aspect to French causative constructions with *faire* as measured by an interpretation and production task?

To summarize, analyses of the results for the present study demonstrated secondary effects for PI. Learners who received PI instruction on French past tense imperfective aspect, were able to process subjunctive mood morphology better than the TI group. The PI group improved between 10 per cent and 20 per cent in both measures.

The most important finding of the present study, arguably, is that PI offers learners cumulative transfer-of-training effects. PI learners trained on verbal morphology gained 11 per cent in form production and 34 per cent in form interpretation on a syntactic construction.

The findings of this investigation (secondary and cumulative) led to the following conclusions:

Participants in the processing group were able to transfer the PI training received for the French imperfect to another linguistic form in French (subjunctive) affected by similar processing problems;

Participants in the processing group were able to transfer the PI training received for the French imperfect to another linguistic form in French (causative with *faire*) affected by different processing problems.

What may account for the result that L2 learners in the PI group benefited from the instructional treatment and were able to transfer the PI training to other features?

First, we believe that we have provided evidence in support to Lee's hypothesis (2004) on possible transfer of training effects. In our study, learners who received PI training on one processing strategy for one specific form were able to appropriately transfer the use of that strategy to another form affected by the same processing problem without further instruction in PI.

Second, the results of this study also provide evidence to another Lee's hypothesis (2004) by showing that learners in the PI group were able to pick up a second processing strategy without any instruction. We believe that L2 learners receiving PI develop other intuitions about how the language works.

Overall, the main results of this study have demonstrated that PI has secondary and cumulative transfer-of-training effects. Learners benefit from PI directly, that is, they improve on the targeted linguistic item, but also indirectly, in that they improve on other linguistic items.

Future research should include delayed post-tests and should investigate whether there are other possible factors which might be considered responsible for the findings of this study. One possible factor, might have been the 'test' factor. The PI group might have used the items in the tests (for the other linguistic features) in order to work out how the language works. In other words, individual item in the 'tests' administrated to the participants, might have worked as a sort of instructional treatment for the PI group.

Note

[1] This chapter uses data also reported in chapter five in Benati, A., Lee, J. (2008). *Grammar Acquisition and Processing Instruction: Secondary and Cumulative Effects.* Clevedon: Multilingual Matters. The current version is a smaller scale and reworked presentation of that study.

References

Benati, A., & Lee, J. (2008). *Grammar acquisition and processing instruction: secondary and cumulative effects.* Clevedon: Multilingual Matters.

Benati, A., Lee, J., & Laval, C. (2008). From Processing Instruction on the acquisition of French imparfait to secondary transfer-of-training effects on French Subjunctive and to cumulative transfer-of-training effects with French causative constructions (pages forthcoming). In A. Benati, & J. Lee (2008). *Grammar acquisition and processing instruction: Secondary and cumulative effects.* Clevedon: Multilingual Matters, pp. 121–157.

Lee, J. (2004). On the generalizability, limits, and potential future directions of processing instruction research. In B. VanPatten (Ed.). *Processing instruction: Theory, research, and commentary* (pp. 311–23). Mahwah, NJ: Erlbaum.

Lee, J., & VanPatten, B. (1995). *Making communicative language teaching happen.* New York: McGraw-Hill.

Lee, J., & VanPatten, B. (2003). *Making communicative language teaching happen* (2nd ed.). New York: McGraw-Hill.

Lee, J., & Benati, A. (2007a). *Delivering processing instruction in classrooms and virtual contexts: Research and practice.* London: Equinox.

Lee, J., & Benati, A. (2007b). *Second language processing: An analysis of theory, problems and solutions.* Continuum: London.

Lee, J., & Benati, A. (2009). *Research and Perspectives on Processing Instruction.* New York: Mouton de Gruyter.

VanPatten, B. (2002). Processing Instruction: An update. *Language Learning,* 52, 755–803.

VanPatten, B., & Cadierno, T. (1993). Explicit instruction and input processing. *Studies in Second Language Acquisition,* 15, 225–43.

Chapter 13

Models of Speaking and the Assessment of Second Language Proficiency

Peter Skehan
Chinese University of Hong Kong, Hong Kong SAR

Abstract

This chapter relates the areas of psycholinguistics and SLA to second language assessment. The chapter outlines the Levelt model of speech production, and covers findings from the field of second language task-based spoken performance. These findings are then related to the stages of the Levelt model, especially Conceptualization and Formulation, and four general types of influence are discussed: complexifying, pressuring, easing and focusing. These influences are related to the tasks that can be used in second language proficiency assessment. It is argued that the four influences in question provide a framework within which assessment choices can be more effectively made.

Introduction

Within applied linguistics, the assessment of oral second language proficiency has been explored in a way which is surprisingly detached from developments in a range of related areas, including second language acquisition, psycholinguistics and our understanding of what is involved in the speaking process. It is the purpose of this article to explore the relevance for such proficiency assessment of theory in the area of first (and second) language speaking, and empirical findings in task-based performance. It will be argued that these two ancillary areas have much to contribute to how we design and evaluate oral assessment procedures.

Models of Speaking

The dominant model of first language speaking is that of Levelt (1989, 1999; Kormos, 2006). This model proposes that there are three general stages in speech production, as shown in Table 13.1.

Table 13.1 The Levelt model of first language speech production

Conceptualization (Message Level of Representation)
- involves determining what to say
- speaker conceives an intention and adopts a stance
- speaker selects relevant information in preparation for construction of an intended utterance
- the product is a preverbal message

Formulation
- involves translating the conceptual representation into a linguistic form
- includes the process of lexicalisation, where words that the speaker wants to say are selected
- includes the process of syntactic planning where words are put together to form a sentence
- involves detailed phonetic and articulatory planning
- includes the process of phonological encoding, where words are turned into sounds

Articulation
- involves retrieval of chunks of internal speech from buffer
- involves motor execution

The first stage, Conceptualization, is concerned with developing and organizing the ideas to be expressed, in a particular situation and with a particular emphasis and stance. The second stage, Formulation, involves lexical selections to match the preverbal message, triggering lemma retrieval from the mental lexicon, and then syntax building from the information retrieved through this retrieval. The third stage is concerned with transforming this form of representation of ideas, lexis and syntax into actual speech.

Fairly obviously, if we are dealing with native language speech, certain assumptions are made. Most central for present purposes is that the Conceptualizer delivers challenges to the Formulator which the Formulator is able to meet, since the driving force for its operation is the mental lexicon, which is extensive, well-organized, and contains rich entries, with semantic, syntactic, collocational and phonological information. It is the capacity to retrieve such rich information very quickly that enables speech production to be so smooth, without requiring consciousness, and with parallel operations. The Conceptualizer can be working on one stage of operation, while the Formulator is dealing simultaneously with previous Conceptualizer operations, as language is being assembled, just as the Articulator can be working on previous Formulator operations.

When we turn to second language speaking, things are very different. The 'driver' for the Levelt model is the mental lexicon, which is the repository of considerable information about each lemma, information which underpins the production of native language speech in real time. With second language speakers, this mental lexicon is

- smaller, so that many lemmas required by the preverbal message, will not be available;
- incomplete, so that where many lemmas are part of the mental lexicon, they are only partially represented, so that for example, limited semantic information may be available, or limited syntactic implication information is available, or no collocational information etc.;
- less organized, so that connections between lemmas do not prime one another, or alternative forms of expression are less available;
- less redundantly structured, in that collocational chunks are less available, so that speech production has to be done more often 'from first principles' on the basis of rule-generated language;

The result of all these omissions is that during speech production, the preverbal message, however impressive, encounters considerable difficulty at the Formulator stage. The smooth process of speech production is disrupted, as second language speakers have to try to find alternative methods of expressing their meanings, or to find ways of using the resources that they have sufficiently quickly so that 'normal' communication can proceed. This is likely to present serious difficulties for the modular, parallel operation of the Levelt model, so that some of the time, this ideal set of interlocking processes is severely impaired.

Task Research

The preceding discussion has been general, and data-free. It has assumed that second language speakers, of different proficiency levels, will encounter difficulties and that it is meaningful to express these difficulties in terms of the Levelt Model. What is necessary to take the discussion further is some empirical method of characterizing difficulty. To this end, we will next review findings from the literature on task-based performance. This literature provides a wide range of generalizations regarding the way task characteristics and the conditions under which tasks are done might have an impact on different aspects of second language performance. These findings can take us beyond the programmatic statements in the previous section.

Broadly, the task findings can be portrayed in terms of the information that tasks are based on, the operations that tasks require to be performed on this information, and the conditions under which tasks are done. These three headings organize the findings which have emerged in the task literature. Regarding information, we can say that

- the scale of the information (e.g. the number of elements, the number of participants) has an impact on performance, with more information leading to performance that is more complex (Michel, Kuiken & Vedder, 2007);
- the type of information has a strong influence, with concrete information being easier to handle than abstract information which in turn is easier to handle than dynamic information (Brown, Anderson, Shillcock & Yule, 1984), and also with there being a tendency for concrete information to advantage fluency and accuracy in performance;
- greater familiarity with the information is associated with higher levels of accuracy and fluency (Foster & Skehan, 1996);
- greater organization and structure in the task information leads to performance which is also more accurate and more fluent (Tavakoli & Skehan, 2005).

There are interesting theoretical issues which relate to this range of findings. For now, we will simply say that these are a set of empirically based generalizations which have relevance for any development of a model of second language spoken performance. In any case, we move on to consider the operations which are carried out on the information in tasks. Here another set of generalizations can be offered, contrasting simple and complex operations. Simple operations, for example listing, enumerating (Willis and Willis, 2007), or retrieving (Foster and Skehan, 1996) or simply describing are associated with higher fluency and accuracy in performance. In contrast, more demanding operations on information, such as sequencing (Willis and Willis, 2007) or reorganizing (Foster and Skehan, 1996), or integrating information (Tavakoli and Skehan, 2005), or reasoning (Robinson, 2001; Robinson and Gilabert, 2007) are associated with greater language complexity. As these different influences suggest, there is something of a contrast here between the performance areas of complexity, on the one hand, and accuracy and fluency, on the other. Complex cognitive operations seem to drive greater language complexity, while simpler operations are more likely to be associated with higher fluency and accuracy.

The final area to consider here is the conditions under which tasks are done. This has provoked considerable research effort. Robinson (2001) reports higher levels of accuracy in his there-and-then condition, that is input absence, contrasted to a here-and-now condition (input presence). A whole series of studies has examined the effect of pre-task planning on performance. The results suggest that such planning is consistently associated with greater complexity and fluency, with these generating sizable effects, while accuracy is generally advantages, but not to the same degree (Ellis, in press; Foster & Skehan,

1999). Yuan and Ellis (2003) have reported that opportunity for online planning, that is more relaxed time conditions during performance, are associated with greater accuracy. Skehan and Foster (1997, submitted) have proposed that requiring second language speakers to do post-tasks which emphasize language form leads selectively to increases in accuracy. Finally, Skehan (in press) proposes that tasks which contain unavoidable and more difficult lexis are associated with lower levels of accuracy and complexity.

Applying the Levelt Model

The generalizations about second language task-based performance provide the basis for examining the relevance of the Levelt model in accounting for the second language case. An initial assessment would suggest that it has to be applicable. Essentially, the model proposes that thought precedes language, and that the functioning of the model is essentially concerned with how Formulator operations, and associated resources, such as the mental lexicon, can enable the thoughts embodied in the preverbal message to be expressed through externalized language. One is drawn into saying that anything other than this would not be satisfactory on general, logical grounds. Communication requires ideas, and the ideas, if they are to be transmitted effectively, require language.

The difficulty, of course, is that first language speakers are able to function in this way because they have mental lexicons which are extensive, elaborate, analysed and accessible. Preverbal message demands can therefore be met, and ongoing speaking in real time is possible. In particular, the different modules within the Levelt model can function in parallel, that is the Conceptualizer may be working on the next preverbal message, while the Formulator is working on the current one, even while the Articulator is giving voice to the previous. This is possible because the different modules can handle the demands which are placed upon them in real-time, and smoothly, such that successive cycles of communication proceed, if not totally effortlessly, at least fairly so.

Problems occur when a second language speaker attempts the same ideas-to-language mapping, but is equipped with a much more limited mental lexicon. The result is, as Kormos (2006) argues, that parallel processing below the level of consciousness is replaced by serial, effortful and conscious attempts to deal with pre-verbal message demands on the mental lexicon – demands which are either beyond it, or which require considerably greater allocation of attention. Messages may then be assembled slowly, or communication strategies used or messages may be modified or even abandoned (Faerch and Kasper, 1983). This is turn brings us back to the question of the applicability of the model. What is argued here is that the model is still relevant (for the general reasons proposed earlier), but that it is inappropriate to regard the model as an 'all or none' affair. The generalizations from the previous section show that performance is systematically influenced by a range of information, operation and condition influences, and that these impact upon complexity, accuracy and fluency aspects of performance. Broadly, it is argued that what we have learned from this research is the conditions which facilitate the relevance of the Levelt model and those that do not. So the question needs to be recast so that we explore not whether there is a simple positive or negative answer to applicability, but rather the influences which make the model a more useful explanatory account and those which suggest that its potential for second language speakers is limited.

So far, in reviewing empirical work, we have presented research in the terms which are typical for task-based performance, distinguishing between information, operations and conditions, as independent variables, and complexity, accuracy and fluency, as the dependent variables. To examine the relevance of the Levelt model, though, it is necessary to consider an alternative perspective, and to organize the findings which have been reviewed in a way more consistent with the model, and transparent in terms of its functioning. This is shown in Table 13.2.

Two introductory points are helpful here. First, the table is organized around the central 'spine' which shows the relevant stages of the Levelt model. There is a section which focuses on the Conceptualizer, and then a separation between the two Formulator stages of lemma retrieval (and access to the mental lexicon), and syntactic encoding (which is driven by the information made available when lemmas are accessed). These three stages organize the presentation of the information from the task-based performance literature. Second, the outer columns are concerned with four general influences on performance, two which indicate difficulty (complexifying, pressuring) and two which are more focused on achievement (easing, focusing).

Complexifying focuses on performance influences which make the message to be expressed more demanding, elaborate or extensive. These influences are mostly relevant for Conceptualizer operations. Pressuring concerns influences

Table 13.2 The Levelt model and task performance

Complexifying/pressuring	Levelt model stage	Easing/focusing
• planning: extending • complex cog. operations • complex info. type	*Conceptualiser*	• concrete, static information • less information • easier cog. operations
• infrequent lexis • non-negotiable task	*Formulator: Lemma retrieval*	• planning: organizing • dialogic
• time pressure • heavy input pressure • monologic	*Formulator: Syntactic encoding*	• planning: rehearsing • structured tasks • dialogic • post-task condition

which make performance more difficult but are not connected with differences in the complexity of the message. In contrast, they are concerned with the time under which a task is done, or the amount or nature or inflexibility of the material which is involved. Easing is, in a sense, the reverse of Complexifying, and entails the ways in which the pre-verbal message can be arrived at in a more direct manner. Finally Focusing (which is not the reverse of Pressuring), concerns the way in which performance conditions themselves introduce some level of Focus-on-Form, thereby privileging performance areas such as accuracy and complexity. This framework is useful for re-presenting the results from the task literature in ways which bring out more clearly how the findings we have can illustrate the differing degrees of applicability of the Levelt model to the second language speaker case. We will explore each of them in more detail.

There are three clear influences on Complexifying. The first involves planning. At the outset, it needs to be said that planning appears more than once in Table 2, reflecting the different things that can happen during planning. Here the facet of planning time which is focused on is when preparation is associated with making the ideas in a task more complex than they otherwise would be. It is clear (Ortega, 2005; Skehan & Foster, 1999; Skehan & Pang, 2008) that this happens some of the time. Speakers use planning time to explore the ideas in a task, and consequently approach the task as more challenging than it otherwise would be. For example, in an Agony Aunt task, planning may be used to generate more complex advice to the writer of a problem letter, or in a narrative it could be used to develop the connections in a picture story series.

A second influence here could be the more complex operations which a task inherently requires if it is to be completed properly. These might be to reorganize the input which is provided, for example Foster and Skehan's (1996) narrative task, where a story had to be invented from a series of pictures, rather than a pre-existing storyline simply narrated. Or there might be the need to integrate information to tell a story effectively, as in Tavakoli and Skehan's (2005) task where background and foreground elements had to be connected to one another. There might also be a greater need to use reasoning, as in Michel et al.'s task (2007) involving selection of a cell phone where there are many features which influence the eventual decision.

The third kind of influence concerns the type of information which is involved. Brown et al. (1984) showed that dynamic information, for example relating to a changing scene, is more difficult to deal with abstract information, which in turn is more difficult to deal with than static information. It seems that the greater difficulty in dealing with such information types is more demanding of memory resources, and where there are also more complex operations involved, this adds to task complexity. It is assumed that all three influences here concern the Conceptualizer stage of speech production and the nature of the cognitive activity implicated in producing the pre-verbal message.

We turn next to a series of influences which increase the pressure on the operation of the Formulator stage. Regarding the lemma retrieval stage, the first influence is the infrequency of the lexis which is involved in a task. It appears that when less frequent lexis is required, this has damaging implications for the complexity and accuracy of the language which is produced (Skehan, in press). This contrasts with native speaker performance, where lexical infrequency is positively correlated with language complexity – less standard lemmas seem to drive more complex syntax in a harmonious way. So tasks which push learners to need more difficult lexis seem to give them lemma retrieval problems which spill over, because of their attentional demands, into other aspects of performance. Lemmas are retrieved slowly and imperfectly, and the additional effort required for this disrupts the parallel processing of the material for speaking.

Similarly, non-negotiable tasks (Skehan and Foster, 2007) also cause pressure. Native speakers, when generating language, are able to draw upon a range of alternative choices relatively effortlessly. So during speech production they can make a range of selections as they are producing an utterance (Pawley and Syder, 1983). Non-native speakers do not have the luxury of such choices, and as a result are less able to adapt if a first lexical or syntactic choice is unavailable in the mental lexicon. Where tasks are negotiable, such speakers can adapt and revise the pre-verbal message so that it meshes more easily with resources which are available. When tasks are non-negotiable, however, as with narratives where the input is given, this is not possible, and disruption of performance results.

These two pressure-inducing factors are concerned with the nature of the meanings that are required for a task. The remaining pressuring influences are, in one way or another, simply associated with time. Most obviously, requiring tasks to be done under timed conditions is going to add to the speaker's problems. Ellis (2005) has reviewed these studies and shown that online planning is a possibility when time pressure conditions are relaxed, with the result that greater accuracy is obtained. When there is greater time pressure, in contrast, the result is that accuracy is lowered. But a related issue concerns whether a task is monologic or dialogic. Monologic tasks are consistently more difficult (with lower accuracy, and sometimes, lower complexity (Skehan and Foster, 2007)). What seems to happen here is that the speaker, being responsible for keeping the discourse going, has to plan, execute, monitor and continue speaking without any respite. The result is that performance is lowered, because online planning opportunities are less frequent. In contrast, a more dialogic condition does enable one speaker to have a break while interlocutors are speaking. As long as the other speakers' contributions are processed sufficiently, there may be spare capacity available while listening to enable a speaker to plan upcoming conversational contributions, as well as potentially use something said by interlocutors if it is appropriate to his or her own contribution. Monologic tasks do not give any easy natural breaks. Dialogic tasks do and so reduce the pressure, overall (Skehan, in press).

We turn next to factors which ease performance. Some of these can simply be dealt with as the reverse of the effects we have already covered on complexifying or pressuring. For example, regarding information, we can say that tasks based on concrete, static information (Foster and Skehan, 1996); tasks involving less information (Brown et al., 1984); and tasks which require simpler operations, such as listing (Willis and Willis, 2007), are likely to be easier, and as a result, Formulator-based aspects of performance (accuracy, fluency) are likely to be raised. Similarly, task conditions which reduce pressure, such as a dialogic task, also make the task easier, as more time is available to plan online. But there are other influences which are not mirror images of what has been said before. For example, planning figures here, but now in different ways. If planning is directed to organizing what will be said, actual performance is eased (Pang and Skehan, 2008). The planning, effectively, handles the wider plan of what will be said, so that during actual performance, major ideas do not have to be developed and the speaker can focus on the surface of language. Similarly, if a task is structured (Tavakoli and Skehan, 2005), speakers are more likely to be able to exploit the macrostructure of the task, and not need to engage in deeper planning. They too can focus on the surface, and are able to mobilize Formulator resources more effectively, and thereby achieve higher levels of accuracy and fluency. Returning to planning, in addition to the functions of extending ideas, which complexifies, and organizing, which eases, planning may be directed to rehearsing language for actual performance (Ortega, 2005). This too eases, but on the assumption that what is rehearsed is both remembered and is actually useful during performance. If these conditions are met, the result is that performance is eased.

So far, we have been looking at the interplay of ideas and their realization through language. Following much of the task literature, we have conceptualized performance in terms of language complexity, accuracy and fluency, and have tacitly assumed in information processing perspective based on limited attentional resources. So the assumption has been that speakers have limited capacities, and that task difficulty, as well as eased performance conditions, influence performance priorities (Skehan, 1998). Performance, in this view, is a reflex of other influences. But there are also studies which suggest that second language speakers, with their limited attentional capacities, may choose to prioritize particular performance areas. We have seen this slightly with the way planning time can be directed towards rehearsal, where speakers use the preparation time in order to be ready with specific language, and as a result target accuracy, or sometimes, particularly complex structures. But there are other ways in which the same selective effect can occur, always with a focus on some aspect of form, either directed towards accuracy or complexity. We have already seen how interactive tasks can help speakers since they provide online planning opportunities (Foster and Skehan, 1996; Skehan and Foster, 1997). But the effects of such tasks may be wider. Dialogic tasks make salient the existence of an interlocutor, and it may be that speakers increase their focus on accuracy precisely because they want to be understood and try to avoid misunderstandings by selectively attending to accuracy and avoiding error (Pang and Skehan, 2008). In this way, they prioritize attentional focus through awareness of their interlocutor's comprehension needs.

These claims, though, are based on interpretations of research studies with different research foci. Two studies, though, specifically examine how speakers may have the capacity to prioritize particular performance areas. Skehan and Foster (1997) showed that using a post-task condition (requiring speakers, post-task, to engage in a public performance) led to higher levels of accuracy on a decision-making task (although not on narrative or personal information exchange tasks). It had been hypothesized that foreknowledge of this post-task condition would lead learners to selectively prioritize accuracy during their task performance. Subsequently, Skehan and Foster (2009) used a different post-task condition, hypothesized to be stronger. They required learners to transcribe one minute of their task performance, a more personally relevant and language-focussed condition and hypothesized that this would have a stronger effect specifically on accuracy. This prediction was borne out, not only for a decision-making task, as in Skehan and Foster (1997) but also for a narrative task. In addition, for the decision-making task, complexity, too, was also significantly raised. These results suggest that effective task conditions can lead speakers to focus on particular aspects of performance, despite the attentional limitations which prevail.

Task Research and Proficiency Assessment

The analysis and review of research presented so far suggests that attentional limitations are vital in understanding performance on second language tasks and that one can categorize the range of different influences as follows:

- Complexification, in that factors such as extension planning, information type and operations upon information push speakers to express more complex ideas. This set of influences impacts on Levelt's Conceptualizer stage.
- Easing, with factors such as the reverse of the last set and which therefore simply reduce the work the Conceptualizer has to do, coupled with other factors, for example organizing or rehearsal planning, dialogic conditions, or structured tasks which give speakers clear macrostructure for what they want to say, or provide more online planning opportunities. The consequence in all these cases is that Formulator operations are eased.
- Pressuring, where input conditions or performance conditions mean that speakers have less opportunity to regroup while speaking, and are deprived of online planning opportunities. This too is a Formulator influence.

- Focusing, where selective aspects of performance are privileged, and so a focus-on-form is injected into task performance so that attention is directed in particular ways, towards accuracy or complexity. Once again this is a Formulator influence.

These are a set of factors which influence what is going to be said and how it is going to be said. What is central to this analysis is the balance between Conceptualizer pressure (or lack of it) and Formulator pressure (or lack of it), and how these two sets of pressures work themselves out during ongoing performance. Complexification gives a limited attentional system more things to do, depriving other areas of resources. Easing has the reverse effect, where ideas are manipulable or packagable more easily, thus releasing attention for use in other aspects of speech performance. Pressuring has the general effect of depriving all other areas of performance of time that would be useful. Finally, Focusing operates differently in that it prioritizes attention allocation, whatever is going on elsewhere.

We now need to switch and try to consider how this analysis might have relevance for the assessment of second language spoken proficiency. Here it is useful initially to revisit some of the basics of language testing – that testing concerns the ways we use the information elicited through tests in order to sample, to make judgements and to generalize about real-world performance. One approach to doing these things is to provide learners with tasks to do, of increasing levels of difficulty, and then observe what is the maximum level of difficulty that can be successfully handled. (This is like treating language proficiency as similar to a weightlifting contest.) This approach makes the unidimensionality assumption – that increasing proficiency means getting better along only one dimensions (as when the bar gets heavier in weightlifting). Sampling, in this view, means assessing learners along this one-dimensional scale of difficulty. But it can be argued that anything interesting enough to be worth measuring is likely to be multi-dimensional (Skehan, 1984), with the result that sampling has to be directed at probing the different dimensions that are important (whatever they may be) and then decisions have to be made about how strengths and weaknesses in performance across these dimensions can be combined to yield an overall judgement of proficiency.

The major insight from the analysis presented in this chapter is that for spoken language performance we have to analyse test tasks first in terms of the influences covered in Table 13.2, and particularly in terms of the demands they make on Conceptualizer and Formulator stages in speaking respectively. What influences the Conceptualizer appears to be different from what influences the Formulator and so Conceptualizer difficulty is not the same as Formulator difficulty. In a sense, it is what the Conceptualizer does that shapes the overall difficulty of the ideas which are expressed in a task, and the influences on the Formulator are then constrained by challenges set by the Conceptualizer, although this stage too is affected by a range of influences. The problem is essentially one of sampling, and what the above analysis does is clarify the basis on which sampling needs to take place. It is a truism of testing that one-item tests are non-functional, and so if we apply this to the assessment of spoken language performance, this means that a series of tasks will be necessary for any effective assessment to be made. The matrix in Table 2 helps clarify how a range of tasks and a range of performance conditions can be sampled as the basis for language testing. Different Conceptualizer influences and different Formulator influences need to be drawn on if any rounded estimate of ability for use is to be provided.

This approach interacts with how performance itself is measured (Pollitt, 1990). Language use, being complex and multidimensional, is not susceptible to simple counting. There needs to be a more complex rating of performance, and this in turn means that one has to decide what areas of performance should be represented in the different rating scales which are used. We have seen that Conceptualizer work is reflected in language complexity, and so this aspect of performance requires valid and reliable rating in terms of what is often termed Range in language assessment, that is use of syntax and vocabulary. But Formulator activity is associated with greater fluency and accuracy, other areas where rating scales exist, with precisely these headings. In other words, a Leveltian analysis of performance suggests that we need separate ratings of language complexity (range), accuracy and fluency if we are to obtain any satisfactory overall assessment of the quality of a second language speaker's performance. Only with such information will we be able to make effective prediction about how second language speakers will use language in the real world.

References

Brown, G., Anderson, A., Shillcock, R., & Yule, G. (1984). *Teaching talk: Strategies for production and assessment*, Cambridge: Cambridge University Press.

Ellis, R. (Ed.) (2005). *Planning and task performance in a second language.* Amsterdam: John Benjamins.

Ellis, R. (in press). The differential effects of three types of task planning on the fluency, complexity, and accuracy of L2 oral production, *Applied Linguistics.*

Faerch, C., & Kasper, G. (1983). (Eds.). *Strategies in interlanguage communication.* London: Longman.

Foster, P., & Skehan, P. (1996). The influence of planning on performance in task-based learning. Studies in Second Language Acquisition, 18 (3), 299–324.

Foster, P., & Skehan, P. (1999). The effect of source of planning and focus on planning on task-based performance. *Language Teaching Research,* 3 (3), 185–215.

Foster, P., & Skehan, P. (2009). *The effects of post-task activities on the accuracy and complexity of language during task performance.* Manuscript submitted for publication.

Kormos, J. (2006). *Speech production and second language acquisition*. Mahwah, NJ: Lawrence Erlbaum.

Levelt, W. J. (1989). *Speaking: From intention to articulation*, Cambridge, MA: MIT Press.

Levelt, W. (1999). Language production: A blueprint for the speaker. In C. Brown and P. Hagoort (Eds.). *Neurocognition of Language* (pp. 83–122). Oxford: Oxford University Press.

Michel, M. C., Kuiken, F., & Vedder, I. (2007). The interaction of task condition and task complexity in the oral performance of Turkish and Moroccan learners of Dutch, Paper presented at the 2nd International Conference on Task-based Language Teaching, Hawaii, U.S.A.

Ortega, L. (2005). What do learners plan? Learner-driven attention to form during pre-task planning, In Ellis R. (Ed.). *Planning and task performance in a second language* (pp. 77–109). Amsterdam: John Benjamins.

Pang, F., & Skehan, P. Using a model of speaking to explore second language learners use of planning time, Chinese University of Hong Kong. Manuscript submitted for publication.

Pawley, A., & Syder, F. H. (1983). Two puzzles for linguistic theory: nativelike selection and nativelike fluency, In Richards J. C. and Schmidt R. (Eds.). *Language and Communication*, London: Longman.

Pollitt, A. (1990). Giving students a sporting chance: Assessing by counting and judging, In C. Alderson and B. North (Eds.). *Language Testing in the 1990s* (pp. 46–59). London: Macmillan.

Robinson, P. (2001). Task complexity, cognitive resources, and syllabus design: A triadic framework for examining task influences on SLA. In Robinson P. (Ed.). *Cognition and Second Language Instruction*, (pp. 287–318), Cambridge: Cambridge University Press.

Robinson, P., & Gilabert, R. (2007). Task complexity, the cognition hypothesis, and second language learning and performance. Special Issue of *International Review of Applied Linguistics for Language Teaching*. Berlin: Mouton de Gruyter.

Skehan, P. (1984). Issues in the testing of English for Specific Purposes. *Language Testing*, 1 (2), 202–20.

Skehan, P. (1998). *A Cognitive Approach to Language Learning*, Oxford: Oxford University Press.

Skehan, P. (in press). Modelling Second Language Performance: Integrating complexity, accuracy, fluency and lexis. *Applied Linguistics*.

Skehan, P., & Foster, P. (1997). The influence of planning and post-task activities on accuracy and complexity in task based learning. *Language Teaching Research*, 1 (3), 185–211.

Skehan, P., & Foster, P. (1999). The influence of task structure and processing conditions on narrative retellings. *Language Learning*, 49, 1, 93–120.

Skehan, P., & Foster, P. (2007). Complexity, Accuracy, Fluency and Lexis in Task-based Performance: A meta-analysis of the Ealing Research. In Van Daele S., Housen A. and Kuiken F., Pierrard M. and Vedder I. (Eds.). *Complexity, Accuracy, and Fluency in Second Language Use, Learning, and Teaching*. Brussels: University of Brussels Press.

Tavakoli, P., & Skehan, P. (2005). Planning, task structure, and performance testing. In Ellis R. (2005) (Ed.). *Planning and Task Performance in a Second Language*, Amsterdam: John Benjamins.

Willis, D., & Willis, J. (2007). *Doing Task-based Teaching*, Oxford: Oxford University Press.

Yuan, F., & Ellis, R. (2003). The effects of pre-task planning and on-line planning on fluency, complexity, and accuracy in L2 monologic oral production. *Applied Linguistics*, 24(1), 1–27.

Chapter 14

Researching Task Difficulty: Towards Understanding L2 Proficiency

Parvaneh Tavakoli
London Metropolitan University, United Kingdom

Abstract

The prime purpose of this article is to put teachers', learners' and research perspectives of task difficulty (TD) together and to investigate whether teachers' and learners' perceptions of and criteria for TD are in line with the available research on TD. A summary of three interrelated empirical studies on learner and teacher perceptions of TD is presented before the findings are discussed in light of the current models of TD. The chapter concludes by arguing that cognitive demands of a task are a significant factor that contributes to TD and should be considered more critically by L2 educators and SLA researchers.

Introduction

Since the beginning of the era in which task-based language teaching and learning aroused attention, a substantial amount of research has gone into investigating different aspects of tasks particularly, with regard to the use of tasks in language pedagogy (Bygate, Skehan & Swain, 2001; Nunan, 1989; Samuda & Bygate, 2008). Tasks have been investigated from rather different but potentially complementary research perspectives such as Psycholinguistic (Long, 1989; Pica, 1994), Cognitive (Robinson, 2001; Skehan, 1998) and Sociocultural (Dotano, 1994; Lantolf, 2000) approaches to task-based research (for a full discussion of the different approaches see Ellis, 2003; Skehan, 2003). Those who have taken a Cognitive perspective have focused on the psychological processes that are typically engaged when learners perform tasks. From a Cognitive perspective, 'task' has been seen as a device that guides learners to engage in certain types of information processing that are believed to be important for effective development of L2 proficiency (Robinson, 2001; Skehan, 1998). Central to this research has been exploring task characteristics and conditions that contribute to task difficulty (TD). Researchers in this area have mainly focused on investigating task characteristics and performance conditions that affect TD through studying learners' performance in tasks (Mehnert, 1998; Robinson, 2001, 2007; Skehan & Foster, 1997; Tavakoli & Foster, 2008; Yuan & Ellis, 2003). In such studies, certain features of tasks are usually manipulated to make the tasks more or less difficult. Then, by studying learners' performance in tasks of different levels of difficulty, the researchers are able to decide whether those task characteristics and/or conditions have contributed to TD and whether those characteristics and/or conditions would guide L2 proficiency in certain directions. Although a considerable amount of effort and time has been put in investigating TD, little is done to find out how learners perceive, define, identify or classify TD. Neither has there been any research exploring teachers' perceptions of and attitudes to TD, how they identify TD or what criteria they consider when they evaluate tasks and examine their difficulty level for their every day classroom practices.

This chapter sets out to provide a new perspective to how TD is determined and defined by teachers and learners across a number of EFL contexts. Central to my argument in this chapter, I will probe into the issue of TD by asking whether teacher, learner and research perspectives share similar views and principles or whether they hold three rather different perspectives to TD. Although the main goal of this chapter is triangulating the available research evidence on TD, my main contention here is that learners' and teachers' perspectives are, to a great extent, underrepresented if not ignored in L2 research on TD. In the sections that follow I will first highlight the main debates on TD and will discuss how the different intersecting areas of L2 education find TD useful. I will then report on three interrelated studies that I have conducted to investigate teachers' and learners' perceptions of TD. The general findings of these studies will then be discussed in light of the wider research debates on the two existing models of TD.

Significance of TD in L2 Education

For some time now TD has been of high importance to language teachers, curriculum designers, language testers and language researchers because it is seen as one of the most important criteria for using and sequencing tasks in a language teaching syllabus (Nunan, 1989, 2004; Samuda & Bygate, 2008; Willis, 1996). The fundamental pedagogic claim of research on TD is that tasks should be designed, and then sequenced for learners on the basis of their difficulty level. Robinson and Gilabert (2007, p. 162) maintain that 'the aim of such *pedagogic task* sequences is to gradually approximate, in classroom settings, the full complexity of real-world *target task* demands.' It is also believed that the sequences of pedagogic tasks should constitute the core of a task-based syllabus (Skehan, 1998; Willis, 1996). Hence, a systematic classification of different task characteristics and conditions that contribute to TD will undoubtedly help L2 educators if appropriate and successful use of tasks is expected in language programs.

Language teachers are well aware that choosing tasks of appropriate level of difficulty is a highly motivating feature of language classrooms. In search of suitable tasks for their language teaching, teachers look into different aspects of TD to determine which tasks are more appropriate for learners of different proficiency levels and which tasks can effectively promote different aspects of their L2 learning. Knowledge of TD will further help syllabus designers and materials developers organize the materials in ELT textbooks and schemes of work. Nunan (2004) argues that 'without some way of determining difficulty, sequencing and integrating tasks becomes a matter of intuition' (p. 85). He contends that 'sequencing linguistic exercises is somewhat more straight forward than sequencing pedagogic tasks because one can draw on notions of linguistic complexity and so on' (Nunan, 2004, p. 85).

More recently, research in language testing has also showed some interest in examining aspects of TD (Elder et al., 2002; Fulcher & Marquez Reiter, 2003; Iwashita, McNamara & Elder 2001; Tavakoli, 2009). The common interest of this group of researchers is to identify whether certain task characteristics and conditions contribute to TD which would inadvertently impact upon language performance and subsequent assessments of language proficiency. It has been argued that without knowledge of task difficulty, the danger is that test scores assigned to learners' performance may not reflect their true language ability and will be difficult to compare with results obtained from similar tasks (Bachman, 2002; Tavakoli & Skehan, 2005). Arguably, the ultimate goal of language testing research on TD is to provide an index of task difficulty with which language testers can chart potential task-based influences on candidate performance and can determine how much of the score assigned to a performance has resulted from the construct-irrelevant variance in L2 performance.

An Overview of TD

One of the earliest studies on TD belongs to Brown, Anderson, Shilcock & Yule, (1984) who investigated the difficulty of speaking tasks and proposed a two dimensional framework: the type of information to be conveyed and the scale of and the interrelationships among the different elements of a task. They argued that *static* tasks, for example describing a diagram, in which the elements remained constant, were easier than *dynamic* tasks, for example telling a story, in which the elements changed. They reported that *abstract* tasks, such as expressing an opinion in which the elements were not concrete, were the most difficult. In an attempt to provide a more comprehensive framework for defining TD, Brindley (1987) pointed out that there were at least three interconnected sets of factors involved in a task that influence TD: learner factors, task factors and text or input factors. Candlin (1987) proposed a set of criteria for identifying TD. The criteria Candlin considered in establishing the difficulty level of a task included the cognitive load and clarity of the goal of the task, code complexity and interpretative density of the language to be used.

Drawing on Candlin's scheme for TD and theorizing his model by taking a cognitive approach to language learning, Skehan (1996, 1998) has proposed a three-way distinction for the analysis of TD. He makes the assumption that human beings operate with limited capacity attentional systems, and that second language learner attentional resources become more limited when they are performing a difficult task. Skehan (1998, p. 99) defines TD in terms of:

1. Code Complexity (linguistic complexity, vocabulary load and redundancy and density)
2. Communicative Stress (time limits and time pressure, speed, number of participants)
3. Cognitive Complexity
   a. Cognitive Familiarity (familiarity of topic, familiarity of discourse genre, familiarity of task)
   b. Cognitive Processing (information organization, information type, amount of computation, clarity and sufficiency of information given)

Skehan argues that the 'major contrasts here are between the language required, the thinking required and the performance conditions for a task' (1998, p. 99). He makes an interesting distinction between Cognitive Familiarity, that is the capacity to access 'packaged' solutions to tasks and Cognitive Processing, that is the need to work out solutions to new problems.

Adopting a different cognitive approach to language learning, Robinson (2001) argues that the human brain has a multiple-resource attentional system, that is depletion of attention in one pool has no effect on the amount remaining in another. Robinson (2001) proposes a three-factor framework for examining and defining TD in which he distinguishes between 'task *complexity* (the task dependent and proactively manipulable cognitive demands of tasks) from task *difficulty* (dependent on learner factors such as aptitude and motivation) and task *conditions* (the interactive demands of tasks)' (2001, p. 287). He maintains that task complexity should be the sole basis of prospective sequencing decisions since most learner factors can only be diagnosed while task performance is in process and therefore cannot be anticipated in advance. Focusing on cognitive factors affecting task complexity, Robinson argues that cognitive factors are either resource-directing or resource-dispersing. The number of elements involved in a task, the amount of contextual support available and the reasoning demand needed from the speaker are all different resource-directing factors. Resource-dispersing factors, however, include the amount of planning time available, task structure, whether the task makes single or dual demands and whether the learner has some prior knowledge. He proposes that any of these factors can be manipulated to increase or decrease the cognitive demand of a task and thus the difficulty level associated with it. In a recent article, Robinson and Gilabert (2007) have slightly modified Robinson's previous model of TD by defining Resource-directing factors as cognitive/conceptual demands and Resource-dispersing factors as performative/procedural demands. This new classification, in effect, claims that Resource-directing factors would 'prime learners – and direct their attentional and memory resources – to aspects of the L2 system required to accurately understand and convey them' (p. 164); whereas Resource-dispersing factors 'make increased performative/procedural demands on participants' attentional and memory resources, but do not direct them to any aspect of the linguistic system which can be of communicative value in performing a task' (pp. 165–66).

Perceptions of TD

Although investigating learner perceptions of different aspects of language teaching and learning has been a burgeoning area of research (Barkhuizen, 1998; Cooper & McIntyre, 1994; Ilins, Inozu & Yumru, 2007; McDonough & Chaikitmongkol, 2007; Mitchell, Brumfit & Hooper, 1994), researching learner perceptions of tasks and TD has not received much attention. Nunan and Keobke (1995) were among the few to explore TD from a learner perspective. In a study of 35 undergraduate Cantonese speaking students, they used a number of reading, listening and speaking tasks and asked the students how difficult they found the tasks and why. The learners in that study identified a number of factors such as lack of familiarity with task types, confusion over task purpose, and the impact and extent of cultural knowledge as the main factors underlying TD.

Robinson (2001), investigating learner perceptions of TD, narrowed his focus to speaking tasks. In his study, he used simplified and complex versions of the same task by manipulating the cognitive demands of the task. The cognitive demand in this study was operationalized through the amount of information and availability of prior knowledge. In the complex version of the task, a large area of a map with which the learners were not familiar was given to them while the simplified version included a smaller area of the map with which the learners were very familiar. The results showed that the learners rated the more complex version of the task as more difficult and more stressful than the simplified version. In addition, they rated their own ability to perform the complex version lower than that on the simplified task. Robinson (2001) concludes that learners' ratings of TD are clearly related to the cognitive demand of the tasks.

Robinson (2007) in a study of 42 Japanese learners of English investigated L2 learners' perceptions of task difficulty. Using a retrospective questionnaire, he asked the participants to rate how difficult they found the task and how stressful performing the task appeared to be. In this study, cognitive complexity was operationalized through the intentional reasoning required in the different oral narrative tasks. The results of data analysis indicated that the participants rated the least complex version of the task as significantly less difficult than other versions. The results also suggested that anxiety was clearly influenced by the intentional reasoning demand of the tasks.

Perceptual Mismatches

Investigating the potential mismatches between teachers' and learners' perceptions of language classroom activities and aims has become a burgeoning area of research in recent years (Hawkey, 2006; Ilin et al., 2007). Kumaravadivelu (2003) summarizes four studies (Barkhuizen, 1998; Block, 1994, 1996; Kumaravadivelu, 1991) in which learners' and teachers' perceptions of classroom events do not match. These studies have investigated teachers' and learners' perceptions of a range of classroom activities and the results have indicated that the same classroom event is often interpreted differently by teachers and learners. Such results clearly demonstrate the existing mismatches between the two groups' perceptions of classroom events which could denote potential problematic areas in language teaching and learning. Second language acquisition research concedes that minimizing this perceptual mismatch is of high significance in language classrooms because it can lead to a more effective pedagogic intervention (Kumaravadivelu, 2003). In addition, recent research has acknowledged that knowing more about teachers' perspectives seems necessary because the structure of teachers' beliefs, assumptions and perceptions play a crucial role in their classroom practices and would consequently have an impact on the learners and the learning process (Kumaravadivelu, 2006).

Creating a Larger Picture of TD

Three different but interrelated studies in which teachers' and learners' perceptions of TD were examined are discussed in this section. The overarching aim of these studies was to investigate what teachers' and learners' perceptions of TD were, whether there was a perceptual mismatch between their view points on TD and whether their perceptions of and criteria for TD were reflected by the principles and claims of the existing research on TD. In all the three studies the same tasks were used, the same procedures were taken and the same design was employed. The main difference between the studies was with regard to the participants who took part in the study and/or the type of the data collected.

Study One reports on a research in which 80 Iranian EFL learners' perceptions of TD were examined by means of a retrospective questionnaire. Study Two was a questionnaire-based investigation of 30 international EFL teachers' perceptions of TD. Study Three was designed to provide an insider perspective to TD (Creswell, 2007; Dornyei, 2007). Since in Studies One and Two quantitative data were collected, the participants did not have an opportunity to express their views, attitudes and experiences of how they feel about and act on TD during task performance. Hence, in Study Three a semi-structured interview was employed to investigate 20 London-based EFL/ESOL teachers' and learners' perceptions of TD, how they identified and defined different aspects of TD, and what criteria they considered in identifying and defining TD. This qualitative study, in effect, was developed to test out the findings of the first and second studies and to extend the current understandings of TD by including learners' and teachers' views on and criteria for TD (for further information see Tavakoli, in press).

Narrative Tasks

Narrative tasks, which are mainly retelling of picture stories or videos to a partner, were used in all the three studies. The cognitive difficulty of the narratives was operationalized through the degree of macrostructure presented in the picture stories. The design of the study allowed for two structured narratives (Football and Picnic) in that they had a clear macrostructure and a fixed timeline underlying the events and two less structured narratives (Unlucky Man and Walkman) which had a loose timeline and an arbitrary sequence of events. The loose structure in Unlucky Man and Walkman, in effect, allowed for some of the pictures to be moved around without the main theme of the story being changed. In Football and Picnic, because the sequence of events was fixed it was not possible to move any of the pictures around (see Tavakoli & Skehan, 2005 for further details).

Procedures

All the learner participants were met separately, in a one-to-one setting in a quiet room. First, the purpose of the research was explained to them. They were provided with the tasks one at a time and were given three minutes to look at each picture story to plan what they wanted to say. Then, they were asked to start narrating the first story. While they had the picture story in hand they narrated it and what they said was recorded. Once the first performance was completed the same procedure was repeated for the other three narratives. In order to avoid any possible sequencing effect, the tasks were given to them randomly. After performing all four narratives, they were either interviewed or given a retrospective questionnaire.

For the teachers, similar procedures were followed. The teachers were asked to look at each of the picture stories one at a time and to consider the picture stories for their L2 learners at an intermediate proficiency level who were going to perform the narratives. After studying the four picture stories, the teachers were either interviewed or given a retrospective questionnaire.

The questionnaires, used in Studies One and Two, simply asked the participants to decide which tasks they found difficult by ranking them from 1 to 4, 1 being very easy and 4 very difficult. They were also given an opportunity to comment about any aspect of the tasks and performing the tasks. The interviews for both groups included a number of different questions about the four picture stories, performing the tasks, how difficult they found each task, which task they perceived as difficult, easy and interesting, why they found some tasks more difficult than others and what factors contributed to this difficulty. Any other relevant discussion and comments about performing the tasks were also welcomed.

Participants

The participants in Study One were 80 female Persian speaking learners of English at a language school in Tehran, Iran. They were at either an elementary or intermediate level of proficiency, were aged between 18 and 45 and had been studying English for at least 18 months prior to the data collection.

In Study Two, the participants were 30 teachers of English studying towards an MA in TEFL at a university in London. They were 21 female and 9 male teachers, aged between 25 and 44, with different types of English language teaching experience, and from a wide range of L1 backgrounds. The majority of the teachers spoke English as a second/foreign language and had taught English in non-English speaking countries. They all spoke at least one second language at an intermediate or a higher proficiency level and therefore saw themselves as second language learners at some stage in their lives.

The participants in Study Three were ten second language learners studying English at an intermediate level at a college in London and10 EFL/ESOL teachers teaching at the same college. The L2 learners were 7 females and 3 males aged between 18 and 33 from a number of different language backgrounds. The teachers were 7 females and 3 males, all native speakers of English aged between 30 and 52. All the teachers had internationally recognized English language teaching qualifications and at least two years of teaching

Table 14.1 Results for learners' perceptions of TD $(N = 80)$

Tasks	Football	Picnic	Unlucky Man	Walkman
	More structured	More structured	Less structured	Less structured
Ratings of TD	1.85	1.79	2.60	2.48

EFL/ESOL experience in the United Kingdom and abroad. They all spoke at least another language at an intermediate or a higher proficiency level and therefore had been second language learners at some stage in their lives. All the teachers and learners in the three studies reported here volunteered to take part in this research.

Study One

The main objective of Study One was to find out whether learners' perceptions of TD were influenced by the degree of task structure (see Tavakoli & Skehan, 2005, for the details). Responding to a retrospective questionnaire, the participants rated the difficulty level of the four narratives on a four-point scale with 1 representing "very easy" and 4 "very difficult". The results are indicated in Table 14.1.

An ANOVA was run to see whether there was any statistically significant difference between the learners' perceptions of TD on the four tasks. The results of the ANOVA showed a statistically significant difference among the ranking of the four tasks ($F = 32.36$, $p < .001$, $\eta^2 = .244$). The analysis of a Scheffe test indicated that the two more structured tasks, that is Football and Picnic were statistically different from the two less structured tasks, that is Unlucky Man and Walkman. In other words, the results indicated that the learners in this study consistently rated the more structured tasks as easier than the less structured tasks by giving them lower ranking. The learners considered Picnic as the easiest and Unlucky Man as the most difficult narratives to perform. It is worth mentioning that the results of other analyses of learners' task performance also indicated that the learners' performance was more accurate and more fluent on the more structured tasks. This clearly suggested that presence of structure in a narrative not only influenced the learners' perceptions of TD but also had an impact on their task performance.

Study Two

Following from the findings of Study One, Study Two was designed to examine teachers' perceptions of TD. The main reason for designing this study was to

Table 14.2 Results for teachers' perceptions of TD (N = 30)

Tasks	Football	Picnic	Unlucky Man	Walkman
	More structured	More structured	Less structured	Less structured
Perceptions of TD	1.80	1.60	2.40	2.90

replicate Study One to a teacher participant group in order to find out whether the teachers' perceptions of TD were similar to those of the learners. The teachers in Study two were asked to respond to a questionnaire by ranking the difficulty level of the four narratives on a four-point scale with 1 representing 'very easy' and 4 'very difficult'. They were also asked to comment on how interesting their learners would find each of the narratives and to make any comments they had about the tasks. The results of the data analysis of Study Two are shown in Table 14.2.

An ANOVA was run to see whether there was any statistical difference between the teachers' perceptions of TD on the four different tasks. The results of the ANOVA showed a statistically significant difference among the teachers' perceptions of the four tasks ($F = 28.46$, $p < .001$, $\eta^2 = .286$). The analysis of a Scheffe test indicated that the ranking of the two more structured tasks was statistically different from the ranking of the less structured ones. As indicated in Table 14.2, the results of Study Two were in line with the findings of Study One. Similar to the learners in Study One, the teachers in this study rated the more structured tasks as easier than the less structured tasks. They also agreed with the learners in rating Picnic as the easiest task to perform. However, unlike the learners, the teachers considered Walkman as the most difficult task. When asked which of the tasks their learners would consider more interesting, they gave a range of different responses. Interestingly, some stated that this mainly relies on the personal preference of the learners and therefore cannot be decided by the teachers in advance of task performance. A few teachers provided extra comments about the tasks, mainly expressing their concern over whether the picture stories were relevant, suitable and engaging to their adult learners. One teacher thought that learners' age and gender would affect their interest in and reaction to the picture stories.

Study Three

The findings of the two previous studies clearly suggested that both the teachers and learners perceived the less structured tasks as more difficult to perform. However, as the findings of both studies were based on a ranking scale questionnaire, it was not possible to gain an in-depth insight to the teachers' and learners' beliefs, perceptions and attitudes. The data collected in those studies did not provide an 'insider meaning' (Dornyei, 2007; p. 38) to issues such as what the learners experienced during task performance, whether and how they were affected by TD, what the teachers thought of and believed about TD, or how TD affected their choice of tasks in their practices. For this reason, a semi-structured interview was used to collect data that could allow for the participants to express their views, beliefs, attitudes and opinions on TD and to explain what criteria they consider in identifying and defining TD. Study Three was designed to answer the following research questions:

1. Which tasks do the teachers and learners perceive as the most/more difficult?
2. What criteria do they consider in identifying and defining TD?
3. Do the teachers' and learners' perceptions of and criteria for TD match?
4. Can these criteria be linked to the two cognitive models of TD, that is Skehan's (1998) scheme and Robinson's (2001) triadic framework? This would allow an in-depth exploration of how these models reflect learners' and teachers' perspectives.

The results of the data analysis showed that both the teachers and learners in Study Three perceived the more structured tasks as easier to perform. The teachers considered Walkman and the learners viewed Unlucky Man as the most difficult tasks. These results supported the findings of Studies One and Two in which the teachers and learners ranked Unlucky Man and Walkman respectively as the most difficult tasks. The results also implied that presence of structure in an oral narrative would have a positive impact on learners' and teachers' perceptions of TD. The analysis of the interview data further showed that teachers and learners had very similar perceptions about TD, defined TD in similar ways and referred to similar criteria for TD. Both groups mentioned six common themes of *cognitive demand, linguistic demand, clarity of pictures/story, amount of information, task structure* and *affective factors* as the most important elements of an oral narrative task contributing to its TD (for details of the data analysis and results see Tavakoli, 2009). *Cognitive demand* was the first most frequently mentioned criterion for task difficulty. Both groups repeatedly referred to cognitive factors such as understanding the story, following the story up and working out what was happening in a story as factors affecting TD. In addition, they considered elements such as coherence, a clear sequence of events and a reasonable interrelationship among different events, classified as *task structure*, as other important factors contributing to TD. Both the teachers and learners considered *linguistic demand*, that is needing certain vocabulary, structures or expressions to properly perform a task, as the second most important factor contributing to TD. The teachers further mentioned criteria such as teachers' role, information grounding and learner-related variables as other factors affecting TD. Interestingly, issues like cultural differences and age and gender-related features of a task were only mentioned by the teachers, that is none of the students expressed any concern about whether a task was more appropriate for a certain age and/or gender group or cultural background. Although there were few perceptual mismatches between the teachers' and learners' criteria for TD, these results clearly indicated that the learners and teachers in this study had very similar views on and criteria for TD.

The fourth research question in Study Three enquired whether the teachers' and learners' perceptions of TD can be linked to the two existing models of TD, that is Skehan's (1998) and Robinson's (2001) models. In the next section, the criteria for TD proposed by the teachers and learners in Study Three are matched against Skehan's and Robinson's models of TD.

Discussion

The prime purpose of this chapter has been to compare teachers', and learners', perceptions of and research perspectives on TD with each other and to see whether the current models of TD conform with the teachers' and learners' perceptions of and criteria for TD. In an attempt to do so, Table 14.3 presents

Table 14.3 Results of Study Three: Teachers' and learners criteria for TD and the two models of TD

Teachers' and learners' criteria for TD	Robinson's Triadic Framework	Skehan's model of TD
Cognitive demand	Cognitive Factors: Resource-directing	Cognitive Complexity (both Cognitive Processing and Cognitive Familiarity)
Clarity of pictures/story	No corresponding factor available	Cognitive Processing (Clarity and Sufficiency of Information Given)
Linguistic demand	No corresponding factor available	Code Complexity (Linguistic Complexity and Variety, Vocabulary Load and Variety)
Amount of information	Cognitive Factors: Resource-directing	Cognitive Processing (Sufficiency of Information Given and Amount of Computation)
Task structure	Cognitive Factors: Resource-directing (Robinson, 2001), Resource Dispersing (Robinson & Gilabert, 2007)	Cognitive Processing (Information Organization)
Information grounding	Cognitive Factors: not clear whether Resource-directing or Resource-dispersing	Cognitive Processing (Information Type)
Learner-related and affective factors	Task Difficulty: both Affective and Ability variables	No corresponding factor available

the findings of Study Three and matches them against the different categories proposed by Skehan's (1998) model of TD and Robinson's (2001, 2007) Triadic Framework.

As indicated in Table 14.3, many of the findings of Study Three relate to both Models of TD, that is Skehan's model and Robinson's Triadic Framework. The two models are similar in considering cognitive factors as a key element contributing to TD. However, the way they define and categorize the cognitive demands of a task appear to be rather different. Attempting to match the themes driven from the data in Study Three to the two models of TD, there are certain categories that can be conveniently linked to Skehan's model. For instance, categories such as *cognitive demand, linguistic demand and clarity of pictures/story* can clearly be linked to Skehan's categories of Cognitive Complexity, Code Complexity and Cognitive Processing. One important finding of Study Three was that the *cognitive demand* and the *linguistic demand* of a task were the two most frequently mentioned criteria for TD. Skehan's model (1998, p. 99) accommodates these two by defining them as 'the language required' and 'the thinking required'. Such a distinction evidently represents the two criteria for TD most frequently mentioned by the teachers and learners in Study Three. However, Skehan's model doesn't accommodate for learner-related and affective factors. In other words, Skehan's model for TD implicitly suggests that learners' likes and dislikes, their preferences, age, gender and cultural background would not have any influence on the difficulty level of the task. This is in contrast with the findings of Study Three in which the teachers and learners expressed concern that learner-related and affective factors would contribute to TD.

As shown in Table 14.3, some of the findings of Study Three are adequately linked to Robinson's Triadic Framework. Within this framework, the category of Cognitive Factors, an aspect of Task complexity as Robinson puts it, can suitably represent a number of criteria driven from the data in Study Three such as *cognitive demand, amount of information, task structure* and *information grounding*. However, the main question is whether these criteria are to be grouped as Resource-directing or Resource-dispersing factors. Given that the distinction made between Resource-directing and Resource-dispersing factors in Robinson's model is not clear, for instance, it is not easy to decide whether *task structure* should be classified as a Resource-dispersing or Resource-directing factor. Although 'task structure' is an aspect of task which is 'cognitive/perceptual' in nature and therefore should be taken as a Resource-directing factor, in Robinson's Framework (2007) it is classified as resource-dispersing. Obviously, systematic research is required to determine which aspects of a task are Resource-dispersing and which Resource-directing. Another difficulty in relating the teachers' and learners' perceptions to Robinson's Framework is that the relationship between cognitive and linguistic demand is not clarified. In this Framework, factors such as reasoning and perspective-taking are considered as 'cognitive/conceptual demands' and variables such as prior knowledge and task structure are classified under 'performative/procedural demands'. This classification does not allow for the inclusion of linguistic demands that a task may impose on the learners. It seems possible to define the linguistic demand as an aspect of "performative/procedural demands" of a task but this is not intended in Robinson's Triadic Framework. Likewise, Robinson's categories of Task Conditions (Interactive factors) and Task Difficulty (Learner factors) cannot accommodate for the linguistic demands of a task. Hence, placing *linguistic demand* in any of the Robinson's categories proves difficult. For the same token, *clarity of the pictures/story* and *information grounding* cannot relate to Robinson's Framework. However, Robinson's Triadic Framework is advantageous for including a range of learner-related variables and grouping them under Task Difficulty. *Affective factors* such as likes and preferences and *learner-related factors* such as age and cultural background can therefore be appropriately linked to Robinson's category of Task Difficulty.

Concluding Remarks

The findings of the three studies reported here strongly suggest that task structure has an impact on teachers' and learners' perceptions of TD. In all these studies, the teachers and learners perceived the more structured tasks as easier to perform. In Study Three, the teachers and learners clearly expressed concern over different aspects of 'task structure' including the timeline underlying the events, the sequence of events, and coherence of the story. Obviously, this has significant implications for language teaching and language assessment. In sequencing tasks and grading their difficulty level, language teachers need to pay attention to how well structured tasks are and to how and where tasks of varying degrees of structure can be used in a syllabus. Similarly, given that structure of a task has an impact on learners' perceptions of TD and task performance, language test designers need to know about the structure of the tasks they use in a test if assessment is to provide a fair and true measure of learners' L2 proficiency.

One significant finding of these studies is that the teachers and learners who participated in this research view *cognitive* and *linguistic demands* of a task as the two most important factors contributing to TD. An important implication of this finding is that language educators may need to think of the cognitive and linguistic demands of tasks in some more depth before including tasks in a syllabus, scheme of work or test. An in-depth understanding of L2 proficiency may not be attainable without knowing what aspects of tasks L2 learners find cognitively and linguistically demanding. The findings of this research suggest that the cognitive complexity of a task should be considered one of the main criteria in sequencing tasks in a syllabus. Another significant implication of this research is for the Cognitive approach to tasks. As discussed earlier, the Cognitive approach contends that knowing what demands a task will make, opens up the possibility of using task design to manipulate learners' attention in ways that may help interlanguage develop (Skehan, 1998). Now that the results of the current research on TD strongly suggest that learners' perceptions of TD are, above any other factors, influenced by the *cognitive demands* of a task, a Cognitive approach to task-based research has more crucial responsibility in exploring the cognitive complexities of tasks that challenge learners during task performance. This does not imply that these findings are not relevant to the Psycholinguistic and Sociocultural approaches to task-based research. On the contrary, the argument is that other research approaches will certainly benefit from the findings of this research since these perspectives are complementary and will need to work in collaboration to achieve their research and/or pedagogic goals.

Another interesting finding of these studies is that the learners' and teachers' perceptions of and criteria for TD proved to be very close to, if not the same as, one another. Unlike some studies that report a perceptual mismatch between the two groups' perspectives (Hawkey, 2006; Kumaravadivelu, 2003), the teachers and learners in these studies indicated that their views and beliefs on TD were very similar. This can perhaps be justified in light of the fact that identifying and defining TD is, to some extent, a process in which individuals draw upon their common knowledge of how the human mind works and the general and linguistic knowledge that a second language learner requires to perform a task in L2. The results of Studies Two and Three further revealed that the teachers agreed with the learners on the criteria for defining and determining TD but went further to include factors such as learners' age, gender and cultural background in the list of their criteria for TD. The striking point was that the learners in these studies did not speak of such elements as factors affecting TD. This can be explained in light of the professional training of the teachers or it may be attributed to the teachers' life and teaching experiences. Alternatively, this could be simply regarded as an area of concern to teachers who have worked in multi-lingual/multicultural environments.

Finally, the directions for future research indicated by the findings of the current research are twofold. Firstly, more research is required to investigate teachers' and learners' perceptions, views and attitudes about a range of pedagogic tasks that are frequently used in different classrooms around the world. Knowing more about the complexities of teachers' beliefs and experiences in choosing tasks and the learners' feelings and challenges in performing the tasks would undoubtedly help explain the intricate nature of TD. Secondly, more research is required to explore task characteristics and features that contribute to the cognitive difficulty of a task. Now that research has evidently shown that cognitive demands of performing a task play an important role in TD it is vital to know what elements contribute to the cognitive demand of task performance.

References

Bachman, L. (2002). Some reflections on task-based language performance assessment. *Language Testing*, 19, 453–76.
Barkhuizen, G. (1998). Discovering learners' perceptions of ESL classroom teaching/learning activities in a South African context. *TESOL Quarterly*, 32, 85–108.
Block, D. (1994). A day in the life of class: Teachers/learner perceptions of task purpose in conflict. *System*, 22, 473–86.
Block, D. (1996). A window on the classroom: Classroom events viewed from different angles. In K. Bailey., & D. Nunan (Eds.). *Voices from the language classroom* (pp. 168–95). New York: Cambridge University Press.
Brindley, G. (1987). Factors affecting task difficulty. In D. Nunan (Ed.). *Guidelines for the development of curriculum resource* (pp. 45–56). Adelaide: National Curriculum Resource Centre.
Brown, G., Anderson, A., Shilcock, R., & Yule, G. (1984). *Teaching talk: Strategies for production and assessment*. Cambridge: Cambridge University Press.
Bygate, M., Skehan, P., & Swain, M. (Eds.). (2001). *Researching pedagogic tasks: Second language learning, teaching and testing*. London: Longman.
Candlin, C. (1987). Towards task-based language learning. In C. Candlin, & D. Murphy (Eds.), *Language learning tasks* (pp. 5–22). London: Prentice Hall.
Creswell, J. (2007). *Qualitative inquiry and research design*. London: Sage.
Cooper, P., & McIntyre, D. (1994). Teachers' and pupils' perceptions of effective classroom learning: Conflicts and commonalities. In M. Hughes (Ed.). *Perceptions of teaching and learning* (pp. 66–95). Clevedon: Multilingual Matters.
Dotano, R. (1994). Collective scaffolding in second language learning. In J. Lantolf, & G. Appel. *Vygotskian approach to second language research* (pp. 33–56). Norwood, NJ: Ablex.
Ellis, R. (2003). *Task-based language teaching and testing*. Oxford: Oxford University Press.
Fulcher, G., & Marquez Reiter, R. (2003). Task difficulty in speaking tests. *Language Testing*, 20, 321–44.
Hawkey, R. (2006). Teacher and learner perceptions of language learning activity. *ELT Journal*, 60, 242–52.
Ilins, G., Inozu, J., & Yumru, H. (2007). Teachers' and learners' perceptions of tasks: Objectives and outcomes. *Journal of Theory and Practice in Education*, 3, 60–68.
Iwashita, N., McNamara, T., & Elder, C. (2001). Can we predict task difficulty in an oral proficiency test? Exploring the potential of an information processing approach to task design. *Language Learning*, 51(3): 401–36.
Kumaravadivelu, B. (1991). Language learning tasks: Teacher intention and learner interpretation. *ELT Journal*, 45, 98–107.
Kumaravadivelu, B. (2003). *Beyond Methods*. New Haven: Yale University Press.
Kumaravadivelu, B. (2006). TESOL methods: Changing tracks, challenging trends. *TESOL Quarterly*, 40, 59–81.
McDonough, K., & Chaikitmongkol, W. (2007). Teachers' and learners' reactions to a task-based EFL course in Thailand. *TESOL Quarterly*, 41, 107–31.

Mehnert, U. (1998). The effects of different length of time for planning on second language performance. *Studies in Second Language Acquisition*, 20, 83–108.

Mitchell, M., Brumfit, C. & Hooper, J. (1994). Perceptions of language learning in English and foreign language classrooms. In M. Hughes (Ed.). *Perceptions of teaching and learning* (pp. 53–65). Clevedon: Multilingual Matters.

Nunan, D. (1989). *Designing tasks for the communicative classroom.* Cambridge: Cambridge University Press.

Nunan, D. (2004). *Task-based language teaching.* Cambridge: Cambridge University Press.

Nunan, D., & Keobke, K. (1995). Task difficulty from the learner's perspective: Perceptions and reality. *Hong Kong Papers in Linguistics and Language Teaching*, 18, 1–12.

Pica, T. (1994). Research on negotiation: What does it reveal about second language learning conditions, processes, and outcomes? *Language Learning*, 44, 493–527.

Robinson, P. (2001). Task complexity, cognitive resources, and syllabus design: A triadic framework for examining task influences on SLA. In P. Robinson (Ed.). *Cognition and second language instruction* (pp. 287–318). Cambridge, Cambridge University Press.

Robinson, P. (2007). Task complexity, theory of mind, and intentional reasoning: Effects of L2 speech production, interaction, uptake and perceptions of task difficulty. *IRAL*, 45, 193–213.

Robinson, P., & Gilabert, R. (2007). Task complexity, the cognition hypothesis and second language learning and performance. *IRAL*, 45, 161–76.

Samuda, V., & Bygate, M. (2008). *Tasks in second language learning.* Basingstoke: Palgrave.

Skehan, P. (1996). A framework for the implementation of task-based instruction. *Applied Linguistics*, 17, 38–62.

Skehan, P. (1998). *A cognitive approach to language learning.* Oxford: Oxford University Press.

Skehan, P. (2003). Task-based instruction. *Language Teaching*, 36, 1–14.

Skehan, P., & Foster, P. (1997). Task type and task processing conditions as influences on foreign language performance. *Language Teaching Research*, 1, 185–212.

Tavakoli, P. (2009). Learner and teacher perceptions of task difficulty. *International Journal of Applied Linguistics*, 19, 2.

Tavakoli, P. (in press). *L2 task performance: Understanding the effects of task design.* System.

Tavakoli, P., & Foster, P. (2008). Task design and second language performance: The effect of narrative type on learner output. *Language Learning*, 58, 439–73.

Tavakoli, P., & Skehan, P. (2005). Strategic planning, task structure and performance testing. In R. Ellis (Ed.). *Planning and task performance in a second language* (pp. 239–77). Amsterdam: John Benjamins.

Yuan, F., & Ellis, R. (2003). The effects of pre-task planning and on-line planning on fluency, complexity and accuracy in L2 monologic oral production. *Applied Linguistics*, 24, 1–27.

Willis, J. (1996). *A framework for task-based learning.* London: Longman.

Chapter 15

On Transfer, Proficiency and Cross-Individual/Aggregate SLA Differences: Examining Adjectival Semantics in L2 Spanish

Pedro Guijarro-Fuentes
University of Plymouth, United Kingdom

Tiffany Judy
University of Iowa, United States of America

Jason Rothman
University of Iowa, United States of America

Abstract

This chapter principally addresses L1 transfer effects via an examination of the acquisition of properties related to the Spanish Determiner Phrase (DP), namely adjectival semantics. We compare the experimental performance of English-speaking and Italian-speaking adult learners of L2 Spanish at various levels of proficiency, reporting findings from two experiments: a Semantic Interpretation Task designed to test whether one intuits interpretational differences of pre- and postnominal adjectives and a Context-based Collocation Task. In line with the developmental sequence predictions of the Full Transfer/Full Access initial state model, the Italian-speaking learners' data compared to the English-speaking learners' demonstrate that L1 transfer is robust and deterministic in adult L2 development. Furthermore, by briefly looking at individual L2 learner and native control data, we highlight and support empirically important epistemological and methodological issues.

Introduction

In search of a better understanding of how adults acquire non-primary mental grammars as well as providing explanatorily adequate accounts of L2 linguistic behavior throughout interlanguage development, a central topic of investigation in many SLA traditions has been that of determining the role/influence of the learner's first language grammar in the L2 developmental process. Within generative SLA, whether it be for the reason of determining the cognitive components that comprise the initial state of adult L2 acquisition (e.g., Epstein, Flynn & Martohardjono, 1996; Schwartz & Sprouse, 1996; Vanikka & Young-Scholten, 1996) or the developmental and ultimate attainment implications of (possible) L1 influence, transfer has constituted one of the core research topics of experimental and epistemological inquiry for well over two decades (see White, 1989, 2003 for details). Adding to this general program, the present study investigates the acquisition of nominal features in Spanish by native speakers of Italian and English, most crucially the availability of semantic interpretations of adjectives strictly delimited by the overt syntactic position of adjectives in relation to their head noun in Romance languages. The L2 speakers' L1s represent typologically different languages whereby Italian and Spanish are similar and English diverges from both for the properties we investigate. This scenario creates an interesting contrast with respect to the adult acquisition of the morphosyntax and semantics of nominals, thereby enabling us to address specific questions about L1 influence.

As we will see, our data support the position that actual linguistic typology and/or the extent to which the adult L2 learner perceives the language distance— that is psycho-typology in the sense of Kellerman (1986)—between his L1 and the target L2 comes to bear on the role of L1 influence, in a positive or negative sense, in L2 acquisition. However, we also intend through our data to weigh in on a second line of inquiry, relating to assumptions that underline the successful acquisition of L2 features, in this case of the Spanish Determiner Phrase (DP), in a hierarchical fashion. In particular, we take the position that *a priori* assumptions that advanced L2 learners, regardless of their L1, could/would perform within the native speakers' range; and, on the other hand, that advanced L2 speakers must outperform Intermediate L2 speakers may need to be reconsidered in the context of the acquisition of different domains of linguistic knowledge, for example, narrow syntax properties (e.g., gender and number) versus syntax-semantic interface properties (e.g., the collocational properties of adjectives in relation to the noun head and the semantic entailments they have). This can be true for several reasons; most important is the fact that aggregate differences may obtain due to the nature and extent of the L2 proficiency gap experienced by the individual L2 speakers that form heterogeneous groups (cf. Rothman & Iverson, 2007a, 2007b) compared to a more linguistically homogenous native speaker control.

Under levels of proficiency, researchers predict developmental stages of language proficiency. However, as we will show it is not always the case that those levels of proficiency are as uniform as one might expect when it comes to the measurement (and thus presumed competence) of particular grammatical properties. The majority of L2 studies include a monolingual group as a baseline control group and for good reason, if for nothing more than control data help us to be assured that the experiments themselves are tenable ones. However, as of late SLA researchers have been challenged to find alternative controls than the "monolingual" baseline inasmuch as recent studies highlight a certain degree of indeterminacy not only on the part of the L2 learners regardless of their proficiency level, but critically on the part of the monolingual controls (see for example, Slabakova, 2006; Fruit, 2006), especially when it comes to the semantic interpretation of certain linguistic phenomena, an effect we will see in the present study as well. These conflicting results call into question the effectiveness of native control comparisons, rather than studying L2 performances within their own right. In that regard, White (2003), following Grimshaw & Rosen (1990), suggests that it is important to demonstrate not that learners perform at the same level as native speakers but rather whether they are aware of distinctions: "Does learners' performance on grammatical sentences differ significantly from their performance on ungrammatical sentences (cf. Grimshaw & Rosen (1990) for related insights on L1 acquisition and Martohardjono (1993, 1998) for L2)?" (White, 2003, p. 26). We will join this position and ultimately argue that (a) L1 transfer is robust and deterministic in the L2 developmental sequence we see in the comparative cross-section we analyze, (b) that even in the case L2 learners seem to perform differently from native controls they can be shown to have the relevant knowledge when they are compared against themselves in counterbalanced conditions and, (c) that being native does not ensure expected native performances at the group or individual level and that this fact has important implications for SLA epistemology.

Related Previous Studies

Herein we review, albeit briefly due to space limitations, some of the previous research on adjectives and related features of nominals in L2 Romance, particularly that which comes to bear most directly on the present research (e.g., Anderson, 2007a, 2007b, 2008; Gess & Herschensohn, 2001; Judy, Guijarro-Fuentes & Rothman, 2008). In particular, Gess and Herschensohn (2001) and Judy et al. (2008) demonstrated that there is no representational problem for English-speaking L2 learners of French and Spanish within the narrow syntax (i.e., the acquisition of gender and number (phi) features associated with nominals) in contra claims by others for the same properties (Franceschina, 2005; Hawkins, 2001; Hawkins & Franceschina, 2004). Alternatively, Gess and Herschensohn (2001) in L2 French and Judy et al. in L2 Spanish found convergence gaps for English-speaking learners between narrow syntactic properties and related syntax-semantic interface properties; for example, even intermediate learners seemed to control interpretive properties of grammatical gender, but failed to show target knowledge of the semantic entailments of different adjectival positions in relation to the noun head. Specifically, Judy et al. provided robust evidence that advanced and, importantly, intermediate English-speaking learners of L2 Spanish demonstrate evidence consistent with having acquired the underlying syntactic representation (i.e., gender features) of the Spanish DP. Employing a grammaticality judgment task with corrections, their participants judged and corrected a total of 40 sentences that pertained to gender feature acquisition. Results concerning both the grammaticality and, crucially, the ungrammaticality of the target sentences were very similar across all three experimental groups. However, only the advanced learners performed like the native controls for the subtle interpretive properties related to adjective-noun collocation, despite the fact that such semantic knowledge should fall out directly from acquiring the syntax of the DP. In line with the general program of Interface Vulnerability (see for example, Sorace, 2005; White, forthcoming), Judy et al. concluded that the difference obtained due to the added complexity inherent to the interface properties of adjectival semantics and not because the underlying syntax is deficient.

Similar conclusions were also reached by Anderson (2001, 2007a, 2007b, 2008) who investigated issues related to learnability (i.e., the effect of explicit teaching in the classroom) and parametric change (i.e., the effect of UG constraints in parameter resetting) in the nominal DP system in L2 French. Specifically, Anderson sought to examine (i) the differentiation between result and process nominals in the licensing of postnominal genitives and (ii) the distinction between prenominal and postnominal adjectives in the two different contexts (i.e., unique vs. non-unique noun referents). Taken together, the results from this series of studies enabled Anderson to conclude that whereas parametric (i.e., representational) change is possible in a *poverty-of-the-stimulus* context, such change is not immediate, straightforward, or perfectly reflected in aggregate group data based on academic course levels. He claims that this is a function of the type of instruction learners receive, the kind of input on adjectival position prevalent in classrooms and the manner in which individual learners interact with that input.

Against this background, our goal is take a fresh look at the data from Judy et al. (2008) adding to it two new L2 groups, intermediate and advanced Italian speakers with two general research issues in mind: (i) the role of transfer in L2 grammar, and (ii) assessment of the target language proficiency and what the notion of optionality/variability means in the context of aggregate analyses. To be fair, we will not limit the discussion of the latter issue to L2 learners, but in the discussion section we will look into how this applies to native controls as well and we will confront some important possible methodological implications this has.

Linguistic Background: DPs Nominals in English, Spanish and Italian

In what follows, we present a linguistic analysis of the Determiner Phrase (DP) in Spanish compared to Italian and English. The Determiner Phrase is a functional grammatical category instantiated in all three languages that regulates the syntactic and semantic properties of nominal elements. Abney (1987) offered the DP-hypothesis, drawing a parallelism between the syntactic structure of noun phrases and that of the sentence. According to the DP-hypothesis, determiners (articles, quantifiers, demonstratives, etc.) head their own functional projection, the DP, which must select an NP as its complement. Essentially, the functional value of proposing the DP lies in its explanation of how reference is added to the complement noun phrase. Although all three languages have DPs, the syntax and semantics of Romance and Germanic DPs are significantly different, ranging from the presence or absence of related grammatical features to interpretive differences that obtain as a result of the difference in related feature composition. The linguistic focus of our present study relates two associated aspects of the morphosyntax of nominals: (i) gender agreement/concord (which exists in Spanish and Italian, but not in English—in Spanish and Italian, gender marking is realized inside the nominal, namely, between the head noun and adjectives); and (ii) the lack of interpretive ambiguity depending on the collocation of adjectives within the Romance DP (i.e., in pronominal and in postnominal positions) as compared to the inherent ambiguity of the one English adjectival position.

English

Following Bernstein (1993, 2001 and works cited within), we assume that English DPs are head-initial, adjectives are based-generated before the noun and concord/agreement is realized syntactically within the DP as shown in (1).

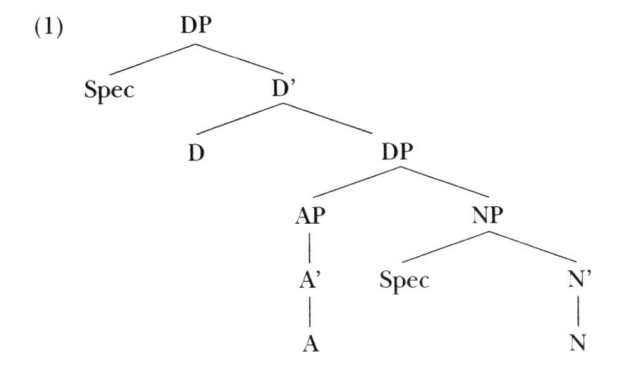

(1)
```
           DP
          /  \
       Spec   D'
             /  \
            D    DP
                /  \
              AP    NP
              |    /  \
              A'  Spec  N'
              |         |
              A         N
```

With regards to morphological agreement, English has limited nominal agreement. Recall that whereas English lacks grammatical gender, English has number inflection, although this is limited to the head noun (i.e., unlike Spanish/Italian it is not realized on adjectives and other D-elements). Besides, the order in the expanded English nominal is fixed: [Det Adj N], that is, determiner, adjective, head noun, as illustrated in (2):

(2) The big books
    Det Adj Noun

Spanish/Italian

Unlike English, Romance languages including Spanish and Italian possess full nominal features (so-called phi features, see Chomsky, 1981, 1995) and overt morphological agreement; in the expanded nominal the different components of the Spanish DP (i.e., determiners, nouns and adjectives) agree with each other in both gender and number. Gender agreement is realized between the head noun and its modifying article and between the head noun and adjectives; that is, if the head noun is feminine (*niña* "girl"), then so are all other elements as illustrated in (3).

(3) La   niña   bonita
    La   ragazza   bella
    The.FEM.SG. girl.FEM.SG.   pretty.FEM.SG

As shown in (3), while determiners precede the noun head, adjectives generally speaking occur after the noun. The so-called ethnic and relational adjectives which convey relations of various types, such as origin and material composition, always follow the noun in a postnominal position (compare (4a) and (4b)). However, most attributive adjectives may also appear prenominally (compare (5a) and (5b)), implying a change in semantic value from the canonical position, captured nicely in the minimal pairs of (6a) and (6b). Therefore, unlike in English where the prenominal position (in most cases the only available position) of these adjectives is inherently ambiguous between a restrictive (intersective) and non-intersective meanings, Spanish and Italian adjectival interpretation is unambiguous, determined directly by the syntax of movement to the adjectives spell-out (or surface) position. We return to this second class of adjectives in greater detail. However, a subset of non-attributive adjectives (namely, temporal modifiers) only occurs pronominally (compare (7a) and (b)).

(4) a. Los hombres japoneses
       Gli uomini giapponesi

b. * Los japoneses hombres
　　　　 * Gli giapponesi uomini
　　　　 "The Japanese men"
(5) a. Una vista bonita
　　　 Una vista bella
　　　 "A pretty view"
　　b. Una bonita vista
　　　 Una bella vista
　　　 "A pretty view"
(6) a. Un niño pobre
　　　 Un bambino povero
　　　 "A poor (not rich) child" (restrictive interpretation)
　　b. Un pobre niño
　　　 Un povero bambino
　　　 "A poor (unfortunate) child" (appositive interpretation)
(7) a. Un mero soldado
　　　 Un puro soldato
　　　 "A mere soldier"
　　b. *Un soldado mero
　　　 *Un soldato puro
　　　 "A mere soldier"

In order to explain the different collocational possibilities of Spanish adjectives, we adhere to Bernstein's (1993, 2001) analysis that proposes that restrictive/intersective adjectives are essentially prenominal in Spanish, but that their postnominal position is derived from noun movement over the adjective, as shown in (8).

Following Bernstein (among others, Cinque, 1994; Picallo, 1991), the head noun moves (as represented by X in (7)) from N to the head of Word Marker Phrase (WMP) and then to Number Phrase (NumP).[1] Following this logic, appositive/non-intersective adjectives are merged higher in the DP, either in Specifier position of NumP or some other functional projection higher above NumP, thus providing the possibility of [Det Adj N] word order even after obligatory noun raising.[2] In summary, Bernstein (1993) asserts that different adjectives emerge in different structural positions: some of them being APs which adjoin to various XPs, whereas others are similar to functional projections in which the head Adj takes a complement. These different structural positions are related to the specific semantic characteristics of the adjectives as shown through examples (4), (5), (6) and (7) above. Because we are dealing with [Det N Adj] and [Det Adj N] orders, the structure given in (7) captures all these possible syntactic structures while assuming that nouns must always raise for feature checking reasons (to value and delete gender and number features).

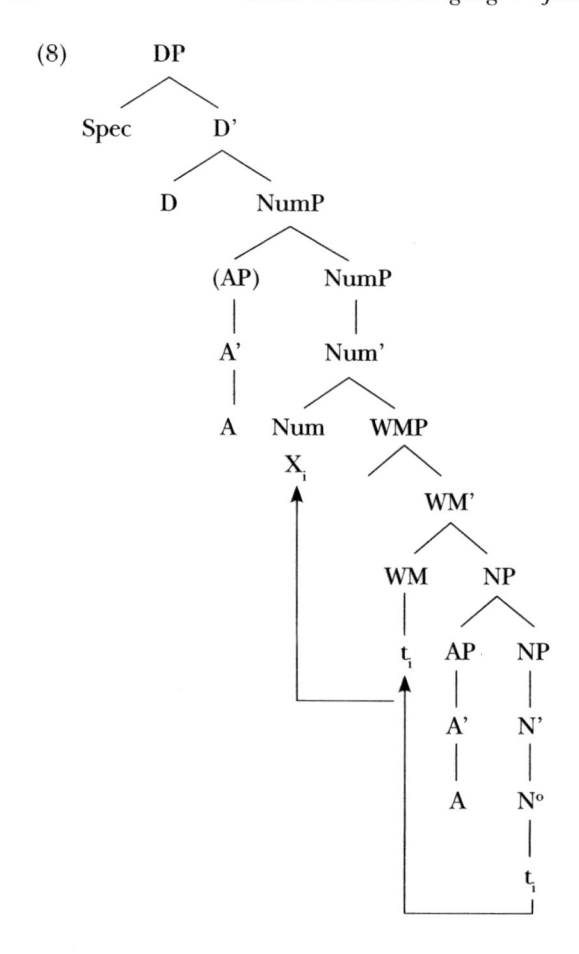

(8)
```
            DP
           /  \
        Spec   D'
              /  \
             D    NumP
                 /    \
              (AP)    NumP
               |       |
               A'     Num'
               |     /    \
               A   Num    WMP
                   X_i   /   \
                        WM'   
                       /   \
                      WM    NP
                      |    /  \
                      t_i AP   NP
                          |    |
                          A'   N'
                          |    |
                          A    N°
                               |
                               t_i
```

Details aside, the resulting distinctive word orders within the DP in Romance and Germanic languages are determined by syntactic position: whereas LF movement in Spanish/Italian is overt and there is no room for ambiguity; LF movement in English is covert creating ambiguity. Let us consider the following example which is a repetition of (6a,b):

(9) [$_{DP}$ a] [$_{NumP}$ [$_{AP}$ poor] [$_{Num}$ +singular]] [$_{nP}$ [$_{AP}$ poor] [$_N$ child]]
    ↓   ↓
    "unfortunate"   "not rich"

Looking at (9), the English phrase "a poor child" is ambiguous because *poor* can be underlyingly linked to either the higher clausal position, that is, NumP, which can only be interpreted as non-intersective, or to the lower clausal position

Table 15.1 Summary of differences and similarities among the three languages under investigation regarding their respective nominal systems

	Spanish	Italian	English
Overt gender on the noun (interpretable gender features)	+	+	−
Overt number on the noun (interpretable gender features)	+	+	+
Overt gender concord (uninterpretable gender features)	+	+	−
Overt/covert number concord (uninterpretable number features)	+	+	+
Prenominal adjectives (via no movement in English; after two types of movement in Spanish/Italian)	+	+	+
Postnominal adjectives (instantiation of WMP and obligatory noun raising in Spanish/Italian only)	+	+	−

in n, which must be interpreted as intersective. In Spanish/Italian, however, N raises to NumP, so that any prenominal adjective must be non-intersective, and any postnominal adjective must be intersective. Thus, the meanings are uniquely determined by the syntactic position of the adjective and, therefore, adjectival interpretation in this respect is a robust indicator of the underlying mental representation of the syntax.

Table 15.1 summarizes the differences and similarities among the three languages under investigation regarding their respective nominal systems.

Learnability Assumptions for the Present Study

While specific lexical/morphological items will have to be learned by both groups of L2 speakers, the target L2 language (Spanish) to be acquired by these two groups creates a nice locus for examining L1 transfer effects since the DP of Italian is identical to that of Spanish for the properties we investigate. Therefore, it is reasonable to assume that Italian speakers are expected to start the task of acquiring L2 Spanish with the target syntax of the DP transferred from their L1. Italian speakers, therefore, should have an advantage over the English speakers of L2 Spanish at early levels of proficiency, even while the learning of new morpho-phonological forms and the mapping of L1 features onto new material are not straightforward endeavors (see Lardiere, 2007; Rothman, 2007). If L2 learners are unable to mentally reconfigure the functional features and categories of their L1, then such advantages for the Italian-speakers are predicted to be indefinite (see Franceschina, 2005; Hawkins & Franceschina, 2004).

On the basis of previous research on the L2 nominal domain outlined above and the assumption that L1 transfer obtains, we can make the following acquisition predictions for the L2 morphosyntax of Spanish nominals:

(10) a. Even though gender and number agreement is morpho-phonologically different between Italian and Spanish, Italian speakers may initially (regardless of their stages of proficiency) have clear advantages over English speakers acquiring gender agreement in the Spanish nominal (an L1 positive transfer effect). Due to possible mapping problems, Italian advanced L2 acquirers might outperform intermediates, but both Italian groups should perform well and do better than the intermediate English-speaking group.[3]

b. Only native English speakers are expected to misinterpret prenominal and postnominal adjectives in Spanish. One cannot appeal to feature remapping problems/delays as an explanation for any differences between the controls and the two aggregate Italian groups here.

c. Advanced speakers, regardless of their L1, should approach native speaker proficiency level, with clear differences between the intermediate group and advanced group for English-speakers. However, we expect aggregate and cross-individual differences that do not match with speakers 'independent' (as measured by a proficiency test) proficiency level nor with their L1s.

Methodology

Participants and Tasks

There were a total of 88 participants in this study. Twelve native Spanish speakers from various Spanish-speaking countries served as the control group. The L2 participants were divided into two proficiency groups based on their performance on a proficiency test. There were 23 Advanced L1 Italian participants and 12 Advanced L1 English participants as well as 12 Intermediate L1 Italian participants and 29 Intermediate L1 English participants. All participants completed a linguistic survey pertaining to things such as language of instruction in high school and university, age of onset of acquisition of Spanish, parents' native language, languages spoken at home and work, length and amount of contact with Spanish, etc.

All participants completed a series of tasks[4] related to the acquisition of the syntax and semantics of Spanish, but due to space limitations and the focus of this chapter only the results of two tasks will be reported: the Semantic Interpretation task and the Context-based Collocation task. For the first task, the participants were instructed to read a short sentence that contained a DP with either a prenominal or a postnominal adjective. Based on this sentence they were then instructed to choose the meaning of the DP based on two interpretations provided to them. Example (11) is a prenominal token (n = 5) and example (12) is a postnominal token (n = 5). The correct interpretation is bolded. In the second task, participants were instructed to read a short context and then place the adjective at the end of the token in either the prenominal or postnominal blank. Example (13) is a prenominal token (n = 5) and example (14) is a postnominal token (n = 5).

(11) Su vecino es un pobre hombre.

| The man is unfortunate. | The man is not wealthy. |

(12) Ella es la persona única de quien te hablé.

| She is the only person that I told you about. | She is the unique person that I told you about. |

(13) Mi mejor amiga se llama Magda. Ella es una persona muy amable y cariñosa. Aunque solo tenemos 22 años, hace mucho tiempo que somos amigas. Magda es una _____*vieja*_____ amiga _____ (viejo).

"My best friend is named Magda. She is a very nice and affectionate person. Even though we are only 22 years old, we have been friends for a long time. Magda is an old friend."

(14) Creo que la gente que tiene mucho dinero puede ser muy arrogante. Pero la semana pasada conocimos a unos millonarios que no son así. Los _____ millonarios _____*simpáticos* (simpático) que conocimos me cayeron muy bien.

"I think that people that have a lot of money can be very arrogant. But, last week we met some millionaires that aren't like that. I really like the nice millionaires that we met!"

Results

The statistical analysis was conducted as follows: a mixed-model ANOVA was computed to compare the five participant groups to each other. If the results from this statistical measure showed there was a main effect, Bonferroni post hoc tests were conducted.

The purpose of the Semantic Interpretation task was to test for accurate semantic interpretations of prenominal and postnominal adjectives. Figure 1 below shows the group average of correct responses (n = 5).

Result: Task 1 (SIT)

	PreAdj-Sem	PosAdj-Sem
■ Native Spanish	4.50	4.28
■ Adv Italian	4.35	4.26
■ Adv English	4.42	3.33
▒ Int Italian	4.17	4.08
Int English	3.38	2.59

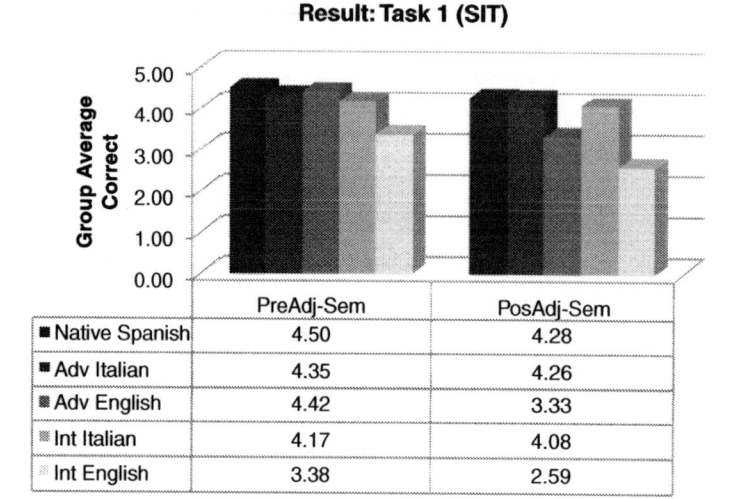

FIGURE 15.1 Semantic interpretation task
PreAdj-sem = prenominal adjective; PosAdj-Sem = postnominal adjective; Native Spanish = control group; Adv Italian = Advanced L1 Italian; Adv English = Advanced L1 English; Int Italian = Intermediate L1 Italian; Int English = Intermediate L1 English

As Figure 15.1 indicates, both Advanced groups and the Intermediate Italian group average correct for prenominal adjectives is very similar to the control group average correct (4.35, 4.42, and 4.17, respectively, compared to 4.50). The Intermediate English group average correct (3.38) is below that of the control group. Both Italian groups perform very similarly to the control group for postnominal adjectives. However, both English groups' average correct is well below that of the control group. As indicated, a mixed-model ANOVA was conducted to determine if the differences among the participant groups were significant. This analysis indicated a main effect for proficiency level: $(4, 83) = 19.12$, $p < .0001$. A main effect was also found for the position of the adjective: $F(1, 83) = 10.90$, $p < .001$. Finally, an interaction between proficiency level and adjective position was also found: $F(4, 83) = 2.85$, $p = .029$.

The Bonferroni post hoc tests revealed a significant difference between the Intermediate English group when compared to all other groups: control group, $p < .0001$; Advanced Italian, $p < .0001$; Advanced English, $p = .001$; and Intermediate Italian, $p < .0001$. No other significant differences were found among the participant groups. Additionally, the post hoc tests revealed that except for the Intermediate English group, no significant difference was found in the way that the groups treated prenominal and postnominal adjectives. This means that, with exception of the Intermediate English group, all participant groups

Results: Task 2 (COL)

	PreAdj-Col	PosAdj-Col
■ Native Spanish	3.08	4.83
■ Adv Italian	4.09	4.52
■ Adv English	3.00	4.50
■ Int Italian	4.08	4.42
■ Int English	1.90	4.10

Group Average Correct (y-axis: 0.00 to 5.00)

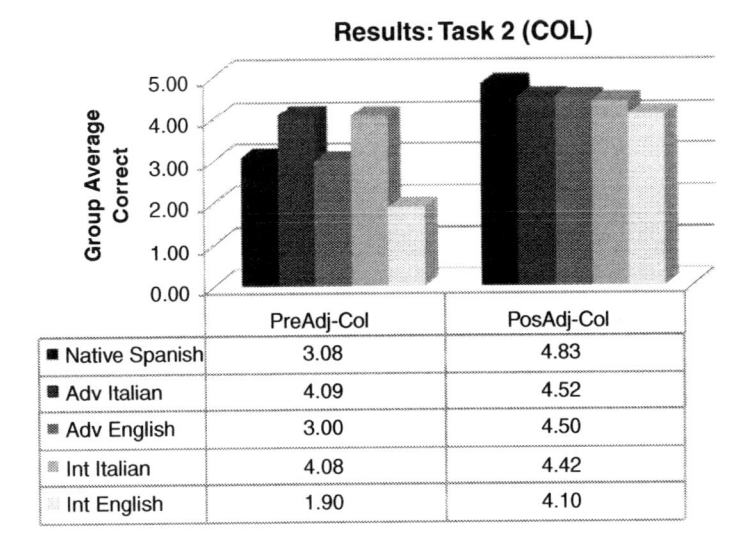

FIGURE 15.2 Context-based collocation task
PreAdj-Col = prenominal adjective; PosAdj-Col = postnominal adjective; Native Spanish = control group; Adv Italian = Advanced L1 Italian; Adv English = Advanced L1 English; Int Italian = Intermediate L1 Italian; Int English = Intermediate L1 English

correctly interpreted both prenominal and postnominal adjectives and were not more accurate in their interpretation of one or the other. Finally, there was no statistically significant difference in the way the two intermediate groups interpreted prenominal adjectives, but there was a statistically significant difference found in their interpretation of postnominal adjectives: $p < .0001$. The Intermediate English group accurately interpreted fewer postnominal adjectives than the Intermediate Italian group. In light of the Intermediate English group performance, it is crucial to highlight the fact that the Intermediate Italian group performed like the control group in all senses on this task. Given that the general proficiency level is the same for both Intermediate groups (hence their classification as "intermediate"), it must be assumed that the Intermediate Italian group performs better than the Intermediate English group based on L1 transfer. As pointed out in Table 15.1, Spanish and Italian share the same properties for nominals, whereas English differs for at least three properties.[5]

The Context-based Collocation task tested for the accurate production (via collocation) of prenominal and postnominal adjectives. Figure 15.2 shows the group average number of correct adjective placements ($n = 5$).

With regards to postnominal adjectives, Figure 15.2 shows that all L2 groups perform similarly to the control group. However, we see an interesting result with the prenominal adjectives: both Italian groups perform basically identically (4.09 versus 4.08) and seemingly perform *better* than the control group.[6] The Advanced English group performs almost identically to the control group (3.00 versus 3.08) whereas the Intermediate English group is far below the control group (1.90 versus 3.08). The mixed-model ANOVA revealed that there was a main effect for proficiency level: $F(4, 83) = 12.96$, $p < .0001$ as well as a main effect for adjective position: $F(1, 83) = 84.35$, $p < .0001$. An interaction between adjective position and proficiency level was also found: $F(4, 83) = 9.83$, $p < .0001$. Bonferroni post hoc analyses revealed a significant difference between the Intermediate English group and all other participant groups: control group, $p < .002$; Advanced Italian, $p < .0001$; Advanced English, $p = .032$; and Intermediate Italian, $p < .0001$. Another interesting result is that a significant difference was found for the control group and both English groups in regard to the placement of prenominal and postnominal adjectives: control group, $p = .0001$; Advanced English, $p = .001$; and Intermediate English, $p < .0001$. That is, these three groups treated prenominal adjectives differently than postnominal ones (in this case, they were more accurate with postnominal adjectives). As was seen in task 1, a significant difference was found between the Intermediate English group and the Intermediate Italian group. In task 2, a significant difference was found for prenominal adjectives, $p < .0001$. This result can be attributed to L1 transfer as the Intermediate Italian group performs more accurately than the Intermediate English group.

Discussion

The goal of this general discussion section is twofold. First, we interpret the data presented in the above section as they relate to the predications we made in section 'Learnability Assumptions for the Present Study' above, detailed in (10a–c). Second, we will address the epistemological questions we have posed in the introduction and see how examining some of the individual data helps us to address important macro issues relevant to SLA broadly defined. Given space limitations, we must be selective and in doing so leave the reader with more questions to ponder than definitive answers; however, such questions are important and ultimately worthy of serious reflection.

All of the predictions we made in section 'Learnability Assumptions for the Present Study' were borne out, to a greater or lesser extent, in the data as was presented numerically in the previous section. It is clear that Italian-speaking learners of L2 Spanish start the process with an advantage in the domains investigated stemming from the similarities between their L1 and the target L2 as compared to the English-speaking groups. As seen above, by comparing the two L2 intermediate groups' aggregate performances on both tasks, we obtain clear and straightforward evidence of L1 transfer effects on L2 development. What is evident across both experiments and across both Italian-speaking aggregates is that they have determinate target knowledge of grammatical gender and adjectival semantic nuances in L2 Spanish. Indeed, it was the case that only the English-speaking learners demonstrated significant differences in these domains, which might indicate representational deficits (e.g., Franceschina, 2005); however, in line with others we contend that any such deficits are an artifact of an ongoing L2 development that corrects itself throughout the L2 acquisition process (cf. Judy et al., 2008) as evidenced by the performance of the advanced English-speaking group for which full convergence was shown to be viable. Taken together, all of the data constitute strong evidence in favor of the Full Transfer/Full Accessibility (Schwartz & Sprouse, 1996) model of the initial state and its subsequent predictions for L2 developmental sequence for L2 Spanish speakers of both L1s under investigation. Whereas the differences between the intermediate groups are consistent with L1 transfer, the performance of the English-speaking advanced group is consistent with full UG-accessibility. This is especially true for the interpretive experiments relating to adjectival semantics since, as detailed above, such knowledge is a very good indicator of the mental syntactic representation one has in this domain.

As it relates to the epistemological issues we endeavored to confront, our last prediction (10c) expected to witness individual performance differences within the groups. This indeed is what occurred and although space limitations do not permit a full analysis of all the raw data, we present here trends and exceptional differences, which we then relate to important implications for general SLA methodology involving tacit assumptions made about group data analyses. We maintain that this discussion is crucial when one keeps in mind the goal of SLA, which is to describe and explain how the individual adult language learner comes to acquire (or not) linguistic systems, which in theory should pertain to every individual learner at least on the cognitive side of the acquisition/learning process. While group experiments are fundamental to our understanding of what ultimately is an individual process, we maintain that one needs to reconsider why the field in general holds individual L2 learners to a standard that might exceed the individual performances of native speakers of the target language or to the trend that emerges of an aggregate set of their peers. This scenario can only be revealed by looking at the individual performances of all participants in a study, including the range of native control performances. Moreover, this issue relates intimately to the notion of linguistic proficiency and how such is measured, that is, the very usefulness of such measures for adult language learners. In an ideal sense, when one assesses L2 proficiency, each categorical label would make exact or good predictions of performance for any given domain and, assuming a tenable methodology, this should be somewhat stable across experiments. Of course, we all know it does not, whereby calling learners "intermediate" L2 learners even when the same objective measures have been used to assess them often results in performances that vary greatly along several axes. In many cases, individual L2 performances correlate more directly to much higher or lower level expectations and this can be true across the same learner's performances that change over short periods of time and/or across empirical methodology. This much is known in general and as such should meet with little controversy; however, what is seldom discussed is the fact that this is also true, to a much lesser extent, for native speaker control participants. An immediate question that emerges is one that ponders the comparative value of the native vs. non-native performance dichotomy in the first place along with the functional value of dividing L2 learners into perceived monolithic categories of proficiency when one knows these categories to be comprised of a significant range of performance variables that seemingly effect native speakers as well.

To make this discussion more tangible, let us turn to some trends we noticed in the individual data of the aggregates we analyzed herein. We note that the native speaker range of performance for all tasks (even the ones not presented here) was as large as the range of advanced L2 learners at the group level. Moreover, at the individual level many intermediate English-speaking individuals performed within the native performances ranges. So, while the English-speaking intermediate group performances were significantly different for many properties, it is not the case that *all* intermediate individuals performed statistically different than all of the native control individuals. Yet a group analysis alone argues for absolute significant differences, inadvertently obscuring a more dynamic and, we would argue, a much more interesting if not complete picture at the individual level. Methodologically, this fact obliges us to consider two questions: (a) if native speakers can vary in their performance at the individual level as well, why do we hold/compare L2 learners both as groups and individuals to a "native" standard that is in fact not steady or monolithic? and (b) how effective are group comparisons if ultimately we want to understand SLA as an individual process?

The answers to the above-posed questions are not uncontroversial and require the rethinking of standard assumption. Minimally, we must reexamine the use of the native control as the default benchmark of SLA comparison. However, there is no debate that scientific experiments must have controls of some sort if for no other reason than to ensure the usefulness of their methodology. So, to challenge the use of native baselines is tantamount to empty lip service if a better control is not offered to replace the existing one. Cook (2003) has argued that childhood bilinguals are a more appropriate control for adult SLA comparison, but such groups invoke a higher level of comparative complexity insofar as they are a more varied group and the possible outcomes limited exposure to input brings to their grammatical systems (see Montrul, 2008 for related issues). In the absence of a better control to offer, we will not suggest that native baseline comparisons should be replaced, but that they must be supplemented with an examination of individual data to determine whether or not all individuals fall within or outside the range of the native controls before making conclusions with respect to so-called grammatical deficiencies. Since no one would label individual native grammars as deficient simply because they fall outside the average of a group of their peers, we need to be cautious when we do just that for groups of L2 learners or L2 individuals compared only to a native group average that inadvertently obscures individual differences within the native group as well. After all, individual L2 learners cannot be held to a higher standard on linguistic measures than the individuals that comprise the control group. The point to be made is that group analyses can inadvertently hide significant idiosyncratic behavior on the part of the adult learner and more importantly on the part of the native controls. Fairly considering individual data as described here as a habit of future SLA studies might lessen the perceived gap of difference between adult learners and native speakers in many domains.

As it relates more directly to proficiency, it might be fair to simply suggest that when individual L2 learners perform significantly outside the expected range of deviation for their assessed level of proficiency that this might simply mean that they are miscategorized and are actually of a higher or lower proficiency level. However, this would only be tenable if performance effects were to obtain with consistency for these learners across the axes of time, methodology and, crucially, across multiple (if not all) linguistic domains tested. As we know, this is not what occurs in the typical case and so the complexity of proficiency and the issues that it brings to be considered are not easily explained by appealing to simple solutions. Perhaps the best way to avoid some of these issues is to develop methodologies of L2 competence assessment that transcend the relative proficiency assessment. This can be accomplished by comparing an L2 learner's individual performance to his/her own performance on counterbalanced methodologies, across time and across space. Ultimately, the goal is to determine the extent to which his/her L2 grammar permits or restricts certain possibilities and to demonstrate not that L2 learners perform at the same level as native speakers or even as other L2 learners at the "same proficiency level," but rather that they are aware of distinctions that make their L2 grammar native-like.

General Conclusions

Bringing together all the experimental data we presented provides strong support for a definitive role for the L1 in the developmental sequence of L2 acquisition, adding to a large and significant literature that has argued and shown this previously. The data of the advanced groups also indicate that full convergence in this domain, irrespective of the L1 at the L2 learners' disposal, is possible. Lastly, a discussion of the individual trends of all groups, but especially the native controls, permitted us to highlight the comparative fallacy between L2 groups and native speaker groups. It was further argued that looking at individual performances of L2 learners and native controls is important and revealing in explicating the actual space that exists between L1 and L2 acquisition as a developmental process and its outcomes.

Notes

[1] We are aware that more recent analyses motivate the placement of the adjectives in terms of the existence of some extra categories, for example, [nP] (e.g., Demonte, 2008).

[2] For feature checking reasons, nouns must raise in Spanish even when they appear overtly to the right of the head noun. This must mean that adjectives in such a position move to a high functional category within the DP-layer.

[3] Details aside, Italian conflates gender and plural number marking in a single morpheme, which constitutes a front vowel [i] or [e] whereas Spanish adds a separate plural marker [s] (or an allomorph) to the constant gender morpheme (or word class marker in the sense of Harris (1995)), usually [a] or [o], to express plural number. This reality requires feature reassembly onto new L2 morphological material, which is not always a straightforward process (see Lardiere, 2007; Prévost & White, 2000).

[4] In addition to the two tasks described, a Grammaticality Judgment/Correction task (GJCT) was also completed by all participants. This GJCT contained a total of 40 sentences that pertained to gender feature acquisition. Twenty of the sentences (ten grammatical and ten ungrammatical) tested for knowledge of agreement between nouns and adjectives while the other 20 sentences (ten grammatical and ten ungrammatical) tested for knowledge of agreement between determiners and nouns. Details aside, the results of this task show that even the Intermediate English learners perform very well with regard to narrow syntax properties. When the results of the GJCT are combined with the results of the two tasks described herein, it seems that the syntax is converged upon fairly early, but that there is a lag in the semantics.

[5] However, if we examine the results of a subgroup of the Intermediate English group, we see that eight participants performed more like the other participant groups; their average number of correct interpretations of prenominal and postnominal adjectives was 4.13 and 3.50, respectively. This fact, combined with the general performance of the group, indicates that even at the intermediate level, the L1 English speakers show a trend towards target knowledge. The Advanced English group supports this claim as they perform like the control group, as we will see, on both tasks.

[6] Again, if we consider individual performance we see that three control group participants performed like the Italian groups (4.00 for prenominal adjectives and 5.00 for postnominal adjectives). Similarly, 7 of the Advanced English group performed like the Italian groups (3.86 for prenominal and 4.86 for postnominal adjectives). Finally, a subgroup of 5 Intermediate English speakers also performed like the Italian groups (3.00 for prenominal and 5.00 for postnominal adjectives). The issues that these results introduce are in the 'Discussion' section.

References

Abney, S. (1987). *The English noun phrase in its sentential aspect.* Doctoral dissertation, Massachusetts Institute of Technology, Cambridge, MA.

Anderson, B. (2001). Adjective position and interpretation in L2 French. In J. Camps., & C.-R. Wiltshire (Eds.). *Romance syntax, semantics and L2 acquisition* (pp. 27–42). Amsterdam: John Benjamins.

Anderson, B. (2007a). Learnability and Parametric Change in the Nominal System of L2 French. *Language Acquisition*, 14, 165–214.

Anderson, B. (2007b). Pedagogical rules and their relationship to frequency in the input: Observational and empirical data from L2 French. *Applied Linguistics*, 28, 286–308.

Anderson, B. (2008). Forms of evidence and grammatical development in the acquisition of adjective position in L2 French. *Studies in Second Language Acquisition*, 30, 1–29.

Bernstein, J. (1993). *Topics in the syntax of nominal structure across Romance.* Ph.D., Graduate Center. City University of New York.

Bernstein, J. (2001). The DP hypothesis: Identifying clausal properties in the nominal domain. In M. Baltin., & C. Collins (Eds.). *The handbook of contemporary syntactic theory* (pp. 536–61). London: Blackwell.

Cinque, G. (1994). On the evidence for partial N movement in the Romance DP. In G. Cinque, J. Koster, J.-Y. Pollock, L. Rizzi., & R. Zanuttini (Eds.). *Paths towards universal grammar* (pp. 85–110). Washington DC: Georgetown University Press.

Chomsky, N. (1981). *Lectures in government and binding.* Dordrecht: Foris.

Chomsky, N. (1995). *The minimalist program.* Cambridge, MA: MIT Press.

Cook, V. (Ed.). (2003). *Effects of the second language on the first.* Cleveland: Multilingual Matters.

Demonte, V. (2008). Meaning-form correlations and adjective position in Spanish. In C. Kennedy., & L. Mcnally (Eds.), *The semantics of adjectives and adverbs.* Oxford: Oxford University Press.

Epstein, S., Flynn, S., & Martohardjono, G. (1996). Second language acquisition: Theoretical and experimental issues in contemporary research. *Brain and Behavioral Sciences*, 19, 677–714.

Franceschina, F. (2005). *Fossilized second language grammars: The acquisition of grammatical gender.* Amsterdam: John Benjamins.

Fruit, M-N. (2006). L2 Acquisition of focus constructions in European Portuguese and the L2 status of the syntax-discourse interface. In M. G. O'Brien, C. Shea, & J. Archibald (Eds.). *Proceedings of the 8th Generative Approaches to Second Language Acquisition Conference (GASLA 2006)*, (pp. 41–50). Somerville, MA: Cascadilla Proceedings Project.

Gess, R., & Herschensohn, J. (2001). Shifting the DP parameter: A study of Anglophone French L2ers. In J. Camps., & C. Wiltshire (Eds.). *Romance syntax, semantics and L2 acquisition* (pp. 105–25). Amsterdam: John Benjamins.

Grimshaw, J., & Rosen, S. T. (1990). Knowledge and obedience: The developmental status of binding theory. *Linguistic Inquiry*, 21, 187–222.

Harris, J. (1995). *The syntax and morphology of class marker suppression in Spanish.* Massachusetts: MIT.

Hawkins, R. (2001). *Second Language Syntax.* Malden, NJ: Blackwell.

Hawkins, R., & Franceschina, F. (2004). Explaining the acquisition and non-acquisition of determiner-noun concord in French and Spanish. In P. Prévost, & J. Paradis (Eds.). *The acquisition of French in different contexts: Focus on functional categories* (pp. 175–205). Amsterdam: John Benjamins.

Judy, T., Guijarro-Fuentes, P., & Rothman, J. (2008). Adult accessibility to L2 representational primitives: Evidence from the Spanish DP. In M. Bowles, R. Foote, & S. Perpiñán (Eds.). *Selected Proceedings of SLRF 2007.* Somerville, MA: Cascadilla Press.

Kellerman, E. (1986). An eye for an eye: Crosslinguistic constraints on the development of the L2 lexicon. In E. Kellerman., & M. S. Smith (Eds.). *Crosslinguistic influence in second language Acquisition* (pp. 35–48). New York: Pergamon.

Lardiere, D. (2007). Feature-assembly in second language acquisition. In J. Liceras, H. Zobl., & H. Goodluck (Eds.). *The role of formal features in second language acquisition* (pp. 106–41). Mahwah, NJ: Lawrence Erlbaum Associates.

Martohardjono, G. (1993). *Wh-movement in the acquisition of a second language: A crosslinguistic study of three languages with and without movement.* Unpublished PhD thesis, Cornell University.

Martohardjono, G. (1998). Measuring competence in L2 acquisition: Commentary on Part II. In S. Flynn, G. Martohardjono., & W. O'Neil (Eds.), *The Generative Study of Second Language Acquisition* (pp. 151–57). Mahwah, NJ: Lawrence Earlbaum.

Montrul, S. (2008). *Incomplete acquisition in bilingualism: Re-examining the age factor.* Amsterdam: John Benjamins.

Picallo, M. C. (1991). Nominals and nominalization in Catalan. *Probus,* 3, 279–316.

Prévost, P., & White, L. (2000). Missing surface inflection or impairment in second language acquisition? Evidence from tense and agreement. *Second Language Research,* 16, 103–33.

Rothman, J. (2007). Pragmatic solutions for syntactic problems: Understanding some L2 syntactic errors in terms of discourse-pragmatic deficits. In S. Baauw, F. Drijkoningen, & M. Pinto (Eds.). *Romance languages and linguistic theory* (pp. 297–318). Amsterdam: John Benjamins.

Rothman, J., & Iverson, M. (2007a). Input type and parameter resetting: Is naturalistic input necessary? *International Review of Applied Linguistics, IRAL,* 45, 285–319.

Rothman, J., & Iverson, M. (2007b). On L2 clustering and resetting the null subject parameter in L2 Spanish: Implications and observations. *Hispania,* 90, 329–42.

Schwartz, B., & Sprouse, R. (1996). L2 cognitive states and the full transfer/full access model. *Second Language Research,* 12, 40–72.

Slabakova, R. (2006). Learnability in the second language acquisition of semantics: A bidirectional study of a semantic parameter. *Second Language Research,* 22, 498–523.

Sorace, A. (2005). Selective optionality in language development. In L. Cornips., & K. Corrigan (Eds.). *Biolinguistic and sociolinguistic accounts of syntactic variation* (pp. 55–80). Amsterdam: John Benjamins.

Vanikka, A., & Young-Scholten, M. (1996). The early stages in adult L2 syntax: Additional evidence from Romance speakers. *Second Language Research,* 12, 140–76.

White, L. (1989). *Universal grammar and second language acquisition.* Amsterdam: John Benjamins.
White, L. (2003). On the nature of interlanguage representation: Universal grammar in the second language. In C. Doughty & M. Long (Eds.). *The handbook of second language acquisition* (pp. 19–42). Oxford: Blackwell.
White, L. (forthcoming). Grammatical Theory: Interfaces and L2 knowledge. In W. Ritchie & T. K. Bhatia (Eds.). *Handbook of Second Language Acquisition.*

Index

bottom-up and top-down process 4, 116–18

cross-linguistic influence 3, 24, 26–30, 33–5, 37–9

Determiner Phrase 233, 237, 238, 239, 240, 241
dictogloss 5, 169, 170, 173–5, 178, 182–5

explicit information 5, 132, 169–71, 173, 175, 180–5

individual variation/linguistic development 4, 6, 45, 46, 48, 50, 53, 55, 56
innate knowledge, generative theories/view 4, 63, 65–8, 72, 76
input processing 3, 6, 9, 16–19
intelligibility of words/extended speech 5, 132, 133, 134, 140–2

L1 transfer/effects on L2 development 6, 233–6, 241, 245–7, 249
learning styles 4, 95–7, 112
lexical development/proficiency/diversity/vocabulary proficiency 4, 95–8, 107–9, 112

meaning-based output instruction 6, 169, 170, 173–5, 178, 181, 182, 184, 185
metalinguistic knowledge/descriptions 4, 79–87, 89–92

native and non-native speech/speakers/performance 5, 147–53, 157, 159–61, 203, 209

priming 3, 9, 10–20
processing instruction 5, 6, 169–74, 178–81, 184, 185, 189–92, 195–201
proficiency/L2 proficiency 3–5, 6, 9, 18–20, 24, 25, 27–30, 33–9, 45, 48–51, 55, 63, 66, 67, 70–3, 76, 77, 80, 81, 112, 119, 128, 133, 147, 148, 149, 154, 157, 159, 161, 162, 169, 202, 212, 216, 218, 234, 235, 247, 249

saliency factors/salience 4, 116, 118, 120, 121, 123, 124, 126
secondary/cumulative effects 6, 19, 189–91, 194, 196–200
speech production (Levelt model) 6, 202, 203, 204, 206, 207
statistical learning/properties 4, 63, 65, 71, 76

task completion/form-focused task 79, 83–7, 90–2
task difficulty 6, 216–2, 224–30

word familiarity/familiarity 3, 24, 26, 29, 34–6, 38, 39
word recognition 4, 116, 118, 120, 123, 125, 127, 128, 134, 141
working memory 4, 45–56, 119, 120